The Economics of UK–EU Relations

Nauro F. Campos · Fabrizio Coricelli
Editors

The Economics of UK–EU Relations

From the Treaty of Rome to the Vote for Brexit

palgrave
macmillan

Editors
Nauro F. Campos
Brunel University
St Albans, UK

Fabrizio Coricelli
Paris School of Economics
Paris, France

ISBN 978-3-319-55494-5   ISBN 978-3-319-55495-2   (eBook)
DOI 10.1007/978-3-319-55495-2

Library of Congress Control Number: 2017938150

Cover credit: Charlotte Allen/Alamy Stock Photo

Printed on acid-free paper

This Palgrave Macmillan imprint is published by Springer Nature
The registered company is Springer International Publishing AG
The registered company address is: Gewerbestrasse 11, 6330 Cham, Switzerland

Contents

List of Figures

List of Tables

Introduction

Nauro F. Campos and Fabrizio Coricelli

The UK referendum on EU membership generated a renewal of academic economists' interest on the political economy of the UK–EU relationship. This is largely because a British exit, or 'Brexit', is one among a constellation of crises currently inflicting upon the EU. Although one among many, Brexit differs in that it can alone ignite other crises. Brexit raises existential questions about the integration project. It asks questions about the value of membership, the dynamics and distribution of its benefits and costs, and the type of integration that can at

N.F. Campos (✉)
Brunel University London, London, UK
e-mail: nauro.campos@brunel.ac.uk

N.F. Campos
ETH Zurich, Zürich, Switzerland

N.F. Campos
IZA Bonn, Bonn, Germany

F. Coricelli
Paris School of Economics, Paris, France
e-mail: fabrizio.coricelli@gmail.com

F. Coricelli
CEPR, London, UK

© The Author(s) 2017
N.F. Campos and F. Coricelli (eds.), *The Economics of UK–EU Relations*,
DOI 10.1007/978-3-319-55495-2_1

least sustain the net benefits we have seen since the 1950s. One of the few benefits of the 'Brexit debate' is that it has fostered a flurry of new research addressing hard and important questions that have not been sufficiently scrutinised before. The aim of this book is to take stock of some of the main lessons.

Nicholas Crafts' chapter provides a historical perspective on the UK–EU relationship. He argues that the impact of EU membership on British growth performance, both past and future, remains controversial. He reviews post-war growth in the UK and its European peer group and considers the implications of economic integration through EU membership. It concludes that the EU has strongly reduced trade costs and had positive impacts on income levels but has not raised trend growth rates. He suggests that the UK's entry into the EU in the 1970s had strong positive effects (he notes per capita GDP net gains of about 8.6%). But domestic supply side policies have been more important for long-run growth performance. The economic benefits of EU membership for the UK have far exceeded the costs of budgetary transfers and regulation. He argues Brexit will probably reduce UK GDP without removing significant constraints on policy that might deliver faster growth. He concluded that "with regards to the future growth of the British economy, it is hard to see a problem to which Brexit is the solution."

Campos and Coricelli complement this analysis by offering new historical evidence on the net benefits of EU membership to the UK stressing the ways in which it could resolve the problem of weak competition. A defining feature of the British performance is its relative decline: After 1945, the six founding members of the European Union grew faster than (and some effectively overtook) the UK, yet there is a turning point when this relative decline stops (although it does not seem to revert). The conventional view is that this occurs in the mid-1980s and the reason is that this is when Mrs. Thatcher implements her package of far-reaching structural reforms. Campos and Coricelli ask whether econometric evidence is supportive of such view, find it is not and ask what else could have played such a role. Theirs amounts to a somewhat dissonant view on post-WWII British relative economic performance. They examine an alternative and much less popular hypothesis: this turning point occurs instead in 1973 when the UK finally joined the European Union and find significant econometric support for 1973. They explain this finding by arguing that EU accession marked the victory of the business groups that wanted to compete at the high-tech end of the very demanding common European market against those business groups which wanted to compete in the comparative-advantage driven mostly former colonies Commonwealth market. These pro-Europe business groups later become the constituency that supported Mrs. Thatcher's reforms without which they would not be nearly as successful.

In his chapter, Macchiarelli presents lessons from the history of European monetary integration. Contrasting optimal currency and optimal control perspectives on European integration to examine the role of European integration for the future of EU–UK relations and, more specifically, the implications of 'completing' the European Monetary Union. He notes that the Financial Crisis exposed the inherent "fragility" of the EMU, calling for the need to put in place a framework to deal with the growing macro-financial and democratic imbalances within the monetary union. This encompassed the creation of a new two-pillar system of financial supervision, i.e. the European System of Financial Supervision (ESFS); the conception of a European liquidity fund, i.e. the European Stability Mechanism; the revamp of macroeconomic policy coordination and fiscal surveillance, i.e. the Fiscal Compact and annex legislations (Two Pack and Six Pack); as well as a renovated role for the ECB in financial stability and supervision, including the banking union. Such reforms, consistent with the idea of 'completing' the EMU (hence, a 'Genuine Economic and Monetary Union') will have an impact on the EU and the single market, with the obvious consequence of affecting the UK as well, and the future of its negotiations. This may well leave the UK in a difficult position, should negotiations fail to deliver a mutually beneficial deal. Provided that European integration worked in the past, the net benefits of staying out of the EU *ex-ante* may be different from the benefits *ex-post*, particularly in the likely scenario the Union will have to move forward to safeguard its integrity. Because a 'Genuine Economic and Monetary Union' (GEMU) would affect the UK irrespective of Brexit, it should be taken into the account for the costs and benefits of EU membership.

The next three chapters highlight a number of individual issues that were important in constructing the UK–EU relationship in the past and will likely continue to be relevant in the future. These are the financial sector, foreign direct investment (FDI), migration and regional policy, regulation and trade. The book dedicate one chapter to each of these important issues.

The chapter by Schoenmaker focuses on the UK financial sector after Brexit, emphasising the issue of "passporting." Part of the UK's attractiveness as international financial centre is the access to the internal market of the wider European Economic Area (EEA). By using a UK licence as European passport, foreign financial firms can offer their financial services throughout the EEA. He argues that if the UK cannot secure a 'Norway' deal and stay within the internal market after Brexit, the UK will lose passporting rights for EU financial services and access to euro clearing and settlement, both of which make London attractive as a financial centre. A substantial part of the UK's wholesale banking and trading sector may move out. Analysing the impact on banking and insurance, he finds that the insurance industry makes very limited use of the passport in comparison to the banking industry. Next, he analyses the impact on wholesale banking and securities and derivatives trading. His findings on wholesale banking and trading are indicative. The early numbers suggest that up to half of the total UK banking system relates to wholesale banking in the City of London. Wholesale banking covers the full remit of trading and derivatives activities and takes place in several currencies (US dollar, euro and pound sterling). Next, he finds that, in particular, the OTC derivatives markets might be affected, as 75% of euro-denominated OTC interest rate derivatives are traded in London.

The effect of EU membership on foreign direct investment (FDI) is a topic of obvious importance but one for which previously we had very few satisfactory estimates. The next chapter, by Bruno, Campos, Estrin and Meng, focuses on FDI and the relationship between the United Kingdom and the European Union. It investigates whether and to what extent foreign direct investment inflows into the United Kingdom are caused by its membership in the European Union (EU). It reports two main sets of econometric estimates, namely synthetic counterfactual method with annual data for large sample of developing and developed countries over

1970–2014 and gravity estimates using bilateral data for 1985–2013. The two sets of estimates strongly concur: EU membership increases FDI inflows by about 30%, a result that is robust to changes in specification, country samples, time windows and the use of different estimators.

Jonathan Portes' chapter focuses on the issue of immigration. Immigration has long been a salient and disputed issue in British politics. This was the case 40 years ago; the government's decision to admit a substantial number of refugees of Indian ethnicity from former British colonies in East Africa was hotly disputed, and then as now a large majority favoured tighter restrictions on immigration. Yet, it scarcely figured as an issue in the 1975 referendum on whether the United Kingdom should remain a member of the European Union (then the European Economic Community). Indeed, if anything, those who thought immigration was too high were slightly more likely to vote to stay in. So, what changed, and how did the UK get to this position? This chapter examines the history of free movement within the EU, and in particular the origins and impact of the decision to allow immediate access to the labour market for workers from the new Member States in 2004. It reviews the economic impacts of recent EU migration and notes they seem to have been relatively benign (even for the low paid and low skilled workers). It then considers the impact of the referendum, and possible options for changes to UK immigration policy after Brexit.

Becker, Egger and von Ehrlich shed light on the effectiveness of EU regional policy with a particular focus on the UK. Some taxpayers in the UK might be concerned whether the EU spends their contributions to the EU Regional Policy budget wisely, independent of whether EU money returns to the UK or not. Also, some UK taxpayers might wonder whether the UK has benefited itself from EU funding. Finally, some UK citizens might be concerned about what would replace EU Regional Policy transfers to some regions in the UK, if the UK were to leave the EU. The chapter addresses all of these questions and complement their analysis with some historical background on EU Regional Policy. The EU spends a large share of its budget on regional policy. The chapter concludes that overall regional transfers across the EU give value for money. However, there is room for further improvement in the design of EU regional transfers to make them more effective. Becker, Egger and von Ehrlich argue that UK regions have benefited from EU regional policy over the last decades and that there is uncertainty for those regions that benefit from substantial amounts of EU funding (e.g. Cornwall) over what would replace those funds after Brexit.

The issue of EU regulation is the subject of the chapter by Springford. He notes that EU's critics argue that increasing costs of regulations from Brussels vastly outweigh the modest benefits they see from membership. Arguments over regulation are a central feature of the British relationship with the EU. Many think that continental Europeans are more inclined to regulate markets than the UK, and that as EU regulation has become more intrusive, the UK is subject to regulations that damage the economy by imposing large and mostly unnecessary burdens on British businesses. However, it is a difficult task to add together the economic effects of all EU rules to calculate a 'net cost (or benefit) of Europe'. Some analysts have added up the costs and benefits of major EU regulations that can be found in UK impact assessments, in which civil servants attempt to quantify the economic impact of individual regulations. However, all impact assessments are highly uncertain estimations, and many do not calculate benefits, as these can be difficult to quantify. Springford presented new evidence that the EU's regulations and directives reduce the cost of trade between member states, noting that the evidence does not support the claim that the EU's rules are an economic straitjacket: repealing them would do little to boost the British economy. In fact, the reverse is more likely. The 2016 referendum result showed that, alongside dissatisfaction at high rates of immigration from newer EU member states, the UK public was persuaded by the Leave camp's appeals to democracy and national self-determination. What is less clear, however, is whether the public understood—or if they did understand, agreed with—the economic rationale behind the EU's attempt to create common regulation. This chapter finally discusses whether the EU's single market process, launched in 1992, has done much to reduce the cost of trade in goods and services across the EU, and whether it has done much to boost trade flows. It also considers whether, if the UK decides to leave the single market as well as the EU, it would be something of liberation to the supply-side of the British economy—a key argument of the Leave campaign. To understand whether an exit from the single market might reduce the cost of regulation, one must establish why regulations exist in the first place; appraise the extent to which the EU has a legitimate interest in regulation; honestly assess the effects of EU regulation on British economic performance; and consider whether the UK would escape the regulatory costs attributed to membership if the country chose to leave the EU.

The last chapter by Mulabdic, Osnago and Ruta focuses on international trade. In particular, it investigates the impact of the exit of the UK from the EU (Brexit) on UK–EU trade relations. Specifically, it applies a standard gravity model to assess the effect that EU membership had on UK trade and then uses the estimates from this analysis to evaluate the future of UK–EU trade relations under different scenarios. The main finding is that as the UK benefited from large trade gains from EU membership, its undoing may lead to substantial trade losses. Differently from previous studies, they use new information on the content of trade agreements to build a measure of "depth" based on the number of provisions these agreements cover, relying on information on goods, services and value-added trade from the World Input Output Database. Deep trade agreements are found to increase goods and services trade by 42% and value-added trade by 14% on average. EU membership had a particularly strong effect on UK–EU services and Global Value Chains (GVC) trade. As a result of its membership, UK services trade more than doubled and UK's backward and forward participation in GVCs increased by 68%. They then evaluate the impact of Brexit on future UK–EU trade under different scenarios and find that UK–EU trade declines under all scenarios, ranging between 6 and 28% for trade in value added, and that this drop is sharper (particularly for services and GVC trade) the lower the depth of the post-Brexit arrangement relative to the depth of the EU agreement. But the tradeoff between the depth of trade agreements and trade intensity will delimit policy choices going forward.

In summary, all chapters warn about the risk of significant economic losses that the UK economy may suffer from exiting the EU. Acknowledging the difficulties in assessing and quantifying the economic effects of Brexit, an unprecedented event, the book provides methodological frameworks and substantial evidence from the experience of EU membership that can help understanding the main channels through which Brexit will impact the UK economy.

UK Economic Growth Performance in a European Context: Has EU Membership Made Much Difference?

Nicholas Crafts

1 Introduction

The growth performance of the UK economy has varied considerably during the post-war period both in absolute terms and, perhaps more significantly, relative to its European peer group. Clearly, many relevant aspects of the economic environment have changed since the early 1950s. Here we focus on the implications of EU membership for growth outcomes. Of itself, this will surely have varied both across countries and over time and could potentially affect growth differentials.

The proximate sources of growth can be found in rates of increase of factor inputs including capital, human capital and hours worked, and of the productivity of those inputs. At a deeper level, economics highlights the importance of micro-foundations of growth in terms of the key role played by the incentive structures which inform decisions to invest, to innovate and to adopt new technology and which depend on an economy's institutions and its policy framework but are also influenced by circumstances beyond policymakers' control such as the scope for catch-up growth. Obviously, there are a large number of supply-side policies that affect growth performance. These include areas such as

N. Crafts (✉)
CAGE, University of Warwick, Coventry CV4 7AL, UK
e-mail: n.crafts@warwick.ac.uk

© The Author(s) 2017
N.F. Campos and F. Coricelli (eds.), *The Economics of UK–EU Relations*,
DOI 10.1007/978-3-319-55495-2_2

9

competition, education, infrastructure, innovation, regulation and taxation. Moreover, even for EU members, to a large extent these are decided
by domestic governments. Nevertheless, openness is an important part of
the picture.

The key idea with which to approach the post-war European experience is catch-up growth. The leader throughout has been the USA but
for much of the period since 1950 Western European countries were
reducing productivity gaps with that country. It is well known that these
gaps provide an opportunity to grow faster than the leader. However,
catch-up growth is not automatic but depends on institutions and policy
frameworks. It is useful to distinguish between catch-up growth in
far-from-the-frontier and close-to-the-frontier economies. In the former,
rapid total factor productivity (TFP) growth can be obtained by reducing
productive and allocative inefficiency and by importing technology. In
the latter, stronger competition in product markets and high-quality
education become more important (Aghion and Howitt 2006), as the
impetus to growth may be expected to switch at least partly from imi-
tation to invention. The process of catch-up growth typically entails a
series of ongoing reforms with the danger that at some point the political
economy of the next step in modernization becomes too difficult.

In terms of short-run static effects, trade liberalization can improve
allocative efficiency and/or productive efficiency, i.e. given existing costs,
factors of production are deployed more efficiently or production costs
are lowered. Insofar as freer trade increases competition in product
markets (through actual or potential entry), it may have both effects as
market power is reduced and price-cost margins fall while managers of
firms are pressured to reduce costs to the minimum feasible
(principal-agent problems are reduced). In terms of long-run dynamic
effects, according to endogenous growth models, it is possible that the
growth rate will rise as a result of economic integration. In a basic AK
model, if investment (or more generally the rate of growth of the capital
stock) responds positively, there is no tendency for diminishing returns
to erode this initial effect so there is a 'permanent' impact on growth.
Perhaps more plausibly, if a larger market and/or more competition in
product markets ensues from economic integration this may raise the rate
of innovation and TFP growth. Even so, in a perhaps more realistic

(semi-endogenous) growth model, the trade liberalization impact on the growth rate would be a transitory phenomenon reflecting a move to a higher level of output rather than faster trend growth.[1]

As we shall see, the most acute phase of British relative economic decline was from the 1950s to the 1970s. Given these insights from growth economics, the subsequent improvement in growth performance suggests that EU membership could have had favourable effects. Support for such an interpretation was recently voiced in Bank of England (2015) which stressed the favourable impact of the greater openness associated with EU membership for the dynamism of the British economy without, however, providing any explicit quantification of its magnitude. However, an obvious alternative hypothesis is that the improved performance was a response to domestic policy reforms, in particular those associated with the Thatcher governments (Crafts 2014). Moreover, those in favour of Brexit might argue that, at least in recent times, European economic integration has had a negative impact by constraining policy innovations that would be good for growth while the positive effects are now exhausted.

Against this background, this paper addresses the following questions: First, what difference has the European Union made to growth outcomes in member countries? Second, in particular, how much has EU membership affected economic growth in the UK? Third, what might be the implications of Brexit for UK growth?

2   European Economic Integration, Trade and Growth: An Overview

We start with a brief descriptive outline of the process of post-war European economic integration. As Sapir (2011) has reminded us, this can usefully be approached using the ideas of Balassa (1961). Balassa distinguished between different degrees of increasingly deep economic integration working up from free trade area to customs union, in which there is also pooling of sovereignty in a common external trade policy, to common market, within which factors of production can move freely, to economic union, in which some economic policies are harmonized, to complete economic integration, where there is political union with a supra-national authority.

In 1958, the European Economic Community was formed by the original six countries following the signing of the Treaty of Rome in 1957. The signatories pledged to lay the foundations of 'ever closer union' among the peoples of Europe and Article 2 committed members to form a customs union, to establish a common market and to harmonize policies. Article 3 spelt out what this would comprise including a common external tariff, a common agricultural policy, the abolition of barriers to trade and of obstacles to freedom of movement of capital and labour, a competition policy regime, and the coordination of policies to avoid balance of payments disequilibria. In contrast, the European Free Trade Association was set up in 1960 with the much more limited aim of establishing a free trade area. The EEC customs union was achieved in 1968 but the common market took much longer and awaited the Single European Act which addressed non-tariff barriers to trade, liberalized trade in services and ended capital controls and was (less than fully) implemented from 1992. The Maastricht Treaty of 1992 was a significant step towards economic union and paved the way to a single currency which further reduced trade costs as well as eliminating exchange rate instability; the Euro started in 1999, initially with 11 countries. Complete economic integration is still out of reach.

Over time, the membership of the EEC/EU expanded considerably through successive enlargements while that of EFTA has shrunk with defections to the EEC/EU. In 1973, the UK and two of its close trading partners, Denmark and Ireland, joined the EU. In the 1980s, the newly democratic Greece, Portugal and Spain acceded and in 1995, following the establishment of the European Single Market, Austria, Finland and Sweden left EFTA to join the EU. In 2004, 8 former communist-bloc transition economies joined the EU together with Cyprus and Malta followed by further transition economies accessions by Bulgaria and Romania in 2007 and Croatia in 2013, while a number of these new members were admitted into the Eurozone soon after accession.

The process of economic integration entailed substantial reductions in trade costs and increased the volume of trade. In both these respects, the EU was much more effective than the alternatives of EFTA or GATT membership. This can be inferred from estimates of the determinants of trade flows based on gravity models, as, for example, in Baier et al. (2008). Two countries both in the EU are estimated to trade with each other by an additional 72–127% compared with countries not in a trade agreement.[2] Their estimates imply that, compared with EFTA membership, being in the EU raised trade by 33%.[3]

Although some endogenous growth models imply that trade liberalization can raise the rate of economic growth, the evidence for European economic integration does not support this prediction. Badinger (2005) approached the issue through growth regressions. He made an index of the level of European integration for each EU15 country from 1950–2000 and in a panel-regression setting with suitable controls examined its relationship with growth and with investment. The integration index, which took account both of GATT liberalization and European trade agreements, shows that 55% of the protectionism of 1950 was eliminated between 1958 and 1975, a figure which then rose steadily to 87% by 2000. The results of the regressions were that changes in integration were positive for growth but that the level of integration had no effect while changes in integration had somewhere between half and three-quarters of their impact through investment with the remainder coming from changes in TFP. For the EU15 as a whole, real GDP in 2000 was estimated to be 26.1% higher than if there had been no economic integration after 1950 with the impact for the UK very similar at 25.5%.

The implication of the results in Badinger (2005) is that European economic integration has had a sizeable impact on the level of income but has not had a permanent effect on the rate of growth. This amounts to rejecting the endogenous growth hypothesis. This is line with recent investigations of the impact of trade liberalizations using difference-in-difference approaches (Estevadeordal and Taylor 2013) but goes against the hopeful predictions of some economists in the 1980s.[4]

A recent method to infer the implications of accession to the EU in the style of 'with-without' comparisons is available in the synthetic counterfactuals method of Campos et al. (2014). This compares growth in each post-EU accession country with growth in a weighted combination of other countries which did not accede and which are chosen to match the accession country before its entry to the EU as closely as possible. A difference-in-differences analysis is then performed to compare the actual and synthetic control series for each country. The results are that EU accession typically has had a substantial and statistically significant impact on growth relative to the counterfactual of staying out. For countries which joined the EU between 1973 and 1995, the average impact of EU membership after 10 years is estimated to have been a 6.4% income gain with the UK showing an 8.6% gain. It seems quite probable that the 10-year impact understates the total since the Single Market surely added to the initial effect during later years and the total cumulative effect is estimated by Campos et al. (2014) to be 23.7%.[5]

An alternative and better-known approach is to use a gravity model to find the implication of EU membership for the volume of trade and then to quantify the effect of expanded trade on the level of income using the estimated relationship in Feyrer (2009) which itself is an improved version of the well-known Frankel and Romer (1999) model.[6] This uses an econometric approach to capture impacts working through improved productivity and a larger capital stock which far exceed traditional welfare triangle gains from improved resource allocation. Feyrer concludes that the elasticity of income to trade is probably between 0.5 and 0.75. The gravity model estimates in Baier et al. (2008) imply that EU15 trade in 2000 was at least 71.6% higher than if there had been no trade agreement with the implication that total EU trade was raised by 25.4%. Based on the lower bound of Feyrer's estimated elasticity, the EU had a positive impact on GDP of 12.7%.

Similarly, this method predicts that EU membership raised UK trade relative to the counterfactual by 33.0% after 15 years. In 1988, EU trade was 51.4% of total so the implication is that joining the EU had raised UK trade by 17.1%. Taking the lower bound of Feyrer's estimated elasticity, this would have raised UK GDP by 8.6%. It should be noted that this is much larger than any reasonable estimate of the membership fee that the UK has paid for EU membership. The main components of this are budgetary transfers, notably including the costs of the Common

Agricultural Policy, and costs of badly designed regulations which have typically amounted to 0.5% and 0.9%, respectively (Crafts 2016).[7] The ex-post benefit-cost ratio of the decision to join the EU appears to have been very favourable.

In sum, there are two main points that emerge from this review of the evidence. First, it is clear that the EU has been exceptionally successful in creating trade. This implies that it has been effective at reducing trade costs and achieving a relatively deep level of economic integration. Second, economic integration and the additional trade that it has generated has been a powerful force that has raised European income levels significantly. However, while the evidence for a levels effect on income from trade liberalization is convincing, there is no reason to believe that economic integration raised the long-run trend growth rate in Europe.

3 The Golden Age of European Growth, 1950–1973

This was a halcyon period when Western Europe was catching up the USA (c.f. Tables 1, 2). During this era of strong β-convergence, which came to an end with the first oil crisis, both real per person and real GDP per hour worked (labour productivity) grew much faster in most European countries than in the USA. The UK experienced relatively slow growth which is only partly explained by its relatively high income level in 1950. A prima facie case for British 'growth failure' is provided by France and West Germany not just catching up but overtaking the UK by 1973.

The Golden Age was a period of macroeconomic stability, notable for the relative absence of financial crises, which followed the traumas of two world wars and the great depression. Some have seen this as an episode of fast growth based on a reversion to the pre-1914 trend line (Janossy 1969) but econometric analysis shows that it was clearly more than this (Mills and Crafts 2000). That said, countries with relatively large scope for post-war reconstruction such as West Germany found that this stimulated their growth in the 1950s (Temin 2002). TFP growth was

Table 1 Rates of growth of real GDP/person and real GDP/hour worked (% per year)

	Y/P	Y/HW
1950–1973		
France	4.02	5.29
Germany	5.00	5.91
Ireland	3.03	4.06
Italy	4.93	5.93
UK	2.42	2.81
USA	2.45	2.57
1973–1995		
France	1.65	2.67
Germany	1.76	2.86
Ireland	2.88	3.37
Italy	2.22	2.30
UK	1.76	2.40
USA	1.81	1.27
1995–2007		
France	1.75	1.75
Germany	1.56	1.70
Ireland	2.59	3.10
Italy	1.18	0.49
UK	2.55	2.17
USA	2.16	2.21
2007–2014		
France	−0.21	0.44
Germany	0.93	0.45
Ireland	−1.45	1.65
Italy	−1.63	−0.11
UK	0.00	−0.12
USA	0.20	1.05

Note Germany is West Germany prior to 1995; Ireland is GNP after 1973. *Source* The Conference Board (2015)

very rapid during the Golden Age especially in countries with low initial productivity levels. This was based to a large extent on reductions in inefficiency (Jerzmanowski 2007), especially based on the structural change associated with the shift of labour out of agriculture.[8] At the same time, technology transfer speeded up as American technology became more cost-effective in European conditions and obstacles to technology transfer were reduced (Nelson and Wright 1992).

Table 2 Real GDP/head (UK = 100 in each year)

	USA	Germany	Ireland	France	Italy
1950	137.8	61.7	49.8	74.7	50.5
1973	138.8	109.4	57.1	106.6	88.4
2007	133.1	107.2	112.8	98.8	97.7
2014	134.9	114.2	100.8	97.3	86.0

Notes Estimates refer to West Germany from 1950–1973. Ireland is based on GNP in 2007 and 2014. Purchasing power parity estimates in $1990GK for 1950 and 1973 and in $2014EKS from Penn World Table for 2007 and 2014. *Source* The Conference Board (2015)

In some countries, especially in Northern Europe, catch-up during the Golden Age was promoted by the development of corporatist 'social contracts' which were based on bargaining equilibria between capital and labour that featured wage restraint in return for high investment (Eichengreen 2007). These arrangements, which also typically entailed a high level of coordination in wage bargaining, were an important stimulus to investment, which allowed new technology to be installed, and growth (Gilmore 2009). This can be seen as an enhancement of 'social capability' under Golden Age conditions. In other countries, for example, Italy, growth was promoted by industrialization based on elastic supplies of labour and undervalued currencies which underpinned investment and allowed the realization of internal and external economies of scale in the industrial sector (Crafts and Magnani 2013). In both cases, there would later be difficulties arising from the institutional legacy, either of the reforms that they had undertaken or of the reforms that they had failed to make.

The evidence suggests that European economic growth was accelerated in these years by trade liberalization which acted to raise the long-run income level. The starting point was the European Payments Union which emerged from the conditionality of the Marshall Plan; a gravity model analysis confirms that the EPU had a large positive effect on trade levels (Eichengreen 1993). The subsequent establishment of the European Economic Community increased trade considerably. Using a gravity model, Bayoumi and Eichengreen (1995) estimated that intra-EEC trade among the original six members was increased by 3.2%

per year between 1956 and 1973 implying that membership of the EEC may have raised income levels by 4–8% by 1970 (Eichengreen and Boltho 2008), and the annual growth rate of real GDP per person by at most 0.5% points. This was a useful bonus but quite modest (about 1/8) relative to the overall growth rate. The total long-term effect of reductions in trade protection, including reduction of external tariffs through GATT, raised European income levels by nearly 20% by the mid-1970s, with a peak effect of perhaps 1% per year (about ¼ overall growth), according to the estimates in Badinger (2005).

During these years, Britain experienced its fastest-ever economic growth but at the same time relative economic decline proceeded at a rapid rate vis-a-vis its European peer group such that by the end of the period Britain had been overtaken by seven other countries in terms of real GDP per person and by nine others in terms of labour productivity. UK growth was slower by at least 0.7% points per year compared with any other country including those who started the period with similar or higher income levels. The proximate reasons for relatively slow labour productivity growth were weak capital per worker and TFP growth compared with more successful economies like West Germany. Maddison (1996) attempted a decomposition of the sources of TFP growth, and he concluded that the shortfall in Britain could not be explained away by lower scope for catch-up or the structure of the economy although clearly very rapid TFP growth in countries like West Germany did reflect reconstruction, reductions in the inefficient allocation of resources and lower initial productivity (Temin 2002).

Britain did not achieve the transformation of industrial relations that happened elsewhere in Europe which implied a considerable growth penalty. When it is not possible to write binding contracts, either the absence of unions or strong corporatist trade unionism would have been preferable to the idiosyncratic British system. This can readily be understood in terms of the Eichengreen model or an extension of it to incorporate endogenous innovation. In Britain, it was generally not possible to make the corporatist deals to underpin investment and innovation because bargaining took place with multiple unions or with shop stewards representing subsets of a firm's workforce who could not internalize the benefits of wage restraint. This exposed sunk-cost investments to a 'hold-up' problem.[9] In the terminology of Hall and Soskice (2001), the UK was a 'liberal market economy', whereas a 'co-ordinated market economy' was the foundation of the Eichengreen model.

Failure successfully to reform industrial relations was a major shortcoming of British governments from the 1950s through the 1970s. However, throughout this period there were continual efforts to persuade organized labour to accept wage moderation in the interests not only of encouraging investment but even more to allow low levels of unemployment without inflation at a time when politicians believed that this was crucial to electoral success after the interwar trauma. At worst, this was tantamount to allowing a de facto trade union 'veto' on economic reforms. In any event, British supply-side policy, which was shaped by the post-war settlement instigated under Labour but largely accepted by the Conservatives, was unhelpful towards growth in several respects. These included a tax system characterized by very high marginal rates described by Tanzi (1969) as the least conducive to growth of any of the OECD countries in his study, missing out on benefits from trade liberalization by retaining 1930s protectionism into the 1960s (Oulton 1976), a misdirected technology policy that focused on invention rather than diffusion (Ergas 1987), an industrial policy that ineffectively subsidized physical investment (Sumner 1999) and slowed down structural change by protecting ailing industries through subsidies (Wren 1996) and tariffs (Greenaway and Milner 1994).

A key feature of the Golden Age British economy was the weakness of competition in product markets which had developed in the 1930s and intensified subsequently. Competition policy was largely ineffective, protectionism continued through the 1960s, and market power was substantial. The evidence on lack of competition and British productivity performance during the Golden Age both shows an adverse effect and also that this worked at least partly through industrial relations and managerial failure (Crafts 2012). Proponents of UK entry into the EEC were basically aware of these issues and saw the increase in competition that it would entail as an antidote to weak productivity performance (Williamson 1971).

The weakness of competition in product markets had potential implications for productivity performance through its interaction with institutions. First, Britain entered the post-war period with an idiosyncratic and unreformed system of industrial relations characterized by craft control, multi-unionism, legal immunities for trade unions and strong but decentralized collective bargaining reflected in increasing trade union density and the proliferation of shop stewards (Crouch 1993). These arrangements in conditions of full employment and weak competition gave trade unions bargaining power and rents to extract while exposing sunk-costs investment to 'hold-up' problems.

Second, corporate governance in post-war Britain was notable for a strongly increasing tendency to the separation of ownership and control, where dominant ownership interests became much less common, which also made it a real outlier within Europe. This reflected the demise of family control, the dilution of equity holdings through mergers, and a tax system which discouraged individual but favoured institutional investors (Cheffins 2008). Given that the market for corporate control through takeovers did not work effectively as a constraint (Cosh et al. 2008), the weakness of competition allowed considerable scope for managerial underperformance.

4   After the Golden Age, Before the Crisis

After the early 1970s, growth slowed down markedly right across Europe. The end of the Golden Age had a number of unavoidable aspects including the exhaustion of transitory components of fast growth such as post-war reconstruction, reduced opportunities to redeploy labour out of agriculture, narrowing the technology gap and diminishing returns to investment. Moreover, the USA itself experienced a productivity growth slowdown. All in all, the scope for catch-up growth was considerably reduced although by no means eliminated. There were big reductions in the contributions of capital deepening and, especially, TFP growth to labour productivity growth (Crafts and Toniolo 2008).

Although there were unavoidable reasons why productivity growth slowed down and European countries generally continued to narrow the productivity gap with the USA, it is clear that productivity performance could have been better after the Golden Age. What accounted for this undue slowdown in productivity growth? One very obvious point is that the fragility of the Eichengreen wage moderation/high investment equilibrium was revealed and it did not generally survive the turbulence of the 1970s, a time when union militancy and union power rose dramatically, as did labour's share of value added, and the rewards for patience fell in conditions of greater capital mobility, floating exchange rates and greater employment protection. At the same time, the corporatist model of economic growth was becoming less appropriate in economies which now needed to become more innovative and less imitative in achieving productivity growth, as Eichengreen (2007) himself has pointed out.

The period from the mid-1960s to the early 1980s was notable for a substantial increase in social protection. This took the place through a general expansion of social transfers financed to a considerable extent by 'distortionary' taxation and, in some countries, increases in employment protection. This can be seen as a legacy effect of corporatist social contracts interacting with the turbulent macroeconomic conditions of the 1970s. Financing this expansion of government outlays by a different tax mix would have been considerably better for growth (Johansson et al. 2008); the similar estimates of Kneller et al. (1999) indicate that the average 10% point increase in the share of direct tax revenues in GDP between 1965 and 1995 could have entailed a fall in the growth rate of about 1% point.

Moreover, high levels of employment protection (if enforced) slow down the process of creative destruction and the labour force adjustment that it entails. The difference in employment protection between France and the USA could account for a difference of 0.5% points per year in labour productivity growth in the 1980s and 1990s according to the estimates in Caballero et al. (2004). This is echoed in recent research. The process of creative destruction clearly works much less well in many European countries than in the USA, as is witnessed by processes of entry and exit of firms and the much stronger growth rate of successful American start-ups (Encaoua 2009). A corollary of this is that, on average, countries in the European Union, especially in Southern

Europe, are much inferior to the USA in shifting employment away from less productive towards more productive firms and this may account for as much as 20% points of the labour productivity gap between the EU and the USA. Barriers to entry and strict employment protection legislation disproportionately reduce the efficiency of labour allocation in high turnover and more innovative sectors (Andrews and Cingano 2014).

It is also relevant to look at the progress that European countries made in the upgrading needed as they moved closer to the frontier, in particular with regard to education and competition the areas stressed by Aghion and Howitt (2006). A measure of cognitive skills shown, based on test scores, correlates strongly with growth performance (Hanushek and Woessmann 2012), and it is striking that even the top European countries were well behind Japan and South Korea. Woessmann et al. (2007) show that the variance in outcomes in terms of cognitive skills is explained by the way the schooling system is organized rather than educational spending.

Strict product market regulation (PMR) has raised mark-ups and lowered entry rates, thus reducing competitive pressure on managers with adverse impacts on both investment and innovation (Griffith and Harrison 2004; Griffith et al. 2010), and reduced European TFP growth relative to the USA in the late twentieth century by around 0.75% points on average based on the estimates in Nicoletti and Scarpetta (2005). Similarly, in many European countries competition policy was much weaker than in the USA. The analysis in Buccirossi et al. (2013) found that this held back TFP growth.

The growth rate of real GDP per hour worked increased in the USA between 1973–1995, and between 1995–2007 from 1.27 per year to 2.21% per year. The acceleration in American productivity growth was underpinned by ICT. In contrast, as is reported in Table 1, the rate of labour productivity growth fell between these two periods in France, Germany and Italy and in each of these countries was lower than the USA after 1995 so that, rather than catching up, now they were falling behind. Growth accounting comparisons suggest that, on the whole, European countries were less successful in taking advantage of the opportunities of the ICT revolution with significantly adverse consequences for productivity performance relative to the USA.

Restrictive regulation of labour and product markets and, in some cases, shortfalls in human capital explain Europe's sluggish take-up of ICT (Cette and Lopez 2012).[10] This reflects shortcomings in domestic policy rather than at the EU level.

Italy has experienced major obstacles to the rapid diffusion of ICT for which it was not well positioned. The effective assimilation of this new technology has been hindered by the small size of firms, oppressive regulation, and shortfalls in human capital by comparison with the European leaders in the take-up of ICT, as microeconomic studies of Italian manufacturing confirm. The take-up of ICT has been strongly correlated with firm size and changes in organizational structure (Fabiani et al. 2005). Managerial selection processes which are insufficiently meritocratic have exacted a heavy cost in the context of the reorganization required to get the productivity pay-off from ICT (Pellegrino and Zingales 2014). Bugamelli and Pagano (2004) found that many firms appeared to be constrained in their ICT investment by the adjustment costs it entailed, especially if their workforce has relatively low levels of human capital. These reflect regulatory burdens which, because they are fixed costs, bear very heavily on the small- and medium-size firms that have been central to Italy's distinctive variety of capitalism.

More fundamentally, Italy's very weak growth performance since 1995 (c.f. Table 1) indicates an inability to make the reforms necessary to sustain catch-up growth in a close-to-frontier economy. In particular, this includes a failure to strengthen competition policy adequately (Buccirossi et al. 2013) and to improve the quality of Italian education (Bertola and Sestito 2013) and is underlined by Italy's dismal showing in the World Bank's *Doing Business* and *Governance Matters* rankings (Crafts and Magnani 2013). Resource misallocation has increased substantially since the mid-1990s and has undermined productivity growth (Calligaris et al. 2016). Italy epitomizes Europe's problem with expediting creative destruction; exit of low productivity firms is much too slow. Participation in the Single Market and joining the Euro were not adequate substitutes for an effective domestic supply-side policy.

From the 1970s through the 1990s, the impetus to economic growth from European integration continued, notably, through enlargements which expanded membership to 15 countries by 1995 and the inauguration of the European Single Market. The synthetic counterfactuals method suggests that the impact of EU accession on economic growth varied considerably across countries but was generally positive (c.f. Table 3) and, in some cases, provided a significant boost to growth. Harrison et al. (1994), working with a CGE model that allows for increasing returns in some sectors, changes in price-cost markups and capital stock adjustment projected that competition and scale effects resulting from the Single Market would raise EU GDP by 0.7% and the total impact on EU GDP of the Single Market would be 2.6%.[11] Ex-post studies have suggested similar effects; for example, Ilzkovitz et al. (2007) estimated GDP had been raised by 2.2% by 2006. Establishing a true Single Market in services could probably double this impact by reducing barriers to entry but governments still have considerable discretion to maintain these barriers notwithstanding the Services Directive (Badinger and Maydell 2009). A recent estimate is that this implementation of this directive has so far raised EU GDP by about 0.8% whereas full implementation would triple this (Monteagudo et al. 2012).[12]

An important aspect of regional trade agreements like the Single Market is that they reduce non-tariff barriers to trade, for example, from regulatory divergence, between trading partners and provide the underpinning for increasingly complex supply chains with stages of production situated in several different locations (Baldwin 2012). In the EU, this is reflected in high shares of value added accruing from producers in other

Table 3 Post-accession differences between level of actual and synthetic GDP per person (%)

	After 5 years	After 10 years	Total
Denmark	10.3	14.3	23.9
Ireland	5.2	9.4	48.9
United Kingdom	4.8	8.6	23.7
Greece	−11.6	−17.3	−19.8
Portugal	11.7	16.5	18.4
Spain	9.3	13.7	19.8
Austria	4.5	6.4	7.2
Finland	2.2	4.0	4.4
Sweden	0.8	2.4	3.2

Source Campos et al. (2014)

EU countries in the output of final manufactures—in over half of EU countries this fraction was over 20% in 2008 (Los et al. 2015).

The impetus from European integration in this period also came from European Monetary Union. The initial impact on growth was probably positive but much less dramatic than early estimates suggested. The currency union effect on trade volumes was initially thought to be very large but better econometrics and the opportunity to examine the actual impact of EMU now suggests that trade volumes probably were only 'mildly stimulated' (Glick and Rose 2015) with the implication that any trade effect on GDP is likely to have been, at best, modest.[13] Clearly, the Eurozone crisis has entailed large GDP losses and may even have adversely affected trend growth so that the recent contribution of European economic integration to medium-term growth performance may even have been negative.[14]

However, it is important not to forget the one very obvious success story from the late twentieth century. It was about 15 years after acceding to the EU that Irish economic growth took off into very rapid (and belated) catch-up growth during its Celtic Tiger phase which lasted untill the early twenty-first century (c.f. Table 1). This picture is reflected in Table 3 which suggests that Ireland dramatically outperformed the synthetic counterfactual economy after the first 10 years. This success clearly was predicated on being within the EU but also was based on the development of appropriate supply-side policies to exploit this opportunity.

A central aspect of the Celtic Tiger economy was the prominence of foreign direct investment (FDI). 'Export-platform' FDI transformed Ireland's revealed comparative advantage, dominated production in high-skill and knowledge-intensive sectors, and by 2000 accounted for almost half of manufacturing employment and 80% of manufacturing exports (Barry 2004). Rapid TFP growth was underpinned by a large ICT production sector based on FDI. Ireland developed a sophisticated industrial policy to select projects for financial support through the Industrial Development Agency and made investments in telecommunications and college education that were conducive to FDI (Buckley and Ruane 2006). Nevertheless, the most important factor in Ireland's success in attracting FDI was the combination of its corporate tax regime together with EU membership (Slaughter 2003).[15] As trade costs fell, the impact of low taxes on FDI appears to have been accentuated significantly, and their relative importance for location compared with proximity to demand increased (Romalis 2007).

EU membership was a necessary but not sufficient condition for the Irish growth model. Both prior to the late 1980s and from the turn of the twenty-first century to the crisis, Irish performance was mediocre at best, reflecting domestic policy errors. Ireland had a malfunctioning labour market and was in macroeconomic disarray prior to a successful stabilization in the late 1980s. Successful economic reform subsequently delivered rapid growth in employment from a combination of large reductions in unemployment, a reversal of net migration flows, and rising labour force participation, especially of women. The NAIRU fell considerably in the context of wage moderation under the auspices of social partnership and increases in human capital per worker (Bergin and Kearney 2004; Walsh 2004). An elastic labour supply underpinned investment and productivity growth (Barry 2002). However, post-2000 Irish TFP growth can only be described as very disappointing. Beyond reduced scope for catch-up, the reasons for this include a reduced contribution from ICT production, a large shift towards construction and non-market services which together accounted for 35.2% of employment by 2007, and excessive capital deepening which contributed to negative TFP growth in manufacturing.[16] The first was largely unavoidable as the weight of the ICT sector declined but the other two reflected policy errors. The loss of international competitiveness, which was a big factor in a major reduction in export growth (Nkusu 2013) and held back output and employment growth in manufacturing, reflected pro-cyclical fiscal policy and, in particular, growth of public consumption (Lane 2009). The construction boom was fuelled by an explosion of mortgages and loans to property development (Whelan 2014).

The post-Golden Age reaction to poor economic performance in the UK was Thatcherism. In many respects, this did represent a sharp break with the earlier post-war period after 1979 and this was certainly true of supply-side policies relevant to growth performance. Reforms of fiscal policy were made including the restructuring of taxation by increasing VAT while reducing income tax rates and to restrain the growth of public expenditure notably by indexing transfer payments to prices rather than wages while aiming to restore a balanced budget. Industrial policy was downsized as subsidies were cut and privatization of state-owned businesses was embraced while deregulation, including most notably of financial markets with 'Big Bang' in 1986, was promoted. Legal reforms of industrial relations further reduced trade union bargaining power which had initially been undermined by rising unemployment. In general, these changes were accepted rather than reversed by Labour after 1997.

Thatcherism was a partial solution to the problems which led to underperformance in the Golden Age, in particular, those which had arisen from weak competition. The reforms encouraged the effective diffusion of new technology rather than greater invention and worked more through reducing inefficiency than promoting investment-led growth. Nevertheless, under the auspices of 'Thatcher and Sons' relative productivity performance improved and labour productivity growth compared favourably with that of other large European countries after the mid-1990s (c.f. Table 1). Clearly, there have been continuing weaknesses in supply-side policy (Crafts 2015). The most obvious is in innovation policy which is reflected in a low level of R & D (Frontier Economics 2014) but education, infrastructure (LSE Growth Commission 2013), land-use planning regulation (Cheshire and Hilber 2008) and the tax system (Mirrlees et al. 2011) also give significant cause for concern while British capital markets remain notably short-termist with a bias against long-term investment (Davies et al. 2014). Addressing these issues well has generally been 'too difficult' politically even though the 'trade-union veto' has long gone.

Before, during and after Thatcher, government policy moved in the direction of increasing competition in product markets. In particular, protectionism was discarded with liberalization through GATT negotiations, entry into the European Community in 1973, the retreat from industrial subsidies and foreign exchange controls in the Thatcher years, and the implementation of the European Single Market legislation in the 1990s. Trade liberalization in its various guises reduced price-cost margins (Hitiris 1978; Griffith 2001). The average effective rate of protection fell from 9.3% in 1968 to 4.7% in 1979, and 1.2% in 1986 (Ennew et al. 1990), subsidies were reduced from £9bn (at 1980 prices) in 1969 to £5bn In 1979 and £0.3bn in 1990 (Wren 1996), and import penetration in manufacturing rose from 20.8% in 1970 to 40.8% by 2000. The downward trend in the markup from the 1970s onwards appears to have intensified further after the early 1990s (Macallan et al. 2008). Anti-trust policy was notably strengthened by the Competition Act of 1998 and the Enterprise Act of 2003 which increased the independence of the competition authorities, removed the old 'public-interest' defence, and introduced criminal penalties for running cartels.

If accession to the EU raised UK GDP by around 8% (c.f. Sect. 2 above), then a major component of this must have come from increased competition in product markets. A computable general equilibrium (CGE) exercise using a model incorporating imperfect competition and scale economies found that the static effects of reductions in market power would have contributed a welfare gain equivalent to 2.1% of GDP (Gasiorek et al. 2002). However, in addition there were favourable impacts on productivity performance consequent on stronger competition and entry threats in product markets. A difference-in-differences analysis found that there was a substantial boost to productivity in sectors which experienced a large reduction in protection (Broadberry and Crafts 2011).[17] Reductions in market power effectively addressed long-standing obstacles to productivity performance from weak management and industrial relations problems in British firms. Nickell et al. (1997) estimated that, for firms without a dominant external shareholder (the norm for big British firms at this time), a reduction in supernormal profits from 15 to 5% of value added would raise TFP growth by 1% point. Increases in competition resulting from the European Single Market raised both the level and growth rate of TFP in plants which were part of multi-plant firms and thus most prone to agency problems (Griffith 2001). The 1980s saw a surge in productivity growth in unionized firms as organizational change took place under pressure of competition (Machin and Wadhwani 1989) and derecognition of unions in the context of increases in foreign competition had a strong effect on productivity growth by the late 1980s (Gregg et al. 1993). This goes a long way to explain the boost to growth found by Campos et al. (2014) or the higher income level predicted by the Feyrer (2009) method.[18]

Three important points that emerge from this review deserve to be highlighted. First, although European economic integration has played a useful role, it has generally been a junior partner in promoting economic growth compared with other influences on productivity performance. Second, in countries where economic growth has been lacklustre in recent times and catch-up of the USA has stalled, there are many ways to address this by improving supply-side policy.[19] The constraints on doing so lie primarily in domestic politics not in restrictions imposed by membership of the European Union. Third, it should be recognized that in the context of the 1970s and early 1980s joining the EU was an integral part of the Thatcher reform programme through its positive effects on competition, as is reflected in strong British support for the legislation to establish the European Single Market.

5 Implications of Brexit

The general assumption in studies of the economic impact of Brexit is that it will entail an increase in trade costs for the UK. In turn, this will imply a reduction in trade volumes and, accordingly, an adverse impact on productivity. The magnitudes of these effects depend on the details of the new trading arrangements that are assumed to supersede EU membership and on model specifications. Two points of clarification are useful at this point. First, it should be recognized that the most important trade costs these days are imposed not by tariffs but by non-tariff measures such as regulations and border costs (Anderson and van Wincoop 2004).[20] Outside the EU Single Market, the UK would potentially be exposed to such costs as well as the common external tariff on trade with the EU. If the UK is outside the customs union, it will also face significant compliance costs from implementing rules-of-origin legislation (CEPR 2013). Second, the UK could seek to negotiate a trade agreement to continue to participate in the Single Market perhaps on a similar basis to Norway, but this would almost certainly entail continuing to pay some of the membership fee in terms of a budgetary contribution together with acceptance of some regulations and, crucially, free movement of people. If establishing control over migration is the reason for Brexit, then that means accepting trade costs which accrue from being outside the Single Market.

Several papers have recently estimated the long-term economic impact of Brexit in terms of a level effect on GDP, and their results are summarized in Table 4. The methodology is typically based on a gravity model estimate of the trade effects of various alternatives to EU membership ranging from remaining in the Single Market à la Norway to trade on an MFN basis as a WTO member. The trade effect is then converted into an impact on GDP using Feyrer's elasticity to obtain the implications for productivity (LSE) or a macroeconomic model (NIESR) or a combination of the two (HMT). NIESR's basic modelling assumes no impact via productivity but an effect of this kind is added in the case of the WTO[a] estimates. Not surprisingly, the impacts depend on what replaces EU membership with the smallest losses accruing if the UK stays in the Single Market and the largest in the absence of new trade agreements.[21] In every case, GDP is reduced by Brexit and by a quite significant amount once productivity losses are taken into account. Even though tariff levels are lower than when the UK was previously outside the EU, much of the gains that EU membership has brought might be lost. On these estimates, the benefit-cost ratio of Brexit does not look promising—this is a very expensive way to save a net budgetary contribution of about 0.5% of GDP.

Some caveats to these conclusions should be noted. First, the gravity-model evidence does not explicitly cover the case of a former EU member which means that the estimated impact on trade of leaving the EU is not known and there is an element of guesswork in implementing a calculation similar to that of footnote 3 above. History does seem to influence trade volumes and, implicitly, trade costs (Eichengreen and Irwin 1998). This suggests that the adverse impact on trade may be lower than the conventional calculations assume.[22] Second, the post-entry trade effect on productivity that the UK experienced in the 1970s and 1980s came largely from increased competition at a time when this addressed a major weakness in supply-side policy. Brexit will probably not have an equal and opposite effect. The UK has addressed some of its problems of corporate governance and industrial relations, and it has a much more effective competition policy regime. On the eve of the UK's entry into the EU, UK (EU) tariffs on manufactures averaged 10% (8%) compared with an average for the common external tariff at 4% today. It is possible that Brexit could be accompanied by a move to unilateral free trade as some of its proponents would advocate (Minford 2015). So, there must be some doubt about the 'dynamic effects' assumed in the studies summarized in Table 4.

An alternative approach explicitly models the static trade effects and considers the 'membership fee' implications of various permutations of Brexit, although without considering the longer term effects that might accrue through capital stock adjustments or TFP impacts. Table 5 sets out some of these estimates. Neither of these studies covers every component of the possible costs and benefits and, of course, different assumptions and modelling techniques have been employed. Nevertheless, some points emerge quite strongly.

First, it is potentially quite costly to leave the EU without negotiating a new trade agreement and taking positive action to reduce barriers to non-EU trade and to deregulate. Here, reducing the membership fee by about 0.5% of GDP through ending fiscal transfers runs the risk of reducing the level of GDP by as much as 2.75% as the economy faces increased tariff and non-tariff barriers to trade. The costs might be more serious if, over time, regulatory divergence between the UK and the EU increases and/or the UK misses out on future deepening of economic integration inside the EU. Conceivably, this might cost a further 2.0% of GDP each year.

Second, proactive use of the freedom to change policy outside the EU could deliver significant benefits that might partly offset the initial costs

Table 4 Recent estimates of the long-term impact of Brexit (%)

	LSE	HMT			NIESR			
		EEA	FTA	WTO	EEA	FTA	WTO	WTO[a]
Trade	−12.6	−9.0	−16.5	−20.5	−13.5	−15.5	−25.0	−22.0
GDP	−7.9	−3.8	−6.2	−7.5	−1.8	−2.1	−3.2	−7.8

Notes Original estimates in Dingra et al. (2016), HM Treasury (2016) and Ebell and Warren (2016). The NIESR estimates do not allow for 'dynamic effects' on productivity except in the column labelled WTO[a]. Source adapted from Ebell and Warren (2016)

of Brexit. These might arise firstly from abolishing regulations relating to social issues, employment, health and safety, environment and climate change. One estimate of the maximum feasible annual gain is 1.3% of GDP (Booth et al. (2015). In addition, aggressive liberalization of non-EU trade whether by unilateral measures or trade agreements could increase GDP by another 0.75% so that the initial annual GDP loss might be reduced to about 0.7% of GDP.[23]

Third, a better version of Brexit from a purely economic perspective would be to negotiate a trade agreement with the EU that would retain access to the Single Market on EEA terms. This would significantly reduce the losses from trade costs on EU trade but would, on the other hand, probably mean accepting a significant budgetary contribution and constraints on deregulation. Booth et al. (2015) estimate that, if supplemented by freer non-EU trade and feasible deregulation, a permutation along these lines could even produce an overall positive outcome of as much as 1% to GDP annually. However, if this package is only available with free movement of people, it might not be in the politically feasible set on exit.

An important omission from Table 5 is that it does not take account of switching costs. The most important of these would come through increased uncertainty which could be expected to reduce investment. Given the difficulty in establishing what Brexit will actually entail, this could be quite prolonged. Over an initial period of 3 years this might cost around 3% of GDP (Emmerson et al. 2016). It is also worth noting that these two studies do not take into account the possibility that regulation has economic impacts going beyond compliance costs.

Regulations which affect decisions to invest or innovate can impair productivity performance and thus impose welfare losses far in excess of compliance costs (Crafts 2006). In this regard, however, it should be recognized that the UK has persistently been able to maintain very light levels of regulation in terms of key OECD indicators such as PMR and EPL for which high scores have been shown to have significant detrimental effects (Barnes et al. 2011). In 2013, the UK had a PMR score of 1.09 and an EPL score of 1.12, the second and third lowest in the OECD, respectively. Land-use planning regulations do have seriously adverse implications for productivity but they result from domestic

Table 5 Welfare effects of Brexit (%GDP)

	Dingra et al. (1)	Booth et al. (1)	Dingra et al. (2)	Booth et al. (2)
Fiscal transfers	+0.31	+0.53	+0.09	+0.22
Regulation				+0.7 to +1.3
Tariff barriers to EU trade	−0.14	−0.95	+0.00	
Non-tariff barriers to EU trade: initial	−0.73	−1.81	−0.34	−1.03
Non-tariff barriers to EU trade: future	−2.05		−1.03	
Reduced barriers to non-EU trade			+0.30	+0.75
Total	−2.61	−2.23	−0.98	+0.64 to +1.24

Notes Dingra et al. (1) and Booth et al. (1) assume UK exits single market; Dingra et al. (2) and Booth et al. (2) assume that UK has a Norway-type relationship with the single market and pays fiscal transfers to ensure market access.
Future costs of non-tariff barriers to EU trade in Dingra et al. accrue from missing out on benefits of further development of EU single market. I have divided the NTB costs into 'initial' and 'future' based on the relative proportions reported in an earlier version of this paper. *Sources* Booth et al. (2015) and Dingra et al. (2016)

policymaking rather than an EU directive. In this vein, it is noticeable that the regulations which it may be politically feasible to remove in the event of Brexit do not include anything which might make a significant difference to productivity performance (Booth et al. 2015).[24]

If Brexit were necessary to allow radical changes to policies which affect the growth rate, then an economic case in favour might be made. Is this an omission in the studies considered in Tables 4 and 5? After all, as was noted earlier, there is much that could be done to improve UK supply-side policy, for example, in the areas of education, infrastructure, innovation and the tax system. However, reforms are not precluded by EU membership. The obstacles to better policy lie in Westminster not Brussels and are related to British politics rather than constraints imposed by the EU. Whereas 40 years ago entry into the EU did help to improve supply-side policy by strengthening competition, today there is no problem area to which Brexit is required to provide an answer.

6   Conclusions

The EU has been a highly successful trade agreement and has raised trade volumes substantially. In turn, this has raised income levels in member countries. Reductions in trade costs have had a transitory impact on the growth rate as income levels adjusted but have probably not had a lasting impact on the trend rate of growth. The stimulus provided by European integration has been significant but, even so, it has been a junior partner to other sources of growth. The success or failure of EU member countries in achieving economic growth has depended primarily on their design and re-design of supply-side policies as the cases of Ireland and Italy clearly demonstrate.

Joining the EU had a positive on the level of GDP in the UK. A reasonable estimate is that the impact was in excess of 8% and that this was several times the annual membership fee which the UK had to pay through budgetary transfers and the costs of unwanted regulation. A key aspect of accession to the EU was that it contributed significantly to strengthening competition at a time when this was important in addressing management and industrial relations problems that were undermining UK productivity performance. This was not an alternative to but an integral part of Thatcherism as a response to relative economic decline.

Brexit will probably be quite costly in terms of an adverse levels effect on UK GDP although the magnitude of this impact is debatable and depends on the alternative trade agreements that are negotiated. A radical reform of supply-side policy could improve UK growth performance but this is not prevented by EU membership. In particular, there is no reason to believe that leaving the EU will lead to a bonfire of growth-inhibiting regulations.

Notes

1. For example, the model proposed by Fernald and Jones (2014) and Jones (2002) to interpret long-run American growth performance and prospects has this property.
2. The estimated magnitudes are sensitive to precise specification but the EU effect is always large.
3. Calculated based on the estimated coefficients in Baier et al. (2008, Table 6, column 3). Both countries in the EU increases trade by $e^{0.54}-1$ but one country in EU and the other in EFTA by $e^{0.14}-1$. If a country stays outside the EU, its trade with EU members is reduced by $(e^{0.14}-e^{0.54})/e^{0.54} = 33.0\%$.
4. For example, Baldwin (1989) argued that the Cecchini Report could be massively underestimating the impact of the European Single Market because the static efficiency gain that it expected would raise the output to capital ratio, and hence for any given savings rate the growth of the capital stock. In a constant returns setting, this could permanently raise the growth rate of GDP perhaps by as much as 0.9% points per year. Sadly, this does not seem to have been the outcome.
5. It seems fair to suppose that the reliability of these estimates decreases as the length of the post-accession period increases.
6. An estimated relationship of the effect of greater trade exposure on income reported by Frankel and Romer (1999) was used by HM Treasury in its analysis of the impact of the UK adopting the Euro, see below.
7. In common with the mainstream economics literature, this estimate of the 'membership fee' assumes that migration has not entailed net costs, see Crafts (2016).
8. For Italy, this may have contributed as much as 1.7% points per year to Golden Age growth based on the decomposition proposed by Broadberry (1998). In France and West Germany, the contributions were smaller (0.52 and 0.77% points, respectively) but still significant (Crafts and Toniolo 2008).
9. In the endogenous innovation framework, the 'hold-up' arises when after a successful innovation workers use their bargaining power to extract a share of the profits. This reduces the incentive to innovate and thus the rate of growth. The more unions are involved in the bargaining, the more profits are reduced. The problem can be eliminated if a

binding contract prevents renegotiation or there is no union or if a cooperative equilibrium is achieved with a single union. For a formal model and empirical evidence, see Bean and Crafts (1996).

10. The main impact of ICT on economic growth comes through its use as a new form of capital equipment rather than through TFP growth in the production of ICT equipment. This is because users get the benefit of technological progress through lower prices and as prices fall more of this type of capital is installed. In a country with no ICT production, adapting the neoclassical growth model to embody a production function with two types of capital (ICT capital and other capital) shows that the steady state rate of growth will be TFP growth divided by labour's share of income plus an additional term which depends on the rate of real price decline for ICT capital multiplied by the share of ICT capital in national income (Oulton 2012). The ICT capital deepening contribution to labour productivity growth during 1995–2007 in France, Germany and Italy was 0.3, 0.5 and 0.2% per year, respectively, compared with 0.9% in the USA (Van Ark 2011).

11. This is well below the optimistic projections of the Cecchini Report issued by the European Commission which projected 4.8–6.4% of GDP before any impact from capital stock adjustment but is in line with other academic ex-ante studies (Badinger and Breuss 2011, Table 14.3).

12. This does not include any impact from capital stock adjustment.

13. Glick and Rose (2015) conclude that results on the trade effects of the Euro are very sensitive to econometric methodology and that all estimates have to be treated with great caution.

14. A recent review of potential output growth by Havik et al. (2014) concluded that trend growth is now much lower than pre-crisis (1.1% per year vs. 2.0% per year for the EA12). This decline in trend GDP growth is mainly driven by reduced labour productivity growth which in turn reflects weaker trend TFP growth.

15. It is clear from the literature that the semi-elasticity of FDI with respect to the corporate tax rate is quite high, perhaps of the order of −2.5 or even −3.5 (OECD 2007). At the start of the Celtic Tiger period, the Irish tax rate for manufacturing FDI was easily the lowest in Europe and a study by Gropp and Kostial (2000) suggested that the stock of American manufacturing investment in Ireland was about 70% higher than if Ireland had had a tax rate equivalent to the next lowest in the EU.

16. The data in EUKLEMS show that in non-ICT manufacturing the capital to labour ratio grew at 9.6% per year during 2001–2007 while TFP growth averaged −1.3% per year.
17. Sectors which experienced a reduction of 10% points or more in the effective rate of protection saw an additional increase of 1.4% points in the rate of labour productivity growth in 1979–1986 over 1968–1979.
18. It also implies that Williamson (1971) was basically right in his assessment of the possibility of benefits from entry into the EEC but nevertheless significantly underestimated their magnitude.
19. See, for example, the analyses in Barnes et al. (2011) and Varga and in't Veld (2014) for quantification of the possible effects of a selection of reforms.
20. For example, the USA faces non-tariff barriers equivalent to a tariff of 14.7% on its exports to the EU (Dingra et al. 2016).
21. This matches the evidence from gravity models of the relative success of the EU and other trade agreements in increasing trade volumes.
22. An interesting example is the ending in 1979 of the long-standing currency union between Ireland and the UK. Econometric analysis suggests that this had no effect at all on trade (Thom and Walsh 2002) even though, on balance, the literature predicts that a significant reduction was to be expected.
23. Minford (2015) argues that the gains from moving to unilateral free trade would be 4% of GDP. This does not seem to be a credible estimate since it is based on modelling techniques which are inconsistent with the trade-creating impact of the EU and the role of distance in trade; see Sampson et al. (2016).
24. The most likely candidates are in the area of social employment and climate change laws.

References

Aghion, P., & Howitt, P. (2006). Appropriate growth theory: A unifying framework. *Journal of the European Economic Association, 4,* 269–314.
Anderson, J. E., & van Wincoop, E. (2004). Trade costs. *Journal of Economic Literature, 42,* 691–751.
Andrews, D., & Cingano, F. (2014). Public policy and resource allocation: Evidence from firms in OECD countries. *Economic Policy, 78,* 253–296.

Badinger, H. (2005). Growth effects of economic integration: Evidence from the EU member states. *Review of World Economics, 141,* 50–78.

Badinger, H., & Breuss, F. (2011). The quantitative effects of European post-war economic integration. In M. Jovanovic (Ed.), *International handbook on the economics of integration* (pp. 285–315). Cheltenham: Edward Elgar.

Badinger, H., & Maydell, N. (2009). Legal and economic issues in completing the EU internal market for services: An interdisciplinary perspective. *Journal of Common Market Studies, 47,* 693–717.

Baier, S. L., Bergstrand, J. H., Egger, P., & McLaughlin, P. A. (2008). Do economic integration agreements actually work? Issues in understanding the causes and consequences of the growth of regionalism. *The World Economy, 31,* 461–497.

Balassa, B. (1961). *The theory of economic integration.* Homewood, IL: Irwin.

Baldwin, R. E. (1989). The growth effects of 1992. *Economic Policy, 9,* 248–281.

Baldwin, R. E. (2012). *Global supply chains: Why they emerged, why they matter, and where they are going* (CEPR Discussion Paper No. 9103).

Bank of England. (2015). *EU membership and the Bank of England.* www.bankofengland.co.uk/publications/Documents/speeches/2015/euboe211015.pdf.

Barnes, S., Bouis, R., Briard, P., Dougherty, S., & Eris, M. (2011). *The GDP impact of reform: A simple simulation framework* (OECD Economics Department Working Paper No. 834).

Barry, F. (2002). The Celtic tiger era: Delayed convergence or regional boom? *Quarterly Economic Commentary, 21,* 84–91.

Barry, F. (2004). Export-platform foreign direct investment: The Irish experience. *EIB Papers, 9*(2), 9–37.

Bayoumi, T., & Eichengreen, B. (1995). *Is regionalism simply a diversion? Evidence from the evolution of the EC and EFTA* (NBER Working Paper No. 5283).

Bean, C., & Crafts, N. (1996). British economic growth since 1945: Relative economic decline and renaissance? In N. Crafts & G. Toniolo (Eds.), *Economic growth in Europe since 1945* (pp. 131–172). Cambridge: Cambridge University Press.

Bergin, A., & Kearney, I. (2004). *Human capital, the labour market and productivity growth in Ireland* (ESRI Working Paper No. 158).

Bertola, G., & Sestito, P. (2013). Human capital. In G. Toniolo (Ed.), *The Oxford handbook of the italian economy since unification* (pp. 249–270). Oxford: Oxford University Press.

Booth, S., Howarth, C., Persson, M., Ruparel, R., & Swidlicki, P. (2015). *What if...? The consequences, challenges and opportunities facing Britain outside the EU*. London: Open Europe.

Broadberry, S. N. (1998). How did the United States and Germany overtake Britain? A sectoral analysis of comparative productivity levels, 1870–1990. *Journal of Economic History, 58,* 375–407.

Broadberry, S., & Crafts, N. (2011). Openness, protectionism and Britain's productivity performance over the long run. In G. Wood, T. C. Mills, & N. Crafts (Eds.), *Monetary and banking history: Essays in honour of forest capie* (pp. 254–286). Abingdon: Routledge.

Buccirossi, P., Clari, L., Duso, T., Spagnolo, G., & Vitale, C. (2013). Competition policy and economic growth: An empirical assessment. *Review of Economics and Statistics, 95,* 1324–1336.

Buckley, P., & Ruane, F. (2006). Foreign direct investment in Ireland: Policy implications for emerging economies. *The World Economy, 29,* 1611–1628.

Bugamelli, M., & Pagano, P. (2004). Barriers to investment in ICT. *Applied Economics, 36,* 2275–2286.

Caballero, R., Cowan, K., Engel, E., & Micco, A. (2004). *Effective labor regulation and microeconomic flexibility* (NBER Working Paper No. 10744).

Calligaris, S., Del Gatto, M., Hassan, F., Ottaviano, G. I. P., & Schivardi, F. (2016). *Italy's productivity conundrum* (European Economy Discussion Paper 030).

Campos, N. F., Coricelli, F., & Moretti, L. (2014). *Economic growth and political integration: Estimating the benefits from membership of the European Union using the synthetic counterfactuals method* (CEPR Discussion Paper No. 9968).

CEPR. (2013). *Trade and investment balance of competence review*. London.

Cette, G., & Lopez, J. (2012). ICT demand behaviour: An international comparison. *Economics of Innovation and New Technology, 21,* 397–410.

Cheffins, B. R. (2008). *Corporate ownership and control: British business transformed*. Oxford: Oxford University Press.

Cheshire, P. C., & Hilber, C. A. L. (2008). Office space supply restrictions in Britain: The political economy of market revenge. *Economic Journal, 118,* F185–F221.

Cosh, A. D., Guest, P., & Hughes, A. (2008). UK corporate governance and takeover performance. In K. Gugler & B. B. Yurtoglu (Eds.), *The economics of corporate governance and mergers* (pp. 226–261). Cheltenham: Edward Elgar.

Crafts, N. (2006). Regulation and productivity performance. *Oxford Review of Economic Policy, 22,* 186–202.

Crafts, N. (2012). British relative economic decline revisited: The role of competition. *Explorations in Economic History, 49,* 17–29.

Crafts, N. (2014). Economic growth during the long twentieth century. In R. Floud, J. Humphries, & P. Johnson (Eds.), *The Cambridge economic history of modern Britain* (Vol. 2, pp. 26–59). Cambridge: Cambridge University Press.

Crafts, N. (2015). UK economic growth since 2010: Is it as bad as it seems? *National Institute Economic Review, 231,* R17–R29.

Crafts, N. (2016). *The growth effects of EU membership for the UK: A review of the evidence* (University of Warwick CAGE Working Paper No. 280).

Crafts, N., & Magnani, M. (2013). The golden age and the second globalization in Italy. In G. Toniolo (Ed.), *The Oxford handbook of the Italian economy since unification* (pp. 69–107). Oxford: Oxford University Press.

Crafts, N., & Toniolo, G. (2008). *European economic growth, 1950–2005: An Overview* (CEPR Discussion Paper No. 6863).

Crouch, C. (1993). *Industrial relations and european state traditions.* Oxford: Clarendon Press.

Davies, R., Haldane, A. G., Nielsen, M., & Pezzini, S. (2014). Measuring the costs of short-termism. *Journal of Financial Stability, 12,* 16–25.

Dingra, S., Huang, H., Ottaviano, G., Pessoa, J. P., Sampson, T., & van Reenen, J. (2016). *The costs and benefits of leaving the EU.* London: London School of Economics.

Ebell, M., & Warren, J. (2016). The long-term economic impact of leaving the EU. *National Institute Economic Review, 236,* 121–138.

Eichengreen, B. (1993). *Reconstructing Europe's trade and payments.* Manchester: Manchester University Press.

Eichengreen, B. (2007). *The European economy since 1945.* Princeton: Princeton University Press.

Eichengreen, B., & Boltho, A. (2008). *The economic impact of European integration* (CEPR Discussion Paper No. 6820).

Eichengreen, B., & Irwin, D. A. (1998). The role of history in bilateral trade flows. In J. A. Frankel (Ed.), *The regionalization of the world economy* (pp. 33–62). Chicago: University of Chicago Press.

Emmerson, C., Johnson, P., Mitchell, I., & Phillips, D. (2016). *Brexit and the UK's public finances.* London: Institute for Fiscal Studies.

Encaoua, D. (2009). Nature of the European technology gap: Creative destruction or industrial policy? In D. Foray (Ed.), *The new economics of technology policy* (pp. 281–314). Cheltenham: Edward Elgar.

Ennew, C., Greenaway, D., & Reed, G. (1990). Further evidence on effective tariffs and effective protection in the UK. *Oxford Bulletin of Economics and Statistics, 52,* 69–78.

Ergas, H. (1987). Does technology policy matter? In B. R. Guile & H. Brooks (Eds.), *Technology and global industry* (pp. 191–245). Washington, DC: National Academy Press.

Estevadeordal, A., & Taylor, A. (2013). Is the Washington consensus dead? Growth, openness and the great liberalization, 1970s–2000s. *Review of Economics and Statistics, 95,* 1669–1690.

Fabiani, S., Schivardi, F., & Trento, S. (2005). ICT adoption in Italian manufacturing: Firm-level evidence. *Industrial and Corporate Change, 14,* 225–249.

Fernald, J. G., & Jones, C. I. (2014). The future of US economic growth. *American Economic Review Papers and Proceedings, 104,* 44–49.

Feyrer, J. (2009). *Trade and income: Exploiting time series in geography* (NBER Working Paper No. 14910).

Frankel, J. A., & Romer, D. (1999). Does trade cause growth? *American Economic Review, 89,* 379–399.

Frontier Economics. (2014). *Rates of return to investment in science and innovation.* London: Frontier Economics.

Gasiorek, M., Smith, A., & Venables, A. J. (2002). The accession of the UK to the EC: A welfare analysis. *Journal of Common Market Studies, 40,* 425–447.

Gilmore, O. (2009). *Corporatism and growth: Testing the Eichengreen hypothesis.* MSc. Dissertation, University of Warwick.

Glick, R., & Rose, A. (2015). *Currency unions and trade: A post-EMU Mea Culpa* (NBER Working Paper No. 21535).

Greenaway, D., & Milner, C. (1994). Determinants of the inter-industry structure of protection in the UK. *Oxford Bulletin of Economics and Statistics, 53,* 265–279.

Gregg, P., Machin, S., & Metcalf, D. (1993). Signals and cycles: Productivity growth and change in union status in British companies, 1984–1989. *Economic Journal, 103,* 894–907.

Griffith, R. (2001). *Product market competition, efficiency and agency costs: An empirical analysis* (Working Paper No. 01/12). Institute for Fiscal Studies.

Griffith, R., & Harrison, R. (2004). *The link between product market regulation and macroeconomic performance* (European Commission Economic Papers No. 209).

Griffith, R., Harrison, R., & Simpson, H. (2010). Product market reform and innovation in the EU. *Scandinavian Journal of Economics, 112,* 389–415.

Gropp, R., & Kostial, K. (2000). *The disappearing tax base: Is FDI eroding corporate income taxes?* (IMF Working Paper No. 00/173).

Hall, P. A., & Soskice, D. (2001). An introduction to varieties of capitalism. In P. A. Hall & D. Soskice (Eds.), *Varieties of capitalism* (pp. 1–68). Oxford: Oxford University Press.

Hanushek, E. A., & Woessmann, L. (2012). Do better schools lead to more growth? Cognitive skills, economic outcomes, and education. *Journal of Economic Growth, 17,* 267–321.

Harrison, G., Rutherford, T., & Tarr, D. (1994). *Product standards, imperfect competition, and completion of the market in the European union* (World Bank Policy Research Working Paper No. 1293).

Havik, K., McMorrow, K., Orlandi, F., Planas, C., Raciborski, R., Röger, W., Rossi, A., Thum-Thysen, A., & Vandermeulen, V. (2014). *The production function methodology for calculating potential growth rates and output gaps* (European Economy Economic Papers No. 535).

Hitiris, T. (1978). Effective protection and economic performance in UK manufacturing industry, 1963 and 1968. *Economic Journal, 88,* 107–120.

HM Treasury (2016). *HM treasury analysis: The long-term economic impact of EU membership and the alternatives.* Cm 9250.

Ilzkovitz, F., Dierx, A., Kovacs, V., & Sousa, N. (2007). *Steps towards a deeper economic integration: The internal market in the 21st century* (European Economy Economic Papers No. 271).

Janossy, F. (1969). *The end of the economic miracle.* White Plains, NY.: IASP.

Jerzmanowski, M. (2007). Total factor productivity differences: Appropriate technology vs. efficiency. *European Economic Review, 51,* 2080–2110.

Johansson, A., Heady, C., Arnold, J., Brys, B., & Vartia, L. (2008). *Taxation and economic growth* (OECD Economics Department Working Paper No. 620).

Jones, C. I. (2002). Sources of U.S. economic growth in a world of ideas. *American Economic Review, 92,* 220–239.

Kneller, R., Bleaney, M., & Gemmell, N. (1999). Fiscal policy and growth: Evidence from OECD countries. *Journal of Public Economics, 74,* 171–190.

Lane, P. (2009). A new fiscal strategy for Ireland. *Economic and Social Review, 40,* 233–253.

Los, B., Timmer, M. P., & de Vries, G. J. (2015). How global are global value chains? A new approach to measure international fragmentation. *Journal of Regional Science, 55,* 66–92.

LSE Growth Commission. (2013). *Investing in prosperity: Skills, infrastructure and innovation.* London: London School of Economics.

Macallan, C., Millard, S., & Parker, M. (2008). *The cyclicality of mark-ups and profit margins for the United Kingdom: Some new evidence* (Bank of England Working Paper No. 351).

Machin, S., & Wadhwani, S. (1989). *The effects of unions on organisational change, investment and employment: Evidence from WIRS data* (Economics Discussion Paper No. 355). London School of Economics Centre for Labour.

Maddison, A. (1996). Macroeconomic accounts for European countries. In B. Van Ark & N. Crafts (Eds.), *Quantitative aspects of postwar European economic growth* (pp. 27–83). Cambridge: Cambridge University Press.

Mills, T. C., & Crafts, N. (2000). After the golden age: A long-run perspective on growth rates that speeded up, slowed down, and still differ. *The Manchester School, 68,* 68–91.

Minford, P. (2015). *Evaluating European trading arrangements* (Cardiff Economics Working Paper No. E2015/17).

Mirrlees, J., Adam, S., Besley, T., Blundell, R., Bond, S., Chote, R., et al. (2011). The Mirrlees review: Conclusions and recommendations for reform. *Fiscal Studies, 32,* 331–359.

Monteagudo, J., Rutkovski, A., & Lorenzani, D. (2012). *The economic impact of the services directive: A first assessment following implementation* (European Economy Economic Papers No. 456).

Nelson, R. R., & Wright, G. (1992). The rise and fall of American technological leadership: The postwar era in historical perspective. *Journal of Economic Literature, 30,* 1931–1964.

Nickell, S. J., Nicolitsas, D., & Dryden, N. (1997). What makes firms perform well? *European Economic Review, 41,* 783–796.

Nicoletti, G. & Scarpetta, S. (2005). *Regulation and economic performance: Product market reforms and productivity in the OECD* (OECD Economics Department Working Paper No. 460).

Nkusu, M. (2013). *Boosting competitiveness to grow out of debt—Can Ireland find a way back to its future?* (IMF Working Paper No. 13/35).

OECD. (2007). *Tax effects on foreign direct investment.* Paris: OECD.

Oulton, N. (1976). Effective protection of british industry. In W. M. Corden & G. Fels (Eds.), *Public Assistance to Industry* (pp. 46–90). London: Macmillan.

Oulton, N. (2012). Long-term implications of the ICT revolution: Applying the lessons of growth theory and growth accounting. *Economic Modelling, 29,* 1722–1736.

Pellegrino, B., & Zingales, L. (2014). *Diagnosing the Italian disease.* Chicago, NY: University of Chicago, Mimeo.

Romalis, J. (2007). Capital taxes, trade costs, and the Irish miracle. *Journal of the European Economic Association, 5,* 459–469.

Sampson, T., Dhingra, S., Ottaviano, G., & van Reenen, J. (2016). *Economists for Brexit: A critique.* London: London School of Economics.

Sapir, A. (2011). European integration at the crossroads: A review essay on the 50th anniversary of Bela Balassa's *Theory of economic integration. Journal of Economic Literature, 49,* 1200–1229.

Slaughter, M. J. (2003). Host country determinants of US foreign direct investment into europe. In H. Hermann & R. Lipsey (Eds.), *Foreign direct investment in the real and financial sector of industrial countries* (pp. 7–32). Berlin: Springer.

Sumner, M. (1999). Long-run effects of investment incentives. In C. Driver & J. Temple (Eds.), *Investment, growth and employment: Perspectives for policy* (pp. 292–300). London: Routledge.

Tanzi, V. (1969). *The individual income tax and economic growth.* Baltimore: Johns Hopkins University Press.

Temin, P. (2002). The golden age of European growth reconsidered. *European Review of Economic History, 6,* 3–22.

The Conference Board. (2015). *Total economy database.* http://www.conference-board.org/data/economy/database/.

Thom, R., & Walsh, B. (2002). The effect of a currency union on trade: Lessons from the Irish experience. *European Economic Review, 46,* 1111–1123.

Van Ark, B. (2011). Up the hill and down again: A history of Europe's productivity gap relative to the United States, 1950–2009. *Nordic Economic Policy Review, 2,* 27–56.

Varga, J., & in't Veld, J. (2014). *The potential growth impact of structural reforms in the EU* (European Economy Economic Papers No. 541).

Walsh, B. (2004). The transformation of the Irish labour market, 1980–2003. *Journal of the Statistical and Social Inquiry Society of Ireland, 33,* 83–115.

Whelan, K. (2014). Ireland's economic crisis: The good, the bad and the ugly. *Journal of Macroeconomics, 39,* 424–440.

Williamson, J. (1971). Trade and economic growth. In J. Pinder (Ed.), *The economics of Europe* (pp. 19–45). London: Charles Knight.

Woessmann, L., Ludemann, E, Schutz, M., & West, M. R. (2007). *School accountability, autonomy, choice and the level of student achievement: International evidence from PISA 2033* (OECD Education Working Paper No. 13).

Wren, C. (1996). *Industrial subsidies: The UK experience.* London: Macmillan.

How Does European Integration Work? Lessons from Revisiting the British Relative Economic Decline

Nauro F. Campos and Fabrizio Coricelli

1 Introduction

Former British Prime Minister David Cameron was determined to change the relationship between the United Kingdom (UK) and the European Union (EU). His Conservative Party's outright and largely unexpected victory in the May 2015 general elections meant a key

N.F. Campos (✉)
Brunel University London, London, UK
e-mail: nauro.campos@brunel.ac.uk

N.F. Campos
ETH Zurich, Zurich, Switzerland

N.F. Campos
IZA, Bonn, Germany

F. Coricelli
Paris School of Economics, Paris, France
e-mail: fabrizio.coricelli@gmail.com

F. Coricelli
CEPR, London, UK

© The Author(s) 2017
N.F. Campos and F. Coricelli (eds.), *The Economics of UK–EU Relations*,
DOI 10.1007/978-3-319-55495-2_3

47

manifesto pledge would be implemented: the UK would embark on a renegotiation of its EU membership terms and those new terms would be submitted to a popular vote—an 'in or out' or 'remain or leave' referendum. It was also promised that voting would take place before the end of 2017 (Copsey and Haughton 2014a, b). This renegotiation concluded in February 2016 with an agreed 'new settlement', and the referendum was set for 23 June 2016. The Leave campaign obtained 52% of the votes. The new Prime Minister Theresa May took office 20 days later, pledging to make the UK the first country ever to leave the EU.

Brexit stands for the British exit from the EU. Why should economists pay attention to Brexit? The answer is not simple. Brexit is one of the multiple crises currently affecting the largest experiment of voluntary economic integration in human history. The European integration project is in poly-crisis mode: the financial crisis, the debt crisis, the economic crisis, the Greek crisis, the populism crisis, the productivity crisis, the terrorism crisis, the refugee crisis and the democratic deficit crisis. But Brexit is a different type of crisis. Brexit raises fundamental questions about the integration project. This was a one-way process towards a well-defined goal, but because of the 'new settlement', no more ever closer union. The possibility that the citizens of the UK could vote of their own free will to leave the EU is disconcerting.

Brexit is different because it asks questions about the value of being in the union, questions about the value of membership, about the value of being integrated and interconnected in the world, about the dynamics and distribution of the benefits and costs of trying to do so, and about the type of integration that can sustain (and hopefully increase) the substantial benefits we have seen since the start of the project in the 1950s. These are existential questions, and they must be answered if the EU is to be after this crisis.

In this chapter, we try to answer three questions: (1) did EU membership significantly affect UK economic performance? (2) How? And (3) why? In addressing these questions, we discuss the implications of our findings for both the UK and the EU. We believe these are important questions. If EU membership turns out to have no discernible economic effect, the case for remaining would be weaker. However, because of the chequered history of the UK–EU relation, if one can show that European integration played a role here, it is likely it played a substantial role everywhere else.

We first briefly discuss the historical context in which the European economic integration project took-off, in order to assess to what extent one can claim that delayed membership was relatively costly to the UK and to what extent the UK joining the EU was beneficial.

We argue that a fundamental yet relatively unappreciated feature of the relationship between Britain and the EU is a turning point. The ratio of UK's per capita GDP to the EU founding members' declines steadily from 1945 until 1972 but is relatively stable between 1973 and 2010.

The conventional view is that this turning point occurs in the mid-1980s and the reason is that this is when Mrs. Thatcher implements her package of far-reaching structural reforms. This paper asks whether econometric evidence is supportive of such view. We find it is not and ask what else could have played such a role. We examine an alternative and much less popular hypothesis: this turning point occurs instead in 1973 when the UK finally joined the EU. Using the whole range of structural break tests, we find substantial econometric support for this turning point to be around 1970.

Such prominent structural break (and to the best of our knowledge not previously detected and analysed) suggests substantial benefits from EU membership especially considering that, by sponsoring an over-powered integration model, Britain joined too late, at a bad moment in time, and at an avoidably larger cost.

If membership has indeed made a substantial difference, the next logical question is how? To answer this, we then discuss the key potential mechanisms through which these benefits took root. The chosen mode of integration (deep instead of shallow) may have played a key role. While international trade may have been the most important driver until the implementation of the Single Market in the early 1990s, foreign investment may have taken this role since. Another contributing factor is that EU accession marked the victory of the business groups that wanted to compete at the high-tech end of the very quality-demanding common European market against those business groups wanted to compete in the comparative-advantage price-driven, mostly former colonies, Commonwealth market. These pro-Europe business groups later become the constituency that supported Mrs. Thatcher's reforms without which we argue they would not be nearly as successful. We discuss the implications of these findings for Brexit and the EU.

This chapter is organised as follows. Section 2 introduces the British relative economic decline and investigates what may have been the main causes of its reversal. It presents evidence from structural breaks econometrics to make the case that EU membership is at least as strong a contender explanation than the much more popular Mrs. Thatcher's structural reforms. In light of results favouring EU membership. Section 3 presents various economic channels or mechanisms of how EU membership benefitted the UK economy. Section 4 provides an overall discussion that stresses the political economy interpretation put forward above as a promising avenue for future research. Section 5 concludes.

2   Why Did Britain Join the EU?

An examination of European economic history provides valuable insight into the UK's eventual accession to the EU. The unprecedented destruction of WWII resulted in a similarly unprecedented recovery effort, which was largely completed by 1950. The period that followed, until 1973, is commonly referred to by economic historians as the Golden Age of European Economic Growth. Reconstruction and catch-up with pre-war levels were broadly completed by 1950 so other factors were at play. Temin (2003) convincingly argues that structural change (labour shifts out of agriculture) was a leading factor.

The UK was one of the only European nations to grow economically during WWII. Compared to the average of the six founding nations of what would become the EU—France, West Germany, Italy, Belgium, the Netherlands and Luxembourg (the EU6), the UK's GDP per capita was roughly 90% larger in 1945, according to Maddison data.[1]

One prominent area of economic history scholarship is 'British relative economic decline' (Bean and Crafts 1996). Economic historians offer a detailed understanding of key turning points in British economic history since the early 1800s. However, this long-term perspective fails to give WWII and European integration (including gains from liberalisation and increased competition) due credit as important factors, although more contemporary, in this process (a notable exception is Crafts 2012).

A requisite for Marshall Plan aid after WWII was economic coordination for recipient countries. It was clear at the outset that there were many areas of agreement but one of discord. The French favoured a customs union, the British a free trade area. The differences are substantial: customs unions entail deeper integration, they require a 'huge political step' (Sapir 2011). Also worth noting is that 'the United States supported the idea of a customs union in 1947, and continue to give backing to French schemes for West European regional organizations' (George 1994, p. 18).

The UK decided not to participate in the European Coal and Steel Community (ECSC), which was a result of the proposed Schuman Plan in 1950 (Dell 1995). The ECSC created a set of institutions to coordinate and integrate coal and steel production among the participating nations, which are the EU6: a 'High Authority to monitor compliance with the terms of the agreement, a Common Assembly of parliamentarians to hold the High Authority accountable, and a Community Court to adjudicate disputes between the High Authority and member states' (Eichengreen 2008). With the EU6's economic recovery almost completed by 1950, per capita GDP in the UK was about 28% above EU6 average.

By the time the Treaty of Rome was signed by the EU6 in 1957, that figure was reduced to 15% (Fig. 1).[2] The integration efforts embodied by these agreements had successes and failures. The primary failures were the proposed political and defence unions; the expansion of the ESCS to become the European Economic Community (EEC) and the creation of a European atomic energy community (Euratom) in the Treaty of Rome are the major successes. Although the UK government was not a party to either of these agreements, in 1960 they proposed an organisation reflecting their desired ideals, the European Free Trade Area (EFTA).

The EFTA was signed in Stockholm in 1960 by Austria, Denmark, Norway, Portugal, Sweden, Switzerland and the UK.[3] Revealingly, the UK began negotiations to enter the EEC in 1961. At that point, the per capita GDP gap between the UK and the EU6 average had fallen to

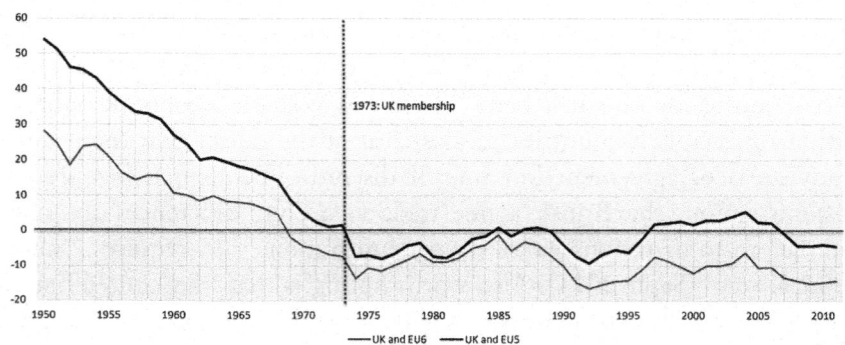

Fig. 1 Percentage difference between the UK's GPD per capita and EU founding members' (EU-6) and EU-5 (excludes Luxembourg) between 1950 and 2011. *Data source* Penn World Tables 8.0

roughly 10%. Nonetheless, French President De Gaulle vetoed the British application after drawn-out negotiations in 1963.

Around this time the UK began coming to realisations about the economic viability of the Commonwealth.[4] It became apparent that they were less competitive and demanding than the developed markets of Western Europe. Additionally, it became apparent that the EEC was economically superior to the EFTA (Aitken 1973; Bayoumi and Eichengreen 1997). Figure 2 shows that the decline over time was much faster for the ratio of the UK to the EU6 than for either Denmark (an EFTA member) or Ireland (not an EFTA member) which were the two countries which joined the EU at the same time as the UK in 1973.

In 1964, Harold Wilson was elected prime minister in the UK and made another failed attempt to revive the Commonwealth-based economy. Subsequently, Britain reapplied for EEC membership in 1967 (Tatham 2009). Once again, De Gaulle vetoes. By this time per capita GDP in the UK was only 6% larger than the EU6 average (Fig. 2).

Georges Pompidou succeeded Charles De Gaulle in 1969 and immediately encouraged Britain to reapply for EEC membership for a third time (Young 1998). Pompidou is also recognised as the creator of a system of individual contributions to the Community budget. In 1969, when the UK officially applies, its per capita GDP had shrunk to be 2% smaller than the average of the EU6.

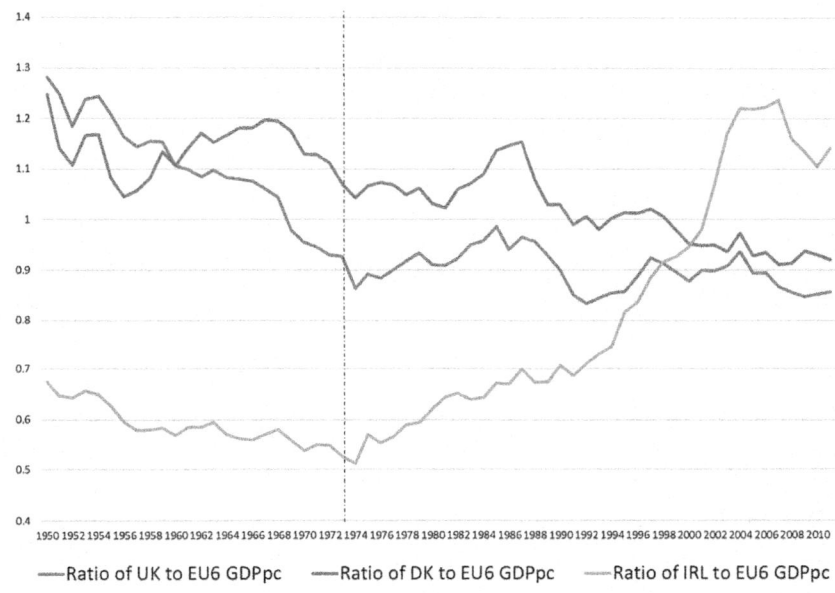

─── Ratio of UK to EU6 GDPpc   ─── Ratio of DK to EU6 GDPpc   ─── Ratio of IRL to EU6 GDPpc

Fig. 2 Per capita GDP 1973 enlargement countries ratios to EU6

Edward Heath succeeded Wilson in 1970, and was known as the staunchest European federalist of all British prime ministers. When the UK joins the EEC in 1973, the EEC funding system operated by collecting revenues from levies on food imports and tariffs on industrial goods. Because the UK was more urbanised and imported more than continental Europe nations, the policy did not suit British interests. 1973 also inaugurates a volatile period with the collapse of the Bretton Woods system and the first oil shock. At this point, the UK's per capita GDP had fallen to a level 7% smaller than the average of the EU6.

The special relationship with the USA, the Commonwealth, and the belief that purely economic integration (FTA) would be superior to deeper, politico-economic alternatives, are often cited as the main reasons for the delay in British membership. Special relation or not, the USA was a resolute supporter of European integration from the outset. With the independence of India, the Suez crisis, and African decolonization, Commonwealth links taper (Darwin 2011; Garavini 2012). Applying for

EC membership 1 year after the creation of EFTA reveals which alternative was perceived as superior.

For the majority of European countries, structural change may well be a very satisfactory explanation for Golden Age growth and catch-up with the USA and perhaps even more so than EU membership. Yet, a stark structural break marks the trajectory of the per capita GDP ratio of Britain to the EU6.[5] The steady decline in the ratio of the UK's per capita GDP to the average of the EU6 from 1945 to 1972 and the relative stability of that ratio from 1973 to 2010 suggest considerable benefits from membership in the EEC/EU. Furthermore, the overpowered integration model employed by Britain suggests the UK joined the EEC too late, in a bad period of time, and at an unnecessarily high price. For this alone, EU membership is an explanation that deserves more careful examination.

We further develop this hypothesis using a standard econometric approach (Campos and Coricelli 2015a, b), namely we study whether there is evidence for structural breaks or turning points at points in time that are often identified as key to understand British relative economic decline. In particular, we would like to see whether breaks could be detected in the run-up to EU accession as well as during the government Mrs. Thatcher so as to draw some comparisons between them.

Using data from the Penn World Tables, version 8, we study GDP, GDP per capita and Total Factor Productivity series, by looking at both the individual UK series and ratios of UK versus the average for the EU6 founding countries.

We subject these data series to a whole range of structural break tests that is the Chow, Zivot-Andrews and Bai-Perron tests (see Hansen 2001 for a non-technical discussion). The seminal Chow framework assumes that the date of the one break it can test for is known beforehand. The Zivot-Andrews test is able to detect multiple breaks simultaneously but still requires that the econometrician knows the exact dates of the turning points. The current and most widely used framework is that by Bai-Perron, which allows the identification of multiple structural breaks and it does not require these to be chosen a priori. It allows the estimations of multiple unknown breakpoints.

For the sake of space, and given that the other results are broadly supportive of our main conclusions, here we only report and discuss the Bai-Perron estimates for the ratio of the UK to the EU6. Other results refer to those for the individual country series, other countries' ratios to EU6, other structural breaks tests and for various changes in the set-up of our Bai-Perron results so as to check their sensitivity (these are available upon request).

Our Bai-Perron results appear robust to various sensitivity tests. We analyse whether results were sensitive to the choice of different maximum number of breaks (the default value of 5 breaks is reported but we also generated results using values above or and below), to different levels of statistical significance for detection of breakpoints (we report results using the conventional 5% but using 1 or 10% generate similar conclusions), to allowing the error distributions to differ across breaks (we report results allowing for this but this does not change our results), to the trimming parameter (default value reported below is 15% but we run results using values above or below) and to the choice of sequential versus global set-up. We find that none of these affect our main conclusions: 1969 remains the key turning point.

Table 1 presents our Bai-Perron results for the ratio between the UK and the EU6 in per capita GDP between 1950 and 2011. The main message is that conventional levels of statistical significance support a main structural break around year 1969. Unsurprisingly, we obtain similar results using both the Chow and Zivot-Andrews tests.

The top of the table summarises the results for different approaches to determining the number of breaks. The 'sequential' result obtains from performing tests from one to the maximum number until the null hypothesis cannot be rejected anymore. The result labelled 'significant' chooses the largest statistically significant number of breakpoints. Both these multiple breakpoint tests indicate that there seem to be five breaks in the annual of the ration of the UK per capita GDP to the EU6 per capita GDP between 1950 and 2011. UD_{max} and WD_{max} show how many breakpoints are detected using the unweighted and weighted maximised statistics. The former indicates one single break, while the later suggest at most three breakpoints. These latter statistics warm against giving too much weight to more than three breakpoints.

Table 1 Multiple breakpoint tests: per capita GDP ratios

Bai-Perron tests of 1 to M globally determined breaks
Sample: 1950 2011
Included observations: 62
Breakpoint variables: C
Break test options: Trimming 0.15, Max. breaks 5, Sig. level 0.05

Sequential F-statistic determined breaks:			5
Significant F-statistic largest breaks:			5
UDmax determined breaks:			1
WDmax determined breaks:			3

Breaks	F-statistic	Scaled F-statistic	Weighted F-statistic	Critical Value
1*	286.0367	286.0367	286.0367	8.58
2*	270.2292	270.2292	321.1311	7.22
3*	270.2397	270.2397	389.0363	5.96
4*	213.0432	213.0432	366.3148	4.99
5*	168.9021	168.9021	370.6343	3.91

| UDMax statistic* | 286.0367 | UDMax critical value** | 8.88 |
| WDMax statistic* | 389.0363 | WDMax critical value** | 9.91 |

Estimated break dates:
1. 1969
2. 1960, 1969
3. 1960, 1969, 1990
4. 1960, 1969, 1981, 1990
5. 1960, 1969, 1981, 1990, 1999

* Significant at the 0.05 level
** Bai-Perron (Econometric Journal, 2003) critical values

The table also shows the individual test statistics (original, scaled, weighted) along with the critical values for the scaled statistics. The original and scaled are the same because there is only one regressor in the model. In each case, the statistics considerably exceeds the critical value thus supporting the rejection of the null of no breaks. The next results show the test results for double maximum statistics. In both cases, the maximised value clearly exceeds the critical value, so that again we reject the null of no breaks.

The bottom part of the table is probably the most intuitive and reports the global optimizers for the breakpoints for each number of breaks. It shows, for example, that if set to detect one and only one break in the per capita GDP series that breakpoint would correspond to year 1969 (for the ratio with the EU5 this year is 1970 instead). This means that there is indeed a break in this series and it is most likely to be around year 1969 (and not around 1979 when Thatcher comes to power nor around 1983 when she starts her second term in government and actually implements her far-reaching agenda of structural reforms). If one allows only two structural breaks to be detected, the Bai-Perron test indicates that these would be 1960 and 1969, again giving little credence to conventional views that entrust 1979 or 1983 or even 1986 which is when her big-bang financial reforms are completed (Young 1998). Moreover, 1960 is the year in which the EFTA Stockholm treaty is signed and 1969 is when De Gaulle finally resigns and Pompidou, his successor, invited the UK to apply for EU membership for a third time indicating that third time around France would welcome and support the UK application. Interestingly, if one allows three breaks to be detected, 1990 is identified as the third most important break (after 1969 and 1960, respectively), again not 1979 (start of Thatcher's first term) or 1983 (start of Thatcher's second term) or 1986 (big bang reforms) which could be more naturally associated with Mrs. Thatcher effects especially given that 1990 is the year Thatcher resigns. Keeping in mind the above caveat of not attaching too much weight to more than three detected breaks, it is only when one allows for four breakpoints that 1 year within her time in office appears as an important break and that is for year 1981.

In a nutshell, our results provide scant support for the still very popular notion that Mrs. Thatcher and her reforms were the main culprit for the reversal in the trajectory of the British relative economic decline. Instead, focusing on the dynamics of per capita GDP they point to EU membership as a powerful alternative explanation.

The results discussed above for *per capita* GDP ratios are very much like those we obtain for GDP ratios as well as for the series for the individual countries. Yet these are imperfect measures of productivity which are a concern given the common expectation that the effects from deep integration are mostly in productivity rather than in gross output terms (Campos et al. 2014). In this light, we try to complement the analysis above by replicating it for a productivity measure.[6]

Here we use the measure of total factor productivity (TFP) available from the Penn World Tables version 8, which is reported as a percentage of the USA TFP level. Table 2 below shows eight 'snapshots' between 1950 and 2014 of the level of TFP in the UK and in each of the EU6 countries with respect to the USA.

Table 2 highlights a number of issues. Chiefly among them is that although it is well established that between the end of WWII and the 1973 accession to the European Community, per capita GDP growth in the UK was faster than that in the USA but slower than in France or Germany, the figures from TFP reveal a much more nuanced picture. Indeed, it is a picture that even in its description reinforces the findings we present above: productivity growth in the UK before 1970 is pretty flat and shows practically no signs of closing the gap with the USA. Notice that this is not the case for any of the EU6 with France deserving special attention having recorded huge gains in productivity before 1970 (Adams 1989).

Overall, these leading European economies starting from 1950 until the mid-1990s were able to close their productivity gap with respect to the USA. Yet this gap has opened up again since.

Figure 3 helps to further understand these developments. It can be seen that except for Luxemburg and the UK there is a visible acceleration of TFP relative gains between 1950 and 1980. This is followed by a flattening out of the gaps with some countries registering levels below their 1970 figures. In particular, for Germany and France the 2010 or 2014 level is clearly above that for 1970, while for Belgium it is barely above but again, only for these three countries these positive gains were not fully reversed between 1970 and 2010. Moreover, as Fig. 3 shows,

Table 2 Total factor productivity (USA = 1) for UK and EU6 between 1950 and 2014

	1950	1960	1970	1980	1990	2000	2010	2014
Great Britain	0.68	0.69	0.71	0.89	0.86	0.92	0.74	0.73
France	0.51	0.68	0.87	1.07	1.02	1.01	0.94	0.95
Belgium	0.71	0.73	0.89	1.21	1.07	1.11	0.91	0.92
Germany	0.41	0.56	0.62	0.81	0.81	0.88	0.82	0.82
Italy	0.57	0.64	0.86	1.14	0.98	0.94	0.81	0.71
Netherlands	0.67	0.72	0.84	1.07	0.95	1.02	0.83	0.81
Luxembourg	0.97	0.99	1.02	1.12	1.12	1.11	0.79	0.78

Source PWT 8

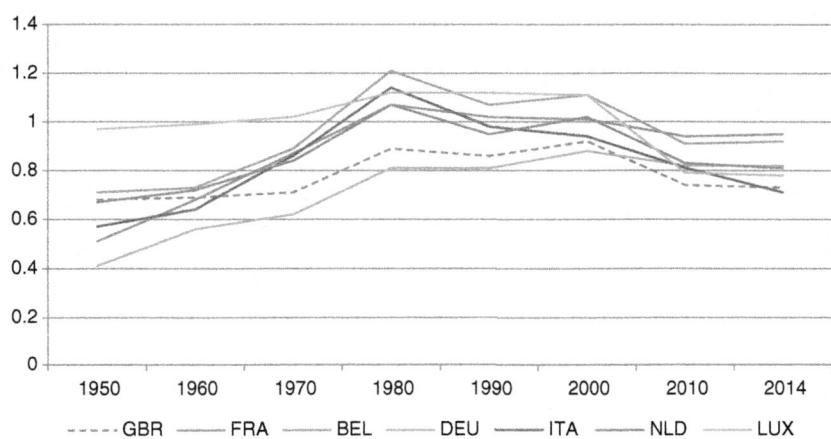

Fig. 3 Total factor productivity (USA = 1): UK and EU6 between 1950 and 2014 (from PWT8)

the least productive economy by this measure in 2010 is the UK, which for 2014 it is only beaten, barely, by Italy.

Given these developments in terms of TFP and the assumption that most deep integration gains are in productivity not gross output terms, it would be particularly valuable to investigate whether there are also detectable turning points or structural breaks in the TFP series. Moreover, it would be useful to examine this issue focusing both on the individual countries and, much more importantly, on the ratios between UK and EU6. The latter of course indicates how close, below or above, is the comparative performance of the UK vis-à-vis the EU6 countries.

Figure 4 displays the ratios of TFP for the three countries that joined the EU in 1973 (UK, Denmark and Ireland) to the EU6 founding members between 1950 and 2011. If one is searching for turning points, the contrast between the per capita GDP (Fig. 2) and TFP (Fig. 4) UK ratios to EU6 countries is extremely revealing. The mere existence of such structural breaks is much clearer than in the case of per capita GDP. Although it seems that the turning point for productivity in Ireland occurs basically with the Single Market, that for both the UK and Denmark seem to have taken place much earlier and coinciding with they joining the EEC in 1973.

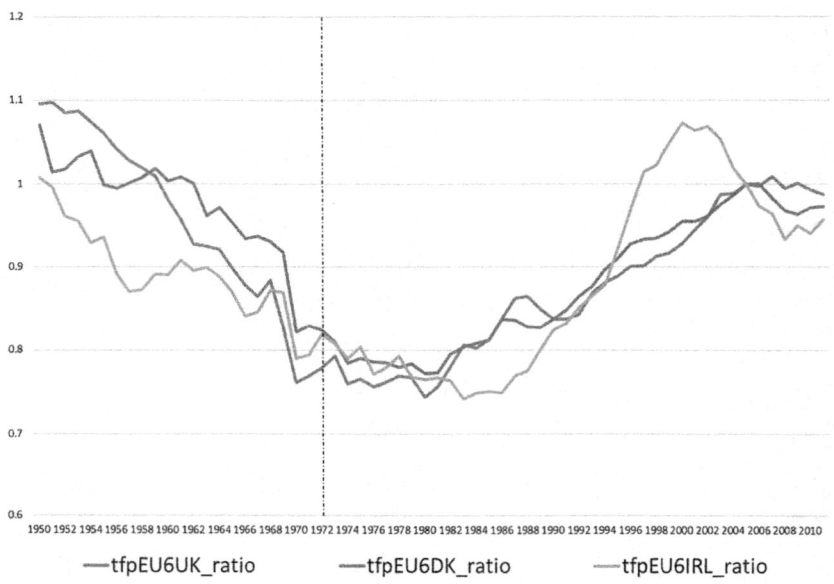

Fig. 4 Total factor productivity 1973 enlargement countries ratios to EU6 (2005 = 1)

Table 2 reports our Bai-Perron estimates and as expected they are even cleaner than those in Table 1 in pointing to a main, dominant structural break in year 1969. The discussion of the econometric diagnostic tests follows very closely that provided above for per capita GDP. If anything, the conclusions emerging from Table 2 are richer and even stronger regarding the prominence of 1969 especially vis-à-vis 1979, 1983 or 1986.

It is worth mentioning that differently from the case of per capita GDP, for TFP all results suggest the existence of five structural breaks but again with 1969 being the dominant one. Another similarity with the per capita GDP results that is worth mentioning is that 1960 again appears to represent a substantial turning point. Once again, the results for more than three breakpoints suggest that years 1986 or 1985 also support a structural break but as before these results are dominated by 1969 and are not clearly related to Mrs. Thatcher's effects. If the latter are so powerful and distinctive to many analysts, we do not believe it would be unfair to expect these tests to reveal two or more dominant breaks during her years in power. For all the data series we have examined, we find no evince of such an outcome occurring.

The results above provide strong evidence supporting the notion that as far as the British relative economic decline is concerned the key date is 1969. This is when De Gaulle resigns and this opens the way to the UK and other EFTA members to successfully apply for EEC membership (Tatham 2009). If this is the case, one has to ask how and why? What are the channels or mechanisms at play? We turn to this question next.

3   How and Why Did Britain Benefit from EU Integration?

If membership in the EU has indeed made a substantial difference to British economic performance (perhaps even more than the much more conventional explanation that is Mrs. Thatcher's reforms), the next logical question is how. Even though not a founding member, the UK is one of the three largest economies in Europe, is a powerful military and diplomatic force, and has a history of being an awkward partner (George 1994). This is an important question because if one can establish convincingly how EU membership benefited the UK, it would strengthen the case that EU membership can generate significant benefits elsewhere.

Campos et al. (2014) estimates that the net benefits of EU membership to the UK are positive, but marginal until around 1986 when the Single Market was introduced. This estimate is derived from the econometric construction of a hypothetical UK that did not join the EU in 1973. Comparing the outcomes from the actual UK experience with the estimated outcomes from the hypothetical model indicates whether EU membership (which is the specified, post-1973 treatment) generates positive or negative net benefits. This analysis considers whether membership paid off, whether these returns are temporary or permanent, and assesses how they changed over time.

Figure 5 shows that, when measured by per capita output, net benefits were at their maximum in the early 1990s and have remained constant since. Conversely, labour productivity benefits (GDP per worker)

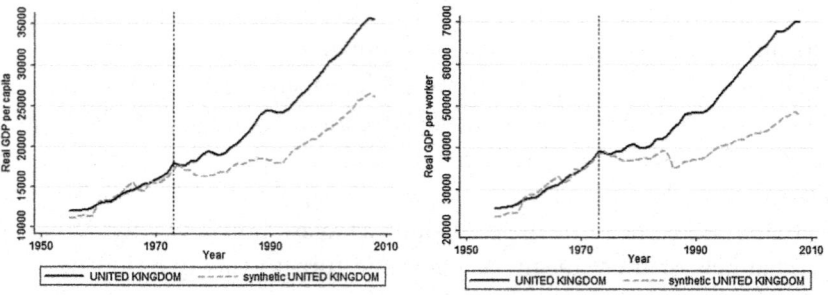

Fig. 5 UK net benefits from EU membership: per capita GDP and labour productivity. *Source* Campos et al. (2014)

increased continually on an annual basis over the same time period. The international evidence on productivity suggests an upward trend break for the USA in the mid-1990s and, at around the same time, a downward break for the euro area (Bergeaud et al. 2016). Table 3 shows the averages of these estimated benefits for the whole period after accession, as well as for its first 5 and 10 years. In order to draw sensible comparisons, it is advisable to focus on the latter. The results summarised in Table 3 indicate that per capita GDP in the UK would be 8.5 or 4.8% lower 10 or 5 years after accession (that is, in 1983 and in 1978,

Table 3 Average effects of EU membership

DIFFERENCE (%) in post-treatment average GDP pc LEVEL between ACTUAL and SYNTHETIC			
	All post-treatment	10 years after treatment	5 years after treatment
United Kingdom	23.694	8.586	4.824
Northern enlargement 1973	32.152	10.760	6.786
Southern enlargement 1981 and 1986	6.133	4.288	3.164
Southern enlargement 1986	19.078	15.099	10.541
Northern enlargement 1995	4.915	4.244	2.491
Eastern enlargement 1998 (anticipation)	14.803	14.803	9.858

Source Campos et al. (2014)

respectively) if the UK had not joined the EEC in 1973. These offer a mixed comparison with latter accessions. They are below the average benefits for the 1973, 1986 and 2004 enlargements, but they are above the average for the 1995 enlargement. In terms of their economic significance, these benefits are substantial and exceed related estimates. Below we argue that the some of the main factors responsible for these benefits are trade, foreign direct investment (FDI) and finance and that these are intrinsically related to European integration (Table 4).

Article 2 of the 1957 Treaty of Rome stipulates that a common market between member states is the primary objective of European Integration (Sapir 2011). The common market aimed to facilitate trade between

Table 4 Multiple breakpoint tests: TFP

Multiple breakpoint tests			
Bai-Perron tests of 1 to M globally determined breaks			
Sample: 1950 2011			
Included observations: 62			
Breakpoint variables: C			
Break test options: Trimming 0.15, Max. breaks 5, Sig. level 0.05			
Sequential F-statistic determined breaks:	5		
Significant F-statistic largest breaks:	5		
UDmax determined breaks:	5		
WDmax determined breaks:	5		
Breaks	F-statistic	Scaled F-statistic	Weighted F-statistic	Critical Value
1*	49.64613	49.64613	49.64613	8.58
2*	97.96414	97.96414	116.4172	7.22
3*	113.8057	113.8057	163.8344	5.96
4*	181.221	181.221	311.5985	4.99
5*	186.8258	186.8258	409.9655	3.91
UDMax statistic*	186.8258	UDMax critical value**	8.88
WDMax statistic*	409.9655	WDMax critical value**	9.91
Estimated break dates:			
1. 1969			
2. 1962, 1996			
3. 1960, 1969, 1994			
4. 1960, 1969, 1986, 2001			
5. 1960, 1969, 1985, 1994, 2003			

* Significant at the 0.05 level
** Bai-Perron (Econometric Journal, 2003) critical values

member states and in turn prevent future conflicts through economic interdependence simultaneously contributing to economic growth (Martin et al. 2012). The benefits of free trade are one of the few commonly accepted elements among economists. Open trade is generally considered to increase competition and innovation, which, in turn, increase welfare and growth.

Although the UK's accession to the EU increased trade openness, it was not in the expected way. According to analysis from Penn World Tables (PWT) trade openness data, the UK experienced a significant increase in its *level* of trade openness after EEC membership. The data indicate that from the late 1950s to 1970s, the UK's trade openness was roughly 40%, and jumped to roughly 55% from 1973 to 2010. In fact, the 1972 value of this ratio is 42.46% while for 1974 it is 58.82%. Note that both PWT and UNCTAD data support this 'level' effect. PWT data reveals another thought-provoking notion, namely that although trade openness in the UK shows no trend since 1973, for Germany it shoots up after 1999.

A common explanation is that the economy specialised in services. However, the latest United Nations Conference on Trade and Development (UNCTAD) data reveal the limits of that explanation. Trade in services in the UK grew in lockstep (from rather similar initial levels) with Eurozone countries despite the noticeable differences in growth of trade in goods.

The answer to the overall growth in trade openness for the UK may be found in intra-industry trade.[7] Overall trade openness among the EU6 grew (from roughly 35% in 1958 to 50% in 1973) but intra-industry trade increased substantially more. Over the same time period intra-industry trade in Italy grew from 42 to 57%, and in the Benelux countries from 62 to 72%. Western Europe's growth in this regard is impressive despite the fact that intra-industry trade was growing globally.[8] UK intra-industry trade saw massive growth after its accession in 1973. In the 1960s, it was below 50%, and grew to more than 70% in the late 1970s and after (OECD 1987).

The traditional argument is that trade is beneficial, but inter-industry trade is even more so. This point has been largely overlooked in the debate about European integration, in general, and that on Brexit in particular. Of course, trade with the Commonwealth adds to the UK's GDP, but trade with the EU has the added benefit of increasing the UK's productivity. Trade with the Commonwealth is primarily inter-industry, and therefore driven by comparative advantage (gains are derived from specialisation and scale), while trade with the EU is primarily intra-industry (gains are derived from competition and innovation). Therefore, it stands to reason that the effects of the latter on UK productivity growth are more extensive and resilient (Fig. 6).

The benefits of FDI are well established. Not only FDI contributes to the diffusion of frontier management practices, increases competition and shores up technological innovation, but it does all this in a relatively more resilient and sustainable fashion (than, for example, portfolio investment).

The UK is one of the main FDI recipients in Europe. Net FDI inflows to the UK were small until the mid-1990s but exhibit two periods of rapid expansion, one in the second half of the 1990s and the other before the financial crisis (Fig. 7). Meanwhile, the share of FDI into services has increased. Despite the obvious importance of the subject and the availability of evidence contrasting the rationales of European and non-European intra-EU FDI (Basile et al. 2008), the literature focusing on potential reasons for foreign investors to choose the UK vis-à-vis Germany or Ireland remains scarce. Yet, at first sight European integration seems to have played a significant role if not with EU membership per se, at least thanks to the establishment of the Single Market.

Figure 7 also presents estimates of the effects of the launch of the Single Market in 1986 on UK FDI net inflows.[9] The dotted line shows our estimates for what would have been FDI net inflows after 1986 if the UK had decided to opt-out of the Single Market. The results show that the Single Market played a key role in mobilising FDI to and from the UK. Perhaps even more interesting is the suggestion that the bulk of these benefits (in terms of additional UK FDI had the UK chosen to opt out instead) happen after the introduction of the common currency (the euro) and, more specifically, between the dot-com bubble and the financial crisis. These results also indicate (much more tentatively of course given that the Financial Crisis has not yet fully concluded) that

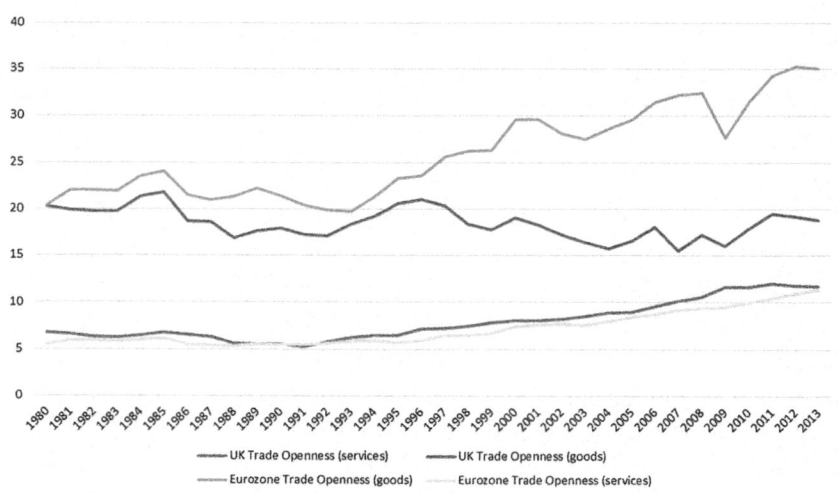

Fig. 6 Trade openness (as % of GDP) in the UK and the Eurozone, 1980–2013. *Source* UNCTADstat

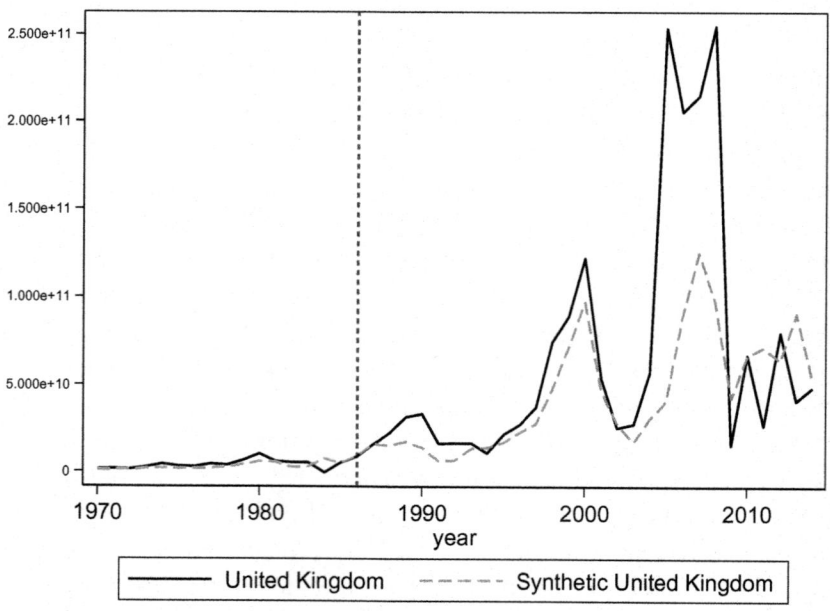

Fig. 7 What would UK FDI net inflows look like had the UK opted-out of the Single Market in 1986? *Source* Authors' estimation based on World Bank (WDI) data

the Single Market stop being such a powerful magnet after 2009, although the net costs since are small vis-à-vis previous gains.

Finally, it is very important to note from Fig. 7 that net FDI inflows to the UK seem much more volatile than one would expect. The main reason for this may be that these figures reflect the high share of the more 'footloose' service sector, especially finance.

Let us now turn to finance because we believe this is also one of the important channels through which the positive effects of EU membership filter through the UK economy. One of the least discussed features of the financial sector in the UK is that is that its relative importance to the British economy hugely outdates the mid-1980s. As pointed out by Burgess (2011) and Haldane et al. (2010), the period in which the growth of aggregate gross value added (GVA) in finance exceeds that of the aggregate economy the most is the period before WWI. Haldane et al. (2010) calculate that this difference for 1856–1913 is of 5% points, with the average aggregate value at 2%. Conversely, between 1914 and 1970, the average annual growth rate of aggregate GVA was 1.9% while that of financial intermediation was 1.5%. Interestingly, between 1970 and 2008 finance GVA again grows faster than that of the overall economy (3.8% against 2.4%). The message that these figures tell is that (a) finance has always been an important sector of the UK economy, because (b) it is one of its most dynamic and (c) when it grows faster it seem to be able to pull the rest of the economy. Schumpeter indeed may have been right.

There seems to be also support to the notion that the UK benefited from EU membership through the positive impact of EU integration on the development of the UK financial sector. The relevance of the EU for the UK financial sector cannot be underestimated. Access to the EU Single Market contributed to strengthening the position of the UK as leading international financial centre.

London has traditionally been the main centre for foreign exchange transactions. However, since the beginning of the 1990s, the share of the UK in foreign exchange transactions has sharply increased, from 25 to more than 40% of the world market.[10] Note that foreign exchange, with daily transactions of more than 6 trillion US$ in 2013, accounts for the largest amount of overall global financial transactions. Although the US

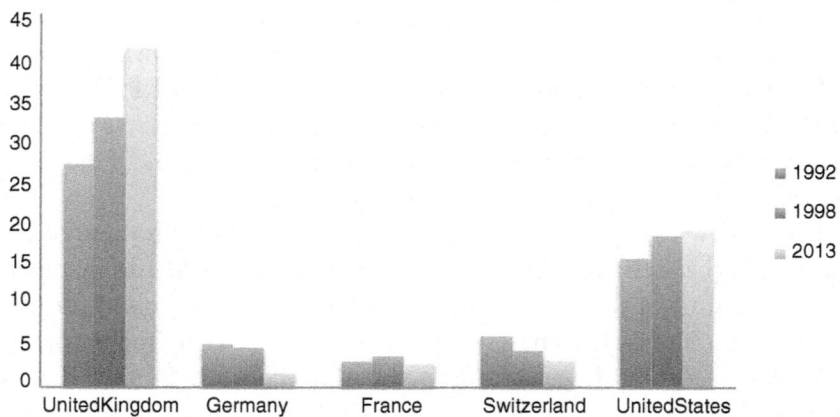

Fig. 8 Foreign exchange turnover: Country shares in total transactions. *Source* BIS (2015)

dollar still dominates, the Euro accounts for more than one third of foreign exchange transactions. As shown in Fig. 8, the UK has substantially gained shares in foreign exchange at the expense of the main Euro area members, Germany and France, but also of Switzerland. Technological factors may explain such phenomenon, but the fact the UK is a EU member certainly played a role.

Clearly, access to the EU Single Market has been one main factor in consolidating the role of the UK as an international financial centre. The comparative advantages of the UK financial sector (tradition, flexible regulation, product diversification, human capital, language, etc.) help the UK to exploit the benefits of EU integration. It is worth noting that, despite being outside the common currency, the UK remains by far the largest player in euro-denominated transactions in the EU.

One other last and final channel that has not received due attention in the current debate on European Integration regards monetary integration, in particular the relation between the euro-ins and euro-outs. We think that one way to start looking into this issue is business cycle synchronisation. We want to make only two observations. One is that synchronisation has increased hugely after the introduction of the euro even for those countries outside of the Eurozone. The second, and related, point is that the effect of the Economic and Monetary Union

(EMU) integration is to pull in the euro-outs, thus reducing the cost of membership (or conversely, increasing the cost of leaving).

The degree of synchronisation of supply shocks indicate that the EU6 plus Denmark constitute the 'core' of the EEC economies, whereas the remaining 'periphery' countries display a lower degree of synchronisation—as was famously argued by Bayoumi and Eichengreen in 1993. It is also noted that demand shocks are lower in and outside of the core.

Although the European Monetary system removed individual monetary policies as a cause of demand shocks, fiscal policies remain independent and contribute to differences in demand between nations. Therefore, it may be valuable to update the famous Bayoumi and Eichengreen exercise by reassessing the extent to which the European Monetary Union has affected the core-periphery dichotomy identified by the data set, which ended in 1988, before the European Monetary Union was implemented.

The results displayed in Fig. 9 indicate that the European Monetary Union has mitigated the trend of core-periphery differences in supply and demand (Campos and Macchiarelli 2016). The European Monetary Union successfully integrated the entirety of the EU, including the UK. After the introduction of the Euro, UK business cycles synchronised with, and the economy became much more integrated with, the rest of the EU.

4   A Political Economy Explanation

Two of the most powerful myths about the relationship between the UK and the European integration project are that the European Single Market (ESM) was a British idea and that Mrs. Thatcher's structural reforms caused the revival of the British economy. Our results above provide new evidence contrary to these myths. They argue that a crucial factor in the British relative economic revival was membership in European Community such that, without EU membership, Mrs. Thatcher's reforms would have been much less effective.

The European Single Market (ESM) and Mrs. Thatcher's reforms are closely related myths because they form the basis of the view (widespread

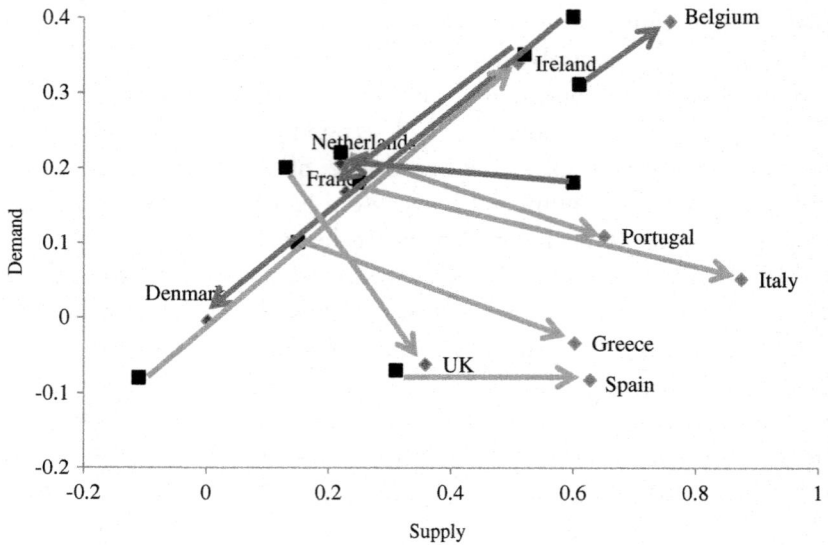

Fig. 9 The dynamics of the correlation of supply and demand disturbances between pre-EMU (1963–1988) from Bayoumi-Eichengreen (1992) and post-EMU (Campos-Macchiarelli for 1991–2014)

in the UK) that those reforms were not only good for the UK but also good for Europe. These supply-side structural reforms are widely seen as arguably the utmost British contribution to the European project (and one can add: a very much under-appreciated contribution at that). The fact that the European Single Market is one of the clearly stated goals of the 1957 Treaty of Rome, which the UK of course refused to sign, is more than obviously suggestive in this case.

Mrs. Thatcher's reforms were implemented in her second term in office. Her June 1983 general election victory was the most decisive since Labour's in 1945. Her first term was marked by the second oil shock and by the Falklands War. The main structural reforms that defined her second term were privatisation, labour, financial and product markets liberalisation, and greater openness to foreign investment.

Our analysis combines the empirical identification of turning points (structural breaks) with an analysis of how and why the benefits from EU membership changed over time using econometric counterfactuals.

One of the main empirical findings is that the turning point around 1973 (which is when the UK joined) is significantly more powerful than the 1983 or 1986 turning points (which correspond to the launch of the massive programme of structural reforms in the UK). Thatcher was right: the lady was not for turning; Europe was. The UK's per capita GDP relative to the EU founding members' declined steadily from 1945 to 1972 but it became relatively stable from 1973 onwards. If Britain joined the EU in an attempt to stop its relative economic decline, it worked. Moreover, it laid the ground for future improvements in relative economic performance (which come to fruition in the Single Market).

One possible explanation is that the success of Mrs. Thatcher's reforms required EU integration. These structural reforms could not have taken place without a large and powerful constituency. In this case, these were British entrepreneurs who would benefit from a much larger, more innovative and more demanding market place (contrast the EU and the Commonwealth in this respect). These entrepreneurs also realised that to be competitive they would need to tap in mobile capital and labour and would need a clear set of common standards and regulations so as to guarantee a level playing-field. Without the support of such powerful constituencies, Mrs. Thatcher's reforms would not have been proposed or fully implemented, and clearly would not have been nearly as successful or influential.

This explanation draws clear parallels to the French experience in the post-WWII period (Adams 1989). Between 1945 and 1957, there was conflict of interest between powerful groups of entrepreneurs against and in favour of furthering European economic integration. Those against tended to export mostly to the former French colonies. Yet these groups lost influence in the run-up to the Treaty of Rome and found themselves locked-in the project even after regaining considerable political influence with De Gaulle appointment in 1958. At that point, they could slow down but they could not reverse the process.

Mrs. Thatcher's reforms were clearly important and together with the Single Market have played an important role in buttressing Bristish economic performance. The results and the interpretation above basically challenge the exclusive prominence of this explanation for the reversal in the long-standing UK relative economic decline. It makes little sense to argue that Mrs. Thatcher reforms were implemented in a vacuum, that is, without the support of powerful constituencies that would benefit from them in the very long-term. EU membership in 1973 marks the undisputable arrival of such constituencies to the centre stage of British politics and policymaking. One further drawback of the dominance of the Mrs. Thatcher and her reforms explanation is that it crowded out research on the emergence of such constituencies. For example, Bean and Crafts (1996) that 'we also anticipate that much more will eventually be written on the implications for growth of the interplay between government and producer interests' (p. 162). Unfortunately, this crucial area of research remains to this day to be fully developed causing an important gap in our knowledge.

5   Conclusions

Why did Britain join? For various reasons. Because De Gaulle left. Because the Commonwealth could not compete. Because Heath defeated Wilson. Because the free trade area integration model sunk. But above all, Britain joined because joining the European project was perceived to be a way to stop its relative economic decline. In 1950, UK's per capita GDP was almost a third larger than the EU6 average; in 1973, it was about 10% below; it has been comparatively stable ever since. On this basis, joining the EU worked: it helped to halt Britain relative economic decline vis-à-vis the EU6.

Focusing on three main areas (trade, FDI and finance), we argue that Britain benefited significantly from EU integration. Leaving the EU (Brexit) is likely to entail heavy losses (Ottaviano et al. 2014) and we expect the severity of these economic losses to increase substantially after the consequences (from the UK leaving the EU) in terms of intra-industry trade, FDI and financial integration are taken into account. And yet these losses may be even larger when we account for interactions among the three areas. These interaction effects should be large for the relationship between FDI and trade (because intra-industry trade often involves FDI), between financial integration and intra-industry trade (because intra-industry trade is credit intensive;

Giannetti et al. 2011), and between financial integration and FDI (because FDI in the UK concentrates in financial services.) Further research on these issues is urgently needed as the current (and almost exclusive) focus on 'UK exports to and imports from the EU' may severely underestimate the true potential benefits from EU membership.

Exit from the EU may have particularly severe effects on the UK financial sector, and through these, on trade and FDI. True that there are already pressures within the EU to reduce the relevance of the UK as the main financial centre for Euro transactions. However, exiting the EU minimises how the UK can influence these decisions. In March 2015 the UK won an important legal battle against the ECB on the location of euro clearing houses, thanks in large part to its EU membership. It is unreasonable to expect the UK will be granted such powers once it is outside the EU.

Britain joined the European project in an effort to mitigate its relative economic decline. At the time of the creation of the project in 1950, the UK's per capita GDP was nearly 30% larger than the average of the founding members, but by time the UK joined in 1973 it was close to 10% smaller. Since then it has stabilised and is reflective of the EU6's growth patterns. In this sense, joining the EU has been successful in curbing its economic decline relative to the EU6.

UK economic performance is of course complex and driven by multiple (not a single) causes. Yet European integration has so far been broadly dismissed as a potential explanatory factor of the UK post-WWII economic performance rebound. We argue it should not and that showing that European integration played a key role in one of its most reluctant partners implies that if it can work there, it can work elsewhere (and probably anywhere).

Notes

1. For international comparisons, the Penn World Tables (PWT) is considered the superior data source. However, it starts in 1950. Data from Maddison goes back much further, so we use his estimate for 1945.

Note that the behaviour of the UK-EU6 ratio of per capita GDPs between 1950 and 2010 is unsurprisingly similar in these two data sources and that, differently from PWT, the Maddison data set does not include Luxembourg. Hence a comparison with all six founding members is not feasible.

2. Because Luxembourg was not such a significant financial centre before the 1980s, Fig. 1 shows two series, one for the ratio of the UK per capita GDP to the EU6 and the other to the EU5 (EU6 excluding Luxembourg). Despite broad similarities, without Luxembourg the decline is steeper before the 1973 and flatter afterwards.

3. These were often referred to as the Outer Seven so as to contrast with the Communities' Inner Six.

4. Euroscepticism was then influential in both the Conservative and Labour parties. During the 1961 parliamentary debate, Harold Wilson is famously on record as saying: "if there has to be a choice *we* are *not entitled* to *sell our friends* and *kinsmen down* the *river* for a *problematical* and *marginal advantage* in *selling washing machines* in *Dusseldorf*." (Gowland and Turner 1999). Young (1998) argues that euroscepticism still resonates within the Conservative party, while for Labour it loses steam in the 1990s.

5. Notice that this has important implications for constructing counter-factuals because of the difficulty in finding pre-entry trajectories comparable to the UK's (Campos et al. 2014).

6. Productivity is also less affected by oil from the North Sea, which may have boosted GDP.

7. See Badwin and Lopez-Gonzalez (2015) and Alfaro et al. (2015), and references therein. Recall that Frankel and Rose (1998) argue the appropriate criteria for (endogenous) optimal currency area membership is intra-industry trade, not bilateral trade (Fidrmuc 2004 offers supporting econometric evidence).

8. Brülhart (2009) shows that the Grubel-Lloyd index (which measures share of intra-industry in bilateral trade) rose from 0.25 in the early 1960s, to 0.4 in 1975, but remained constant at 0.52 for 1990 and 2006.

9. These are estimates from the Synthetic Counterfactual Method pioneered by Abadie and Gardeazabal (2003). These results are based on a simple model focusing on market size, per capita GDP and trade openness as key determinants of location choice and a similar donor

pool to Campos et al. (2014). Larger weights were estimated for USA, Canada and New Zealand.

10. Data from Lane and Milesi-Ferretti (2007) corroborates this point.

References

Abadie, A., & Gardeazabal, J. (2003). The economic costs of conflict: A case study of the Basque country. *American Economic Review, 93,* 113–132.

Adams, W. (1989). *Restructuring the French economy: Government and the rise of market competition since World War II.* Washington, DC: Brookings Institution Press.

Aitken, N. (1973). The effect of the EEC and EFTA on European trade: A temporal cross-section analysis. *American Economic Review, 63*(5), 881–892.

Alfaro, L., Antràs, P., Chor, D., & Conconi, P. (2015, November 14). Make or buy decisions over upstream and downstream inputs: An investigation of firm boundaries along value chains, *VoxEu.*

Baldwin, R., & Lopez-Gonzalez, J. (2015). Supply-chain trade: A portrait of global patterns and several testable hypotheses. *The World Economy, 38*(11), 1682–1721.

Basile, R., Castellani, D., & Zanfei, A. (2008). Location choices of multinational firms in Europe: The role of EU cohesion policy. *Journal of International Economics, 74*(2), 328–340.

Bayoumi, T., & Eichengreen, B. (1997). Is regionalism simply a diversion? Evidence from the evolution of the EC and EFTA. In T. Ito & A. Krueger (Eds.), *Regionalism vs multilateral arrangements.* Chicago: NBER/University of Chicago Press.

Bean, C., & Crafts, N. (1996). British economic growth since 1945: Relative economic decline... and renaissance? In N. Crafts & G. Toniolo (Eds.), *Economic growth in Europe since 1945.* Cambridge: Cambridge University Press.

Bergeaud, A., Cette, G., & Lecat, R. (2016). Productivity trends in advanced countries between 1890 and 2012. *Review of Income and Wealth, 62*(3), 420–444.

BIS. (2015). *Triennial central bank survey: 2013.* Basel: Bank for International Settlements.

Brülhart, M. (2009). An account of global intra-industry trade, 1962–2006. *The World Economy, 32*(3), 401–459.

Burgess, S. (2011). Measuring financial sector output and its contribution to UK GDP. *Bank of England Quarterly Bulletin 2011, Q3*, 234–246.

Campos, N., & Coricelli, F. (2015a, December 11). Some unpleasant brexit econometrics, *VoxEu*.

Campos, N., & Coricelli, F. (2015b, February 3). Why did Britain's join the EU? A new insight from economic history, *VoxEu*.

Campos, N., Coricelli, F., & Moretti, L. (2014). *Economic growth and political integration: Estimating the benefits from membership in the European Union using the synthetic counterfactuals method* (CEPR Discussion Papers 9968).

Campos, N., & Macchiarelli, C. (2016). Core and periphery in the European Monetary Union: Bayoumi and Eichengreen 25 years later. *Economics Letters, 147*(1), 127–130.

Copsey, N., & Haughton, T. (2014a). Farewell britannia? 'Issue Capture' and the politics of Cameron's 2013 EU referendum pledge. *Journal of Common Market Studies, 52*(1), 74–89.

Copsey, N., & Haughton, T. (2014b). Farewell Britannia? 'Issue Capture' and the Politics of David Cameron's 2013 EU Referendum Pledge. *Journal of Common Market Studies, 52*, 74–89.

Crafts, N. (2012). British relative economic decline revisited: The role of competition. *Explorations in Economic History, 49*(1), 17–29.

Darwin, J. (2011). *The empire project: The rise and fall of the British world system 1830–1970*. Cambridge: Cambridge University Press.

Dell, E. (1995). *The Schuman plan and the British abdication of leadership in Europe*. Oxford: Clarendon Press.

Eichengreen, B. (2008). European integration. In D. Wittman & B. Weingast (Eds.), *Oxford handbook of political economy*. Oxford: Oxford University Press.

Fidrmuc, J. (2004). The endogeneity of the optimum currency area criteria, intra-industry trade, and EMU enlargement. *Contemporary Economic Policy, 22*(1), 1–12.

Frankel, J., & Rose, A. (1998). The endogeneity of the optimum currency area criteria. *Economic Journal, 108*(449), 1009–1025.

Garavini, G. (2012). *After empires: European integration, decolonization, and the challenge from the global south 1957–1986*. Oxford: Oxford University Press.

George, S. (1994). *An awkward partner: Britain in the European community* (2nd ed.). Oxford: Oxford University Press.

Gianetti, M., Burkart, M., & Elligsen, T. (2011). What you sell is what you lend? Explaining trade credit contracts. *Review of Financial Studies, 24*(4), 1261–1298.

Gowland, D., & Turner, A. (1999). *Reluctant Europeans: Britain and European integration 1945–1998.* Abingdon: Routledge.

Haldane, S., Brennan, S., & Madouros, V. (2010). What is the contribution of the financial sector: Miracle or mirage? In A. Turner et al. (Ed.), *The Future of Finance: The LSE Report.* London: LSE.

Hansen, B. (2001). The new econometrics of structural change: Dating breaks in US labor productivity. *Journal of Economic Perspectives, 15*(4), 117–128.

Lane, P., & Milesi-Ferretti, G. (2007). The external wealth of Nations Mark II. *Journal of International Economics, 73,* 223–250.

Martin, P., Mayer, T., & Thoenig, M. (2012). The geography of conflicts and fee trade agreements. *American Economic Journal: Macroeconomics, 4*(4), 1–35.

OECD. (1987). *Structural adjustment and economic performance.* Paris: OECD.

Ottaviano, G. I. P., Pessoa, J. P., Sampson, T., & Van Reenen, J. (2014). *Brexit or Fixit? The trade and welfare effects of leaving the European Union.* CEP/LSE, CEPPA016.

Sapir, A. (2011). European integration at the crossroads: A review essay on the 50th anniversary of Bela Balassa's theory of economic integration. *Journal of Economic Literature, 49*(4), 1200–1229.

Tatham, A. (2009). *Enlargement of the European union.* Amsterdam: Kluwer European Law Collection.

Temin, P. (2003). The golden age of European growth reconsidered. *European Review of Economic History, 6,* 3–22.

Young, H. (1998). *This blessed plot: Britain and Europe from Churchill to Blair.* New York: Overlook Press.

European Monetary Integration and the EU–UK Relationship

Corrado Macchiarelli

1 Introduction

The idea of "ever closer" union is ill-defined, owing to the uncertainty that surrounds it. Still, paraphrasing Jean Monnet, Europe always established itself through discrete and evolutionary steps, where the need for more integration, particularly during crises, has met with the majority of political (rather than economic) support. European integration has never been a jump forward all at once: on the contrary, the very limits one stage exposed led—in many instances—to the necessity for the next step. In this context, British attitude towards Europe is no exception. While the UK's support has always been volatile and influenced by the particular interests of the country in safeguarding trade and sovereignty (see also Ramiro Troitiño 2016), the UK–EU relationship has historically been strong and incremental. This suggests that the multi-layer crisis we are living, and, as a consequence the tightening of the UK–EU

C. Macchiarelli (✉)
Economics and Finance, Brunel University London, London, UK
e-mail: Corrado.Macchiarelli@brunel.ac.uk

© The Author(s) 2017
N.F. Campos and F. Coricelli (eds.), *The Economics of UK–EU Relations*,
DOI 10.1007/978-3-319-55495-2_4

79

relations, is not too telling about the E(M)U and the EU–UK relations' future success. The size of the recent crisis may well act as a catalyst for reforms; something not new in the European integration process.

Since the sign up of the Maastricht Treaty, there have not been many "stops" in European integration, the most severe one being the global economic and financial turmoil taking central stage in Europe. The crisis exposed the inherent "fragility" of the EMU (De Grauwe 2016a), calling for the need to put in place a framework to deal with the growing imbalances of macro-financial and democratic nature within the monetary union. Since 2010, the exceptional effort that has been put in place has translated into reforms both on the legal and the institutional sides (see ECB 2011b). Particularly, the creation a new two-pillar system of financial supervision (see de Larosière Group 2009), i.e. the European System of Financial Supervision (ESFS); the conception of a European liquidity fund, i.e. the European Stability Mechanism; the revamp of macroeconomic policy coordination and fiscal surveillance, i.e. the Fiscal Compact and annex legislations (Two Pack and Six Pack; see ECB 2010); together with a renovated role for the ECB in financial stability and supervision (see Gerba and Macchiarelli 2015), including the historic agreement on a banking union for Europe (see Macchiarelli 2016). These initiatives, which were further developed in the Five President's report, paved the way for a renovated European integration process, which, if successful, will have no precedent in the history of European integration since the introduction of the euro.

Such reforms, consistent with the idea of "completing" the EMU (hence, a "Genuine Economic and Monetary Union"; see Juncker et al. 2015) would not only affect the EMU Member States' governance, but they would also help close the "credibility" breaches left by a "Europe in search for its own identity". Advancing in the European integration process will have an impact on the EU and the single market, with the obvious consequence of affecting the UK as well, and the future of its negotiations (see also Sapir and Wolff 2016). This may well leave the UK in a difficult position, should negotiations fail to deliver a mutually beneficial deal. Provided that European integration worked in the past, the net benefits of staying out of the EU *ex ante* may be different from the same benefits *ex post*, particularly in the likely scenario the Union will have to "comprehensively" move forward to safeguard its integrity.

2 European Economic Integration

2.1 Lessons from the Inter-war Period

It is useful to start the analysis by looking at the European sovereign debt crisis through the lenses of the pre-Bretton Woods' period. During the gold standard, the US became a big sink for gold reserves for the rest of the World. Such a strict convertibility of US dollars into gold makes an interesting parallel with the modern EMU, as both systems involve acceptance of monetary and fiscal orthodoxy (Bordo and James 2013). In the gold standard, the *monetary constraint* was the convertibility of claims into gold. In the modern EMU, orthodoxy is imposed by the ECB's strict inflation target. By the same token, *fiscal orthodoxy* implies both regimes to depend on the avoidance of fiscal deficits which would otherwise jeopardize the price stability objective. During the gold standard, most countries had little room to raise money through taxation, causing a concrete constraint on spending (Bordo and James 2013). In the EMU, the constraint is explicit, with a set-up centered on the idea of "tying one's hands" (Giavazzi and Pagano 1988), i.e. guarding against government failure by agreeing on strict fiscal rules (e.g. the 1997 Stability and Growth Pact) letting, at the same time, markets find their *equilibria* (Fuest and Peichl 2012; see also De Grauwe 2016a).

During this period many countries, such as Argentina, Brazil, Chile, Italy and Portugal, experienced "sudden stops" of capital inflows (Bordo 2006), whenever capital markets proved not to be deep enough to borrow in their own currency (i.e. an "original sin"; Eichengreen and Hausmann 1999; Bordo and Meissner 2007). This situation is reminiscent of the condition of many euro area countries during the sovereign debt crisis since 2010, with the Member States being confronted with market drying out, as the result of a flight-to-quality of capital—facilitated by the single currency (see De Grauwe 2016a)—towards their "safer" EMU peers.

By the end of 1913, the classical gold standard was at its high but WWI caused many countries to suspend or abandon convertibility, because of this asymmetric adjustment problem (Bordo and Meissner 2007). The limits of the gold standard can be summarized as a series of impossible trinities (or political trilemmas, Rodrik 2007; Bordo and Meissner 2007), the most interesting one being the *political economy* trilemma. This principle states that fixed exchange rates, free capital flows, and democratization cannot be observed simultaneously. Here, the lack of democratization is understood as the removal of macroeconomic policy tools from the hands of "democratically accountable governments" (Scharpf 2011).[1] This has become (regrettably) relevant for deficit countries within a monetary system. Surplus countries, such as France and the US, at that time, could count on the active monetary policy pursued by their central banks in sterilizing the gold inflows through bonds' sales. This was instrumental in preventing increases of the money stock. Deficit countries, including the UK, on the contrary, faced pressure to deflate, when capital market dried out, in order to generate a medium-term surplus (Eichengreen and Temin 2010). Given the impossibility to counteract imbalances with the remaining policies, countries were thus forced to "bring down" their economies; something similar to what Scharpf (2011) calls "bankruptcy-cum-devaluation" in today's terms.

With time, attempts to keep gold parities that were too stringently imposed made several economies to suffer, including the US itself, which collapsed in 1929. The Bretton Woods system (1944) that followed recognized the need to fix the exchange rate, however, under non-total parities. All parities were expressed with respect to the US dollar, with a ±1% margin. The dollar was itself convertible into gold at $35/ounce. Although there were a few realignments, the system worked until the 70s, being to a large degree the basis of the post-WWII recovery. The Bretton Woods agreement led to the creation of the International Monetary Fund (IMF), whose role was to provide short-term balance-of-payment assistance—using deposits from all members—to countries in deficit. The creation of a liquidity fund after WWII was not accidental as it reflected the inherent asymmetry of the exchange rate parity system: with countries running a surplus having little problem in maintaining the exchange rate at the agreed parity, and countries in deficit eventually running out of reserves, with the obvious route to devaluation.

2.2   From the Treaty of Rome to the Vote for Brexit

During the 40s, despite British attitude towards integration remained positive—it is of 1946 W. Churchill's famous speech on the "United States of Europe"—it underlined its skepticism with the major priority of the country in retaining sovereignty. The UK withdrew from the latest stages of negotiations of the first European Community, the European Coal and Steal Community (1951)—created to seal a long-term deal between France and Germany—and from the newly created European Economic Community (EEC), formed with the Treaty of Rome in 1957.

Out of the EEC, the UK decided to join Austria, Denmark, Norway, Portugal, Sweden and Switzerland and create the European Free Trade Agreement (Treaty of Stockholm 1959). The creation of the EEC, on the one side, and the EFTA, on the other side, gashed Europe in two. With the EFTA, the UK was mainly interested in a different model for integration, based on trade and common agreements. The start of the so-called UK "relative economic decline" (Fig. 1), compared to France and Germany, in particular, saw the UK to later apply to the EEC in 1961, leaving Ireland, Norway and Denmark no alternative than applying as well (Ramiro Troitiño 2016). The UK's application was rejected in two instances, in 1963 and later in 1967, by the French President C. De Gaulle on the ground of different views on the Common Agricultural Policy. The UK would be able to join the EEC only in 1973 with the change of French presidency. The UK's political demand of joining was by itself driven by two main internal reasons. First of all, there was the necessity to self-legitimate the surrender of the UK's economic centrality in Europe. Second, the UK government viewed the continuation of the integration path as a way for own future economic development and political security.

The US decision to abandon the gold standard in 1971 (the so-called "Nixon Shock"), brought Bretton Woods to an end. This stemmed by and large from pressure induced by the US expansionary policies in the late 1960s and early 1970s, coupled with rising unemployment rate and an increasing current account deficit as a part of the financing of the Vietnam War. With a degree of integration of around 78% and an even

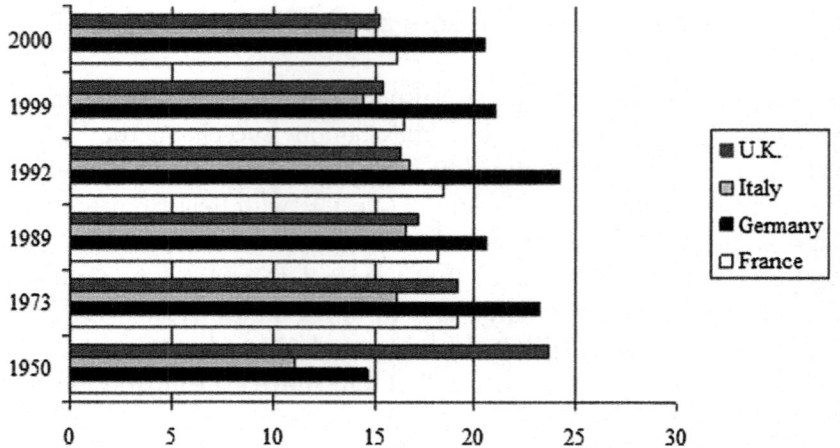

Fig. 1 GDP evolution in Germany, France, Italy and the UK's relative decline. *Source* Data from Valli (2002). *Note* Data are in PPP for all countries but Germany. German data refer to the Federal Republic between 1950 and 1989

higher degree of intra-investment dependence, Europe was too closed and focused on "internal affairs" to allow for a system of perfectly flexible exchange rates. Moreover, the estimated European trade elasticities with respect to the exchange rate were too high, so that excessive exchange rate fluctuations would have had significantly hurt the trade shares of European countries (Macchiarelli and Sangalli 2007). In this context, the Werner proposal paved the way for a model of economic and monetary union in Europe for the first time. The 1970s' Plan envisaged a union to be achieved in three evolutionary phases, to be completed by 1980, including the four freedoms of movement of goods, services, labor and capital, and the total and irreversible convertibility of currencies. At the same time, it recognized the need "for the development of [a] political union which in the long run it [the economic and monetary union] will be unable to do without" (Commission of the European Communities 1970, p. 26).

Despite the extraordinary federal reach of the proposal, any possibilities to develop the Plan further were abandoned under the exceptional volatility of exchange rates of those years. The dollar became effectively floated and the best countries could do was a joint float against the US, with the limited fluctuation of each EC currency with respect to each other. This formed the base for the Smithsonian Agreement, created in December 1971, by the ten largest EC members. By that time, the Community had been enlarged by the entry of Denmark, Ireland, and the UK (Mayes 2011). This early period is known as the "snake in the tunnel," as the Smithsonian Agreement permitted not only exchange rate fluctuations of 2.25% of each currency with respect to the others, but also a ±4.5% fluctuation limit, representing the "tunnel" (Mayes 2011). Market volatility and the supply side shocks of the mid-70s made France, Ireland, Italy and the UK struggle to remain in the snake and exit quite early under the impact of the first oil price crisis. The system continued with Belgium, Luxembourg, Denmark, West Germany, and the Netherlands only, until 1979 (Mayes 2011).

The mid-70s are critical years for the UK and its relationship with Europe. In 1975, the UK's National front rallied against Europe, with Labor voting to leave the EEC after only 2 years of membership. However, a referendum embraced the European cause and membership to the EEC, all in the same year.

By 1978 the need to achieve exchange rate stability within the Community, and the realization of the risks of asymmetric shocks coming from excessive exchange rate volatility itself (Mundell 1973), resulted in the then French President V. Giscard d'Estaing and the German Chancellor H. Schmidt putting forward a plan for the creation of a European Monetary System (EMS). This was essentially the result of a political decision. The EMS was initially thought as a way to provide a response to the constraints implied by the macroeconomic impossible trinity. The idea was to make participant countries commit to a system of fixed but adjustable pegs. The key difference from the snake was that instead of being a dollar-based system it reflected purely intra-Community exchange rate "controlled" fluctuations. At the heart of the system were the Exchange Rate Mechanism (ERM) and the European Currency Unit (ECU), the latter being a weighted sum of the nine component currencies. Within the ERM, the same 2.25% bands were kept, except for Italy, for which a ±6% band was agreed. The system encouraged coordinated foreign exchange interventions and interest rate changes when a country approached the permitted limits. Besides, the EMS conceived issuance of "private" ECU bonds and related instruments, which large corporates and governments found cheaper and convenient to adopt (Mayes 2011). J. Callaghan's Britain decided to opt out of the EMS in 1978, until Thatcher would open to the possibility of it, with the UK's inclusion more than ten years later, in 1989.

Frequent realignments (11 only in between 1979 and 1987; see Eichengreen and Wyplosz 1993) and inflation beginning to take hold turned out soon to alter the symmetric structure of the agreement. The idea was that any countries having troubles keeping within the bands should have started to intervene when the currency had diverged by at least 75% of the tunnel's edge. When this edge was reached, all such interventions were supposed to be symmetric. In practice, however, the encumbrance of adjustment was primarily placed on depreciating currencies. With West Germany's deflating maneuver having begun in the mid-1970s, the Deutschmark enjoyed higher (than the rest of the EC countries) credibility, soon emerging as the center of the system. Despite the mark's centrality was thought as a way to warrant the system's standing, the EMS gradually started to resemble a "Deutschmark area," with West Germany leading, and setting its own interest rate for domestic purposes, and the other countries following (Mayes 2011).

The capital market liberalization of the early 90s, together with the unification of the East with the West, posed a major challenge. In 1992 only, there were 12 realignments. The German reconsolidation, above all, resulted in a large fiscal idiosyncratic shock. High public and private capital inflows to the East (see also Mundell 1994; Hunt 2008), as well as the new Deutschemark's attractiveness, created strong appreciation pressure. Initially, the EMS prevented the Deutschemark from appreciating. However, the EMS was only temporarily able to prevent the massive capital inflows (Sinn 1996). The contingent Bundesbank's decision to raise interest rates to contain pressure on German price levels exacerbated the asymmetry of the shock, especially as Europe was entering a recession (Velis 1995). For Germany's ERM partners not sharing this need, the appropriate strategy would have been to devalue, but within the ERM this was not straightforward. The system began to fall apart as markets speculated against each of the deficit countries, in turn, forcing them out of the system. As explained by Mundell (1994), "a Europe-wide monetary policy would have cushioned the impact of the German unification shock over the EMS part of the continent. It would have led to more inflation than the Bundesbank wanted, and more deflation than her partners wanted, but a more balanced equilibrium for the fixed exchange rate mechanism". Speculation escalated with the pound sterling being first dismissed from the ERM ("Black Wednesday", 16 September 1992), followed by Italy one day later. Spain, Portugal and Ireland although forced to devalue, continued in the ERM. France, Denmark and Belgium remained facing severe market pressure. In 1993, under continued speculation, the permitted fluctuation bands were broadened to $\pm 15\%$, or largely enough to cope with the misalignment and alleviate market stress.

The idea of fixing the exchange rates came back as part of the idea to move to a monetary union under the terms set by the Maastricht Treaty signed in 1992. In 1988, particularly, the Delors' committee set up a framework of economic and monetary integration to be achieved in three stages, echoing the Werner Report, the main idea being that "a single market required a single currency". The project was a very ambitious one, especially because of the turbulent phase (i.e. the concomitant crisis of the EMS; see Eichgreen and Wylopsz 1993) in which it was presented. With the Report, an 11-year transition period began before the introduction of the single currency, with national coinages ceasing to legally exist on 1 January 2002. The starting point was participation into the Exchange Rate Mechanism (ERM), followed by the narrowing of exchange rate bands during the second stage. Stage 1 (to be completed by 1990) mostly concentrated on fiscal consolidation, coordination of macroeconomic policy and performance, completion of the single market, and, finally, greater financial integration and coordination of national monetary policies. During phase 2 (up until 1994), a European System of Central Banks (ESCB) was created, and attention was given to harmonizing the monetary policy tools among the Member States. This second stage also saw the birth of the European Monetary Institute (EMI), then European Central Bank. Shifting control of monetary and exchange rate macroeconomic policies from national to the newly born European central bank was a fundamental step of stage 3. During this third phase (ending on 1 January 1999) exchange rates were irrevocably fixed.

The criteria for the run up to stage 3 of the EMU were set in the well-known Maastricht criteria (Treaty on the European Union, Maastricht Council, December 1991). While achieving an immediate monetary integration would have probably been desirable in a long-run perspective (Eichgreen and Wylopsz 1994), it seemed unrealizable from both a political and economic perspective. The Maastricht Treaty was successful in correctly signaling a "convergence of preferences" among member states, by setting up a clear timeline for integration. That is why Maastricht has to be primarily understood as a political process, which flourished particularly thanks to the "bargain" between Germany and France (Baun 1996).

The collapse of the EMS in 1992 was giving clear evidence that monetary convergence was any longer sufficient neither to guarantee the credibility of fixed exchange rates nor to prevent systematic imbalances to occur. This is why the Maastricht criteria created the occasion to outwit the foregoing stability condition in inflation rates, requiring additional convergence in interest rates and exchange rates (Macchiarelli and Sangalli 2007), as well as fiscal policies. The latter particularly, reflected the idea of acquiescence to clear fiscal targets, i.e. *fiscal orthodoxy* (see Bordo and James 2013) which—together with an explicit provision to discourage governments to resort to price rises for debt financing (i.e. "no monetary financing"—Art. 123 TFEU)—was seen as a way to reduce the risk of high inflation (see Giavazzi and Pagano 1988; Chari et al. 2015). In this respect, the Maastricht criteria—albeit controversial in today's terms (De Grauwe 2016a)—were numbers reflecting political realities at that time, and not just discrete targets (Klein 1998).[2]

Already in 1988, Thatcher announced Britain's intention not to join the European economic and monetary integration plan. That was followed by severe political turmoil in the UK, with the Secretary of State for Trade and Industry, N. Ridley, being forced to resign in July 1990 following a controversial interview, and the UK's deputy Prime Minister, G. Howe, resigning in November of the same year because of his disagreement with Thatcher's opposing policy towards the single European currency. Thatcher will resign 3 weeks later.

With the first 11 countries signing up to the euro, on stage 3 of the EMU, Britain stayed out. In the negotiations leading up to Maastricht, the UK was granted an opt out clause. Technically, it was not eligible because of 2-year ERM criterion; in practice, it would have been almost certainly granted admission based on the standard macroeconomic convergence indicators (see also Ramiro Troitiño 2016). Looking at the period averages reported in Table 1, in the decade elapsing in between stage 1 and 3 of the EMU, the UK performed quite well with respect to the Maastricht criteria. The pattern of short-term interest rates at 1-month maturity (Fig. 2) after the euro suggests—however—a monetary policy stance which is specific to the country (see also Holden 2009). Chiefly, with the decision to stay out, the United Kingdom retained sovereignty and the right to conduct autonomous monetary and exchange rate policy. This was different for the euro area, where monetary policy decisions were indeed delegated to the Governing Council of the ECB for all euro area countries; a stance now identified with the much-discussed term "one-size-fits-all" (see Peersman and Smets 1999; Nechio 2011) (Table 2).[3]

During the first years after the introduction of the euro, the British pound appreciated against the new currency, to some extent following the strong US dollar (Fig. 2). For the pound, sizeable fluctuations have persisted through the whole sample period as the pound has appreciated even more before the vote of June 2016, largely driven by "safe-haven" effects. In the debate about monetary union membership, one concern for the UK was to maintain the credibility of monetary and exchange rate policy. The numbers in Tables 2, 3 and Fig. 2 suggest that "borrowing

Table 1 The orthodoxy in the Maastricht criteria

"Monetary orthodoxy"
Inflation rate not exceeding 1,5% of the mean of EC countries with lower inflation.
The interest rate on long-term Government Securities not greater than 2% with respect to the mean of the three least inflation countries.
Exchange rate within the ERM fluctuations margins for at least 2 years.
"Fiscal orthodoxy"
Gross public debt not exceeding 60% of GDP, or converging at a "satisfactory pace".
Public deficit not exceeding 3% of GDP.

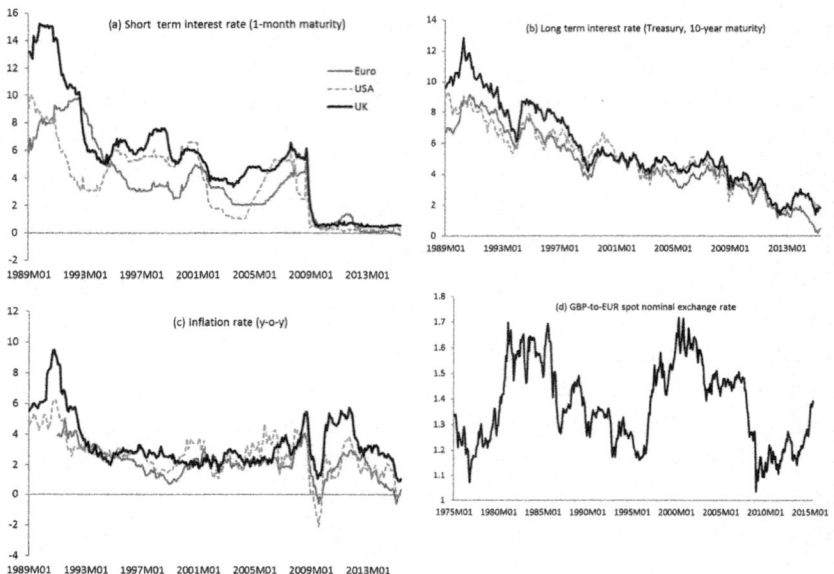

Fig. 2 Macroeconomic and international finance indicators for the UK in comparison with the euro area and the US. *Source* Datastream, BoE, and ECB data. *Note* Data for the euro area use ECB's vintage data prior to Jan. 1999 or, for Treasury bonds, Germany's. Last observation is May 2015

credibility" was indeed never a concern for the UK, which fared relatively well in keeping inflation in check, with the possible exception of the immediate post-crisis period.

In 1997, the UK committed itself to joining in principle the single currency, but with a number of caveats (the so-called G. Brown's Five Tests), the main one being that EMU membership should have been achieved in the national interests. In 2003, a review by the UK Treasury concluded that the investment and financial services tests were met, but the convergence and flexibility tests were not. Thus, the Treasury's assessment, i.e. that "a clear and unambiguous case for UK membership of EMU has not *at the present time* been made and a decision to join now would not be in the national economic interest",[4] reduced membership to a technical matter, showing once again British relation to the integration process as a very pragmatic one, with the country expecting an

Table 2 Macroeconomic convergence

	Period averages					
	Euro area		UK		Euro area unweighted	
	1989–1998	1999–2007	1989–1998	1999–2007	1989–1998	1999–2007
Real GDP growth	2.3	2.2	2.1	2.7	2.9	3.0
Employment growth	0.1	1.0	−0.1	0.2	0.4	0.8
Inflation	3.7	2.1	3.7	1.6	4.0	2.4
Inflation deviation	2.0	0.6	1.8	0.6	2.4	0.8
Fiscal balance	−4.3	−1.8	−3.7	−1.3	−4.0	−0.8
Gross public debt	80.2	71.8	53.4	47.5	73.3	56.8
Trade balance	1.0	1.6	−1.1	−2.2	1.7	2.9

Source OECD data from Holden (2009). *Note* inflation deviation refers to the absolute value of annual deviation from the ECB's target of 2%

Table 3 Standard deviation and correlation of economic cycles

	Jan 1989–Dec 1998	Jan 1999–May 2015	Jan 1999–Jul 2007
ST.DEV. (UK)	1.119	1.609	1.166
ST.DEV. (EUR)	1.741	2.859	1.332
ST.DEV. (US)	0.918	2.105	1.306
CORR (EUR, UK)	0.300	0.865	0.627
CORR (EUR, US)	0.291	0.872	0.604
CORR (UK, US)	0.508	0.786	0.511

immediate, or anyway short term, payback for its contribution.[5] This is something dating back already to 1984 with Thatcher's infamous "I want my money back" struggle to reduce Britain's EEC budget participation. It is in this environment that the then Prime Minister T. Blair committed to a referendum on Europe's Constitutional Treaty in 2004, which happened to never occur. Ten years later, on January 2013, Prime Minister D. Cameron promised a second time to give the British people the "simple choice" by the end of 2017 between staying in the EU under the UK's renegotiated terms, or leaving. The European Union Referendum Bill became law in May 2015, resulting in the June 2016 historic vote to leave.[6]

3   Understanding Integration

By looking at the history of previous monetary systems in Europe, there is something to learn about the state of health of the monetary union today. Undoubtedly, the relaxation of fluctuation limits during the EMS has generally provided countries with the needed flexibility to adjust to shocks. However, this has to do more with the EMS set-up rather than fixing of the exchange rate itself.

During the 70s inflation was the major spectrum to fight, especially after the supply side shocks of those years. In both the EMS and the EMU, the asymmetry of the adjustment problem forced a strategy of disinflation on deficit countries—appealingly exploiting the lessons from the German *Bundesbank*—which soon proved not sustainable. This strategy has historically exposed the system's difficulty in managing idiosyncratic shocks, maintaining, at the same time, credibility. Particularly, there are two main channels through which credibility problems may arise both in a system of *fixed exchange rates without a currency* (Macchiarelli and Sangalli 2007)—like the EMS—and in the system of *a currency without a nation*—like the EMU. In both systems, these can be identified as (see also Weber 1991; Salvatore 1997; De Grauwe and Ji 2015):

1. Adjustment costs and
2. Liquidity or coordination costs.

In the history of monetary integration, countries losing the ability to use the exchange rate suffered from costly adjustments *ex post* mainly in terms of unemployment. As far as the EMS is concerned, De Grauwe (1994) shows how both the average unemployment rate and the inflation differential with respect to the reference currency had a significant impact on the credibility of the system. It is thus clear that the convergence of inflation rates pursued during the 1980s, although necessary for the well functioning of the system, was not sufficient to prevent speculative crises, particularly in the lack of structural reforms. The liquidity problem for the EMS was, on the contrary, a typical $n-1$ problem in which choosing the appropriate monetary policy prevailing through the system resulted in a coordination failure (De Grauwe 1994), i.e. whenever the member countries felt that the monetary stance undertaken by the leading currency may not have been representative of the system as a whole. The EMS suffered from a lack of credibility because it was set-up on a union in which national currencies were to be maintained with "irrevocably" fixed exchange rates. This was just inefficient in dealing with asymmetric shocks (De Grauwe 1994; De Grauwe and Ji 2015).

As for the EMU, the aforementioned adjustment problems can be understood as a moral-hazard problem. The very disappearance of the exchange rate led to protectionism, access to larger than domestic capital markets (the so-called "common pool" problem; see, *inter alia*, Kontopoulos and Perotti 1999; Wyplosz and Kostrup 2010), and a higher capacity to borrow, overall weakening incentives for structural reforms (see Calmfors 2001). Such weak leverage for adjustment exacerbated divergence issues in some countries, resulting into higher than necessary adjustments' costs later on (see De Grauwe 2016a). That is to say that the creation of a currency union in Europe weakened the incentive for a market-based flexibility that could have offset (or at least limited) the loss of exchange rate as an adjustment tool (see also Bean 1992; De Grauwe 2016a).

The liquidity problem in today's terms is slightly different than the one countries were confronted with during the EMS. This problem has to do instead with the "fragility" of a system centered on n Treasuries and 1 central bank. Hence, the problem of a currency with "too many countries" (see also De Grauwe 2016a; De Grauwe and Ji 2015). In this system, not only countries will issue debt in a currency they have no control of (a situation reminiscent of the gold standard's "original sin", as we recalled), but also the presence of a "lender of last resort" for sovereigns is not granted. As explained by De Grauwe (2016a), differently from a stand-alone country such as the UK, the Treasury of any EMU member states not only will not benefit from the exchange rate tool in cushioning shocks—thus preventing capital flights-to-safety towards other EMU countries—but also they will not have the unconditional backup of their national central bank. Simply because in the EMU there is no effectively functioning national central bank, with the exception of the ECB. The ECB could certainly intervene and act as a "lender of last resort", as it did exceptionally (see Gerba and Macchiarelli 2016). However, the European Bank will have the major constraints deriving from the complexity of the governance framework of the monetary union (Gerba and Macchiarelli 2016): again 1 central bank and n Treasuries. In the jargon of game theory, the problem with this set-up is that the Member States' fiscal authorities will be better off if the ECB intervenes, obviating the need for fiscal intervention. Likewise, the ECB will be better off if the governments agree to use their fiscal stimulus, thus alleviating the pressure on the ECB itself (see Onorante 2007; Alcidi and Giovannini 2013). Once again, this gives rise to coordination failures.

3.1 Theory Behind Economic Integration

From a theoretical standpoint, the "economics" of European integration can be understood under two broad headings. The first is the optimal control approach or the *political economy* of strict fiscal rules (see Fuest and Peichl 2012; De Grauwe 2016a), discussed earlier. This approach tends to identify in the moral-hazard implicit in pooling the exchange rate and monetary policy competencies as the main problem within a currency union. A second popular set of tools is the Optimum Currency Area (OCA) first developed in the 1960s (Mundell 1961; McKinnon 1963), and centered on the idea of trade openness, the flexibility of (labor and product) markets, and business cycle's symmetry. The UK's attitude towards the EU has historically put much emphasis on the former.

The main research question driving the scholarship on OCA has to do with the costs and benefits of sharing a currency (Alesina and Barro 2002). The main cost is the loss of monetary policy and exchange rate autonomy, the latter being particularly relevant in the presence of asymmetric shocks. Benefits are mostly in terms of reduction of transaction costs and exchange rate uncertainty, and of increasing price transparency, trade, and competition. Other recent work calls the attention to the role of *credibility* shocks. If there are varying degrees of commitment, countries with dissimilar credibility shocks, which exacerbate time inconsistency, may find profitable to join a currency union (Chari et al. 2015).

The existence of idiosyncratic shocks alone is not sufficient to establish the case for retaining separate currencies. Nominal exchange rate realignments are only helpful in facilitating adjustment when nominal wages and/or prices are not flexible. In other words, the pattern of asymmetric shocks across countries depends on the degree of *nominal* inertia.[7] De Grauwe and Mongelli (2005) have studied the interactions between symmetry, flexibility, and integration in an OCA framework. For both pairs "symmetry versus. flexibility" and "symmetry versus. integration" the relation is downward sloping (Fig. 3).[8] Focusing on the degree of economic integration and symmetry and how it evolves over time, there are different views on such evolution (as illustrated by arrows around the EU and Euro circles in the Figure; see also Krugman 1993). In Fig. 3, the downward sloping OCA line shows the minimum combinations of symmetry and openness that countries must have in order for a monetary union to provide positive net benefits.

A similar relationship exists between symmetry and flexibility. In particular, countries or regions located below the OCA line do not have enough flexibility given the level of symmetry they face. Countries to the right of the OCA line have a lot of flexibility given the level of symmetry they face. Ultimately, the empirical evidence about how many countries in the E(M)U form an OCA is not clear-cut. Particularly, for the UK the empirical evidence based on these three factors is rather mixed (see De Grauwe 2016a; Campos et al. 2014; Campos and Macchiarelli 2016b; Pesaran et al. 2007; Holden 2009).

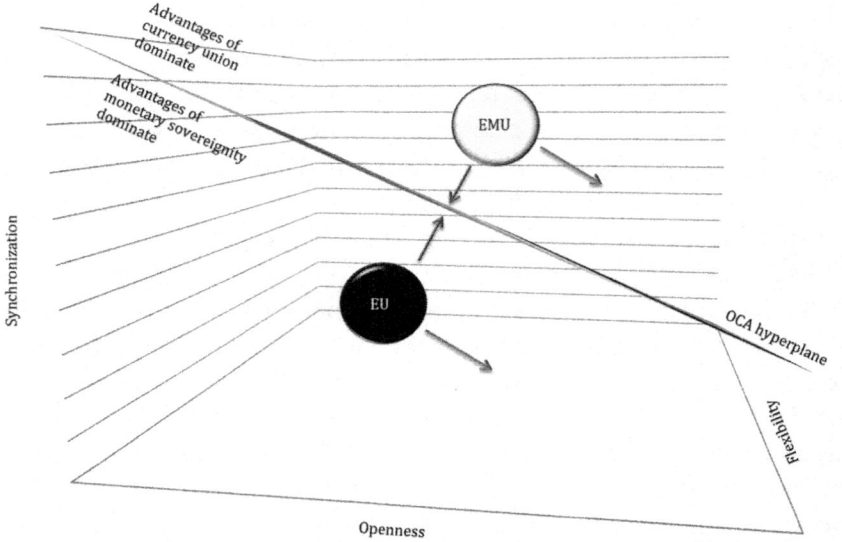

Fig. 3 The interaction between synchronization and openness. *Source* Campos and Macchiarelli (2016a) based on De Grauwe and Mongelli (2005)

3.1.1 Openness

While one would expect a monetary union to have a positive effect on trade, given a reduction in transaction costs and exchange rate risk, as well as higher price transparency, as discussed, the size of the estimated effect of currency unions on trade varies. Seminal work by Frankel and Rose (1998) suggested possible endogeneity of currency unions, i.e. where more openness did not have to be met *ex ante* but rather will *ex post*. However, recent econometric evidence reports "no substantive reliable and robust effect" of currency unions on trade, overall challenging this wisdom (Glick and Rose 2016). Yet, the degree of openness is, *vice versa*, likely to increase the benefits. The evidence suggests there are large differences in the openness of EU countries with the rest of the Union. For the UK, trade of goods between the UK and the rest of the EU is typically low (De Grauwe 2016a), whereas much of the trade share is accounted by financial services (Source: Office for National Statistics).

3.1.2   Flexibility

The lack of independent monetary policy within a monetary union raises the call for labor market flexibility. In particular, in Mundell's (1961) and McKinnon's (1963) original framework the degree of labor market flexibility matters for determining whether a monetary union is attractive to countries (De Grauwe 2016a). When it comes to flexibility, one can distinguish between (i) the pace at which people transition in and out of work, or across sectors, and (ii) wage flexibility. Looking at standard indicators for flexibility, such as individual protection, the use of temporary work and collective dismissal, the UK typically scores low on the protection of individuals, along with other Anglo-Saxon economies, standing in contrast to other continental European countries such as in Germany, Italy and France where protection is significantly higher. The same contrast is true also for temporary work, with very a strict regulation in Spain, France and Italy, differently from Anglo-Saxon economies (2013 OECD's data from the Chartered Institute of Personnel and Development). As underlined by Holden (2009), despite the UK labor market being among the most flexible in Europe, the 1993 Treasury Assessment based on the five Tests highlighted skepticism as to whether flexibility would have been sufficient to cope with a monetary union (Holden 2009). The second key aspect of the labor market flexibility is wage setting. The UK has started an important process of decentralization of wage setting since the 70s (Source: Golden et al. 2006) suggesting a greater degree of moderation (see Calmfors and Driffill 1988; Driffill 2006), hence normally being better positioned in facing supply side shock within a monetary union (see also De Grauwe 2016a).

3.1.3   Symmetry

The efforts to create a European monetary union have sparked increased interest in measuring the synchronization of the business cycles since the beginning of the 1990s. A high level of convergence among the national business cycles, which is the absence of sharp asymmetrical shocks between one country and the euro area, is an important criterion for an OCA. The extent of synchronization between the euro area and the UK studied here can be determined by the correlation of the cyclical components (HP-filtered) in their industrial production (Fig. 4). The cyclical component is calculated as the difference between industrial production growth and an estimate of the trend. Since the euro introduction, the UK's volatility has been considerably lower (Table 3), with this stability being typically attributed to strong domestic demand, with private and public sector consumption and capital investment on new construction contributing to stabilization (Moser et al. 2004). Table 3 also shows that, since the start of EMU, the business cycle of the UK has been correlated considerably with that of the euro area. What is striking is the low level of the correlation for the United Kingdom and the euro area at the beginning of the series, before the EMU (Massman and Mitchell 2002; Campos and Macchiarelli 2016a), something possibly attributed also to the UK sterling dismissal from the EMS in 1992. These fluctuations in the real activity-gap have become smaller over time (see Campos and Macchiarelli 2016a), with correlation being stronger in the second half of the sample. Several studies show that the convergence between the Eurozone and the UK has increased since the EMU (e.g. Angeloni and Dedola 1999; Campos et al. 2014; Canova et al. 2005; European Commission 2008; Massman and Mitchell 2002). In spite of more synchronization, there are still sizeable differences, particularly in the extent monetary policy (captured by short-term interest rates) has been conducted. Assuming a lower interest rate in the UK during the mid-2000, mimicking the ECB's path would have clearly stimulated the late 2000s bubble in property prices further, presumably making the 2008–2009 bust sharper (Holden 2009). However, all such conjectures are purely speculative, as well they present an obvious endogeneity problem. By the design of the EMU, the ECB is constrained to a "one-size-fits-all" monetary policy—the latter being likely to increase the costs of joining the EMU the most de-synchronized are the Member States' cycles. Nonetheless, should the UK have joined, the optimal monetary policy response of the ECB would have possibly been different, reflecting the size and the importance of the UK economy as well (see also Nechio 2011; Peersman and Smets 1999).

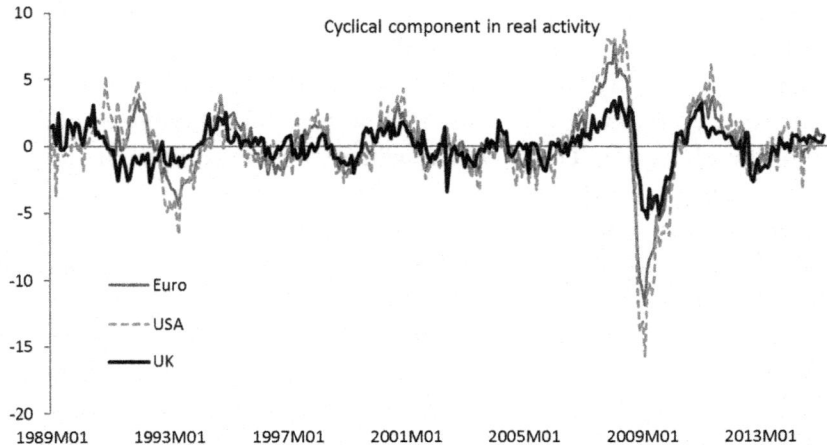

Fig. 4 The UK vs. the Eurozone and the US cycles. *Source* Datastream. Author's calculations

3.2 The EMU Convergence Criteria: A Second Look

Although it is unclear what the prospects for the UK will be outside of the EU, a continuation of the process of European integration, in theory, would be weighed based on the Maastricht convergence criteria. The problem with these criteria has always been political. The Maastricht Treaty was, in fact, paying attention to the idea that, in order to join the new arrangement, countries had to converge sufficiently in their monetary and fiscal policies. Already at the time of their adoption, the unstable conjecture inherited from the EMS crash have probably been "the driving factor in widening the perception that the required criteria were almost paradoxical" (Macchiarelli and Sangalli 2007; see also De Grauwe 2016a). The political paradox was, *inter alia*, accentuated by the evidence that many countries were finding it difficult to fulfill these criteria using policies of fiscal stabilization which were accompanied by economic stagnation, thus keeping actual budget deficits high (as a % of GDP), in spite of any significant attempts to cut public spending (Macchiarelli and Sangalli 2007). Once again, political support among member states remained the strongest in pursuing these goals, above and beyond economic reasons. That is what historically lacked in the UK.

Some (e.g. Baldwin and Wyplosz 2006) have argued that the necessity of the stringent convergence criteria, conceptualized through the adoption of the Maastricht Treaty, was a main attempt to compensate for the fact that Europe was indeed not an OCA. In this respect, the main concern for any enlargements of the monetary union to any other country, including the UK, would be again represented by the costs of adjustment in order to deal with asymmetric shocks. In the absence of sufficient labor market flexibility and/or of fiscal transfers at the euro area level, many countries would suffer from severe adjustment problems. As the crisis made very clear, the lack of such adjustment mechanisms, in the presence of asymmetries, has made adjustment costs *ex post* very high in order for the integrity of the monetary union to be preserved (see Scharpf 2011; De la Dehesa 2012).

Already since before the start of the EMU, this conception of asymmetries has spurred an alternative approach to European integration: the possibility of a two-tier or "multi-speed Europe." Not least, during the recent (at the time of writing) EU6 Summit in Brussels, the limitations of a treaty commitment to pursue the "ever closer union" of the peoples of Europe were reaffirmed as a part of a package to facilitate Cameron's campaign before the referendum. While acknowledging that the Union "allows for different paths of integration", however, European negotiators (French and Belgium in particular) were against the idea of a "pic-n-mix" Europe by adding a clear restatement of the principle that all countries— unless they have an explicit exemption like Denmark (or Britain, before the referendum)—must ultimately join the single currency.

From an economic viewpoint, it is true that smaller groups of selected countries may be better candidates in forming an OCA, given the homogeneity that characterizes them (see also De Grauwe 2016a). Looking at the early evidence on the degree of synchronization of shocks across countries before the EMU (1963–1988), it seems that, with respect to the supply side, one can identify a "core" region-Germany, France, Denmark and Benelux, where the shocks are highly correlated, as well as a "periphery" region where the correlation with the anchor region is much lower (Bayoumi and Eichengreen 1993). With respect to demand shocks, there is more of a difference: the correlation with Germany is much lower, even for the other countries of the European core. The EMU may have eliminated independent national monetary policies as a source of idiosyncratic demand shocks, but national fiscal policies remained independent so the cross-country correlation in movements in demand may well persist (see also ECB 2011a). Using Bayoumi and Eichengreen (1993) criterion on the supply-side core-periphery divide, Campos and Macchiarelli (2016b) show that the UK has moved from the periphery (1963–1988) to core (1989–2015) (Fig. 5). The results for the UK are admittedly not strong. Said that, however, a new, smaller, periphery has emerged (Spain, Portugal, Ireland

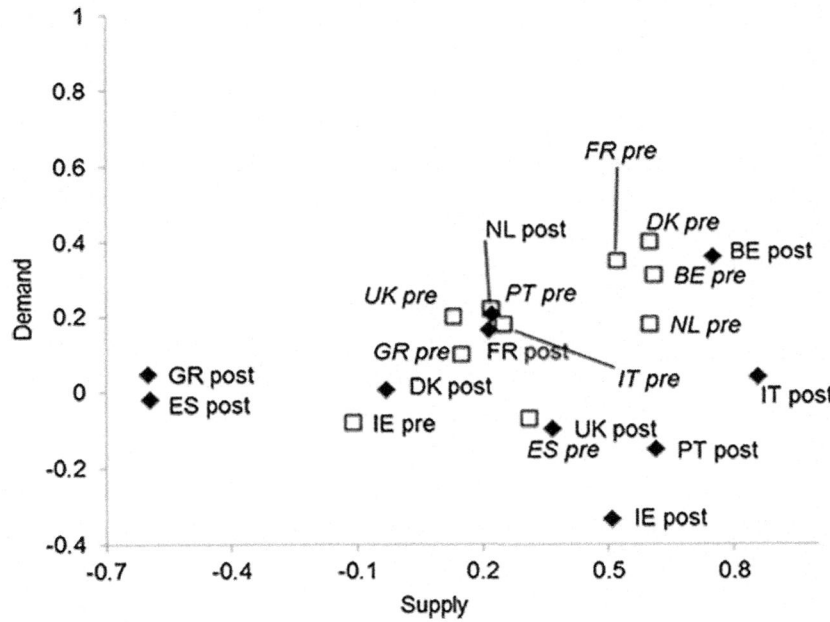

Fig. 5 The role of asymmetries 25 years before and after the EMU. *Source* Campos and Macchiarelli (2016b). *Note* list of countries—*BE* Belgium, *DK* Denmark, *ES* Spain, *FR* France, *GR* Greece, *IE* Ireland, *IT* Italy, *NL* Netherlands, *PT* Portugal, *UK* United Kingdom. The correlation for demand and supply shock is presented with respect to the anchor region (*DE* Germany)

and Greece). Thus, the EMU has actually *weakened* the core-periphery pattern, resulting into countries being more integrated over time.

To conclude, while the hypothesis of a "multi-tier" Europe cannot be dismissed based on the little evidence available, there is a second (and opposite) alternative to a "multi-speed" line of work: a process of reform and—possibly—deepening. This is the spirit of the five Presidents Report, which we will cover in the next section.

4   Towards a GEMU

The five President Report is a far-reaching initiative for a "deeper and fairer" Union, focusing on four key policy areas (Juncker et al. 2015; see also Begg 2014): an integrated financial framework to ensure macro and micro financial stability and supervision at the euro area level; an integrated fiscal framework with the dual goal of delivering discipline and developing new common fiscal policy instruments; an integrated economic policy framework to ensure macroeconomic policy coordination, fairness and competitiveness; and finally, enhancement of democratic legitimation (see also Scharpf 2011).

The key question the Report seeks to answer is: where did the EMU fail and how can it be fixed? (see Pisani-Ferri 2012, 2013; De la Dehesa 2012; De Grauwe 2016a; Scharpf 2011). The Report consists of "short-term", "medium-term" and "long-term" reforms; i.e. as clearly a fiscal or a political union will take longer, given the transfer of sovereignty they involve, than (the existing) bank supervision (see Macchiarelli 2016), or coordination of macroeconomic and fiscal policies, which are short to medium-term measures. The timeline of the five President Report, particularly, reads as follows:

A *first phase* (between now and early 2017) of "deepening by doing", building on the existing EMU framework and instruments, including legal provisions, with a view to boost competitiveness and structural convergence, achieving budgetary discipline at national and the euro area level, completing financial integration (i.e. a capital market Union, federal Resolution and European deposit insurance are on the way), and increasing democratic accountability. A *second phase* of "completing

EMU", including medium to long-term reforms, also of legal nature, with a set of commonly agreed benchmarks for convergence. A *third phase* (to be completed by 2025) of furthering integration—this phase will not exclude other EU countries from joining.

4.1 Is "Completing" the EMU Compatible with Dropping the "Ever Closer Union" Clause?

The key question, in the light of the state of the EU–UK negotiations before June 2016, is whether "completion" of the Union would be compatible with the dropping of the clause of "ever closeness". Let me start by saying that the answer to the above question should be negative. This does not mean intermediate solutions cannot be found in seeking an agreement with the UK. Particularly, there are at least two arguments for the answer above, both falling under the remit of political economy.

The first motivation is *political*.

Many parties have voiced concerns that a British exit could be the beginning of the end for Europe, or—not least—lead to a stall in integration. In their view, the UK could be followed by other countries, creating a legal precedent in the European integration path, within the remit of Lisbon's Article 50. Let us not forget, however, that the UK's vote to leave was the peak of an iceberg, preceded by a period during which Europe has been gripped in waves of Euro-skepticism (see also Mongelli 2013). This trend is strictly linked to the notion of Weber's credibility (Weber 1991); the latter always having been considered a key issue in Europe's identity. Low credibility has been cyclical in the history of European integration, in some sense accompanying the recessive phases of the economic cycles (Macchiarelli and Sangalli 2007) whenever those translated into crises challenging the prevailing paradigm or exposing the system's inherent fragilities. This continuous search for credibility has worked as an accelerator to the process of integration, leaving in most cases European countries no chances but joining in (Macchiarelli and Sangalli 2007). The underlying logic to the convergence criteria has to be evaluated in the light of the will of conditioning expectations concerning the future path of the European economic and monetary union (i.e. a "convergence of preferences"). The question of *a currency without a nation*, together with that of "betrayed expectations" in terms of post-euro introduction growth, is nowadays the most compelling elements holding the EMU's credibility down (Macchiarelli and Sangalli 2007). Particularly, the realization that the positive cycle after the period of very slow growth characterizing the mid-2000s was by and large "bubbly," and coming at the exposes of a growing north–south divide (see De la Dehesa 2012), raised many questions concerning the long-term viability of the European project.

Agreeing to the idea of transition to a GEMU, albeit sounding unprecedented, could indeed ensure that needed convergence in a political sense, in a period in which the credibility of the Union is at stake and its democratic base drifting away. The UK never really bought into the European project with a view of being a part of an "ever closer" union, but rather to balance power within Europe. This explains why British attitude has frequently been based on dismissing or openly rejecting further steps of integration.

There is little clarity about what new relationship the UK and the EU will seek within each other. However, concerns about preserving and defending European integration should be the point starting from which the EU will need to negotiate a new agreement with the UK (see Oliver 2016). That is to say that it is now crucial for Europe to provide an alternative model of integration for countries like Sweden, Denmark Poland or other "pre-ins," avoiding unleashing centrifugal forces which could unravel the Union itself. At the same time, further integration would prevent a "controlled" disintegration path through a multi-speed approach. Providing this alternative model is thus not imaginable without committing to transitioning to a GEMU.

The second motivation is *economic*.

Let us start with the conceptualization of the EMU's sovereign debt crisis as a vicious circle, the so-called "doom loop." The sovereign debt crisis that started in 2010 exposed the very "fragility" of the EMU architecture (De Grauwe 2016a), highlighting the danger of an unfinished set-up at the core of the "wrecking spiral" (Macchiarelli 2016) between public and private debt. Following on from our previous discussion, the "doom loop" took place when one or more conditions were met:

Liquidity costs

(a) Lack of fiscal discipline
(b) Excess of private debt

Adjustment costs

(c) Lack of structural reforms

The accumulation of imbalances that characterized the pre-2010—facilitated by the ECB's "one-size-fits-all" policy, and loose financial market regulation (see Pisani-Ferri 2012, 2013; De la Dehesa 2012; De Grauwe 2016a)—resulted into countries being unable to stall the crisis, needing a coordinated support at the European level. For banks, for instance, last resort guarantees from governments to their own financial institutions (see also Gros and Schoenmaker 2014) resulted in higher public debt and generally large costs to taxpayers (see Macchiarelli 2016). In several cases, e.g. Spain or Ireland, this resulted in a self-reinforcing amplification effect relating to the classical problem of (ir)rational runs in which the market can push an economy into a "bad" equilibrium (see also De Grauwe and Ji 2013; De Grauwe 2016a). This amplification within the EMU had to do (Macchiarelli 2016), at first, with a collapse of confidence in certain markets and financial institutions at the same time, and the broader fragility of systems, because of increased risk or asymmetry of information (see also IMF 2013). Secondly, the interaction between bond prices (via banks' balance sheets) and borrowing constraints, where—to make things easy—the fire sale of government bonds and rising of risk premia had a negative effect on the banks' net worth, with an ensuing liquidity dry-out and freezing of lending to the real economy. Figure 6 summarizes this discussion.

As Macchiarelli (2016) shows, should the five President Report not be adopted, there would be relatively little change compared with the position reached as a result of the governance changes already introduced since 2010 (see ECB 2011a). This could result into the GEMU not

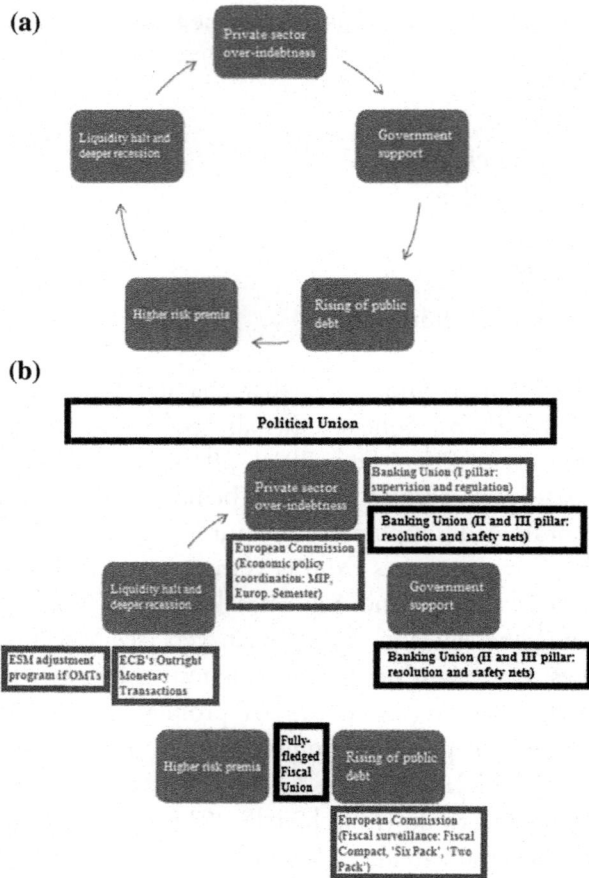

Fig. 6 A representation of the crisis 'doom-loop' a and how a 'comprehensive' GEMU would break it. *Source* Macchiarelli (2016). *Note* The Figure includes the main reforms of the European economic governance framework already in place (*grey*) and measures not yet in place (*black box*), as a part of the 5 President Report. The Figure does not consider measures which are temporary in nature such as unconventional monetary policy

making it through to stage 2, resulting into the aforementioned "doom loop" not being completely broken (see also Begg 2014). A "Comprehensive GEMU" (Begg et al. 2014), on the contrary, would include an extensive and progressive adoption of the additional transfers of power to the European level, resulting not only in an extraordinary development in a federal sense, in the long term, but also in the loop being finally broken (Fig. 6).

As a matter of fact, the Union has very little options outside transitioning to a GEMU. Otherwise the EMU would be characterized by yet another "impossible trinity" (Pisani-Ferri 2012)—absence of co-responsibility over public debt, strict "non-monetary financing" rule (Art. 123 TFEU) and the combination of free capital movements and national responsibility for supervising and, if needed, rescuing banking systems—which the five President Report is committed to break. This will chiefly be through the introduction of a fiscal and a banking union. A political union will be then required not to violate the archetype of "no taxation without representation".

It is worth noting that these reforms, however, implemented, would not only affect the EMU Member States' macroeconomic, financial, fiscal, and political governance, but they would have an impact on the EU and the single market, with the obvious consequence of affecting the UK as well, and the future of its negotiations (see also Sapir and Wolff 2016). In the best case scenario, advancing in the European integration process may result in some of the "euro-outs" to make use of their option to opt in going ahead. This may leave the UK in a difficult position, should EU negotiations fail to deliver a solution convenable for both. Provided that European integration worked in the past, the net benefits of staying out of the EU *ex-ante* may be different from the same benefits *ex post*, particularly in the likely scenario the Union will have to "comprehensively" move forward for its own survival.

5   Looking forward

Seeking immediate benefits from membership to the European project has its limitations. Historically, even in continental Europe, more integration in a federal sense was limited to the extent that the interests of the EU itself (or, joint EU utility) did not necessarily match the sum of the utility of individual Member States (or, aggregate utility). This has had significant implications for the process of EU integration as a whole

(Begg et al. 2014). The crisis is gradually changing this predicament, as the skewed design of the system (a strong monetary leg and a weak economic leg, or the ECB's "institutional loneliness" as the former ECB's Governing Council member, T. Padoa-Schioppa, eloquently put it)[9] resulted in larger costs for the EU if taken together.[10]

Most views are that the outcome of the referendum—a reflection of "British exceptionalism"—will cost heavily economically, mainly to Britain. The EU would feel some knock-on costs as well, with the EU reduced weight on the international political grounds (Butler et al. 2016). Brexit will certainly change both the internal and external *equilibrium*, with some EU non-euro area member states such as Poland, Denmark and Sweden, but also other "pre-ins," feeling they will lose grip in shaping euro zone policies (Oliver 2016), especially against an enhanced role of Germany and the other euro area member states. This may trigger further skepticism, should the EMU fail to provide an attractive alternative model for integration. Deeper integration should carry on to the point of making euro-outs use their option to opt in; something which is indeed not excluded by phase 3 of the Presidents Report. Any suboptimal solutions may be costly for the future of Europe's integration path.

There is no definitive study on the consequences of the impact of EU membership on the UK (see Fig. 7). Hence, in terms of the UK withdrawal, much will depend on how successful the current Prime Minister, T. May, will be in framing the outcome of the renegotiation. In this respect, there is evidence suggesting that May's job will not be the easiest one. Indeed, as Goodwin and Milazzo (2015) points out, when voters were last asked about the future of Britain's relationship with the EU (in 2014), using a question moving away from the usual binary "remain-or-leave" scenario, a majority (40%) were willing to remain within a *reformed* EU with reduced powers.[11] This is all not surprising, but it suggests PM May may have a hard time to renegotiate an agreement keeping the UK strong, with the right of entry to many of the EU benefits. Something the EU certainly cannot afford.

While it is difficult to quantify now whether or not the UK would flourish outside the EU, it is safe to play an exercise in reverse. Withdrawal is likely to have an impact, particularly on some sectors, like

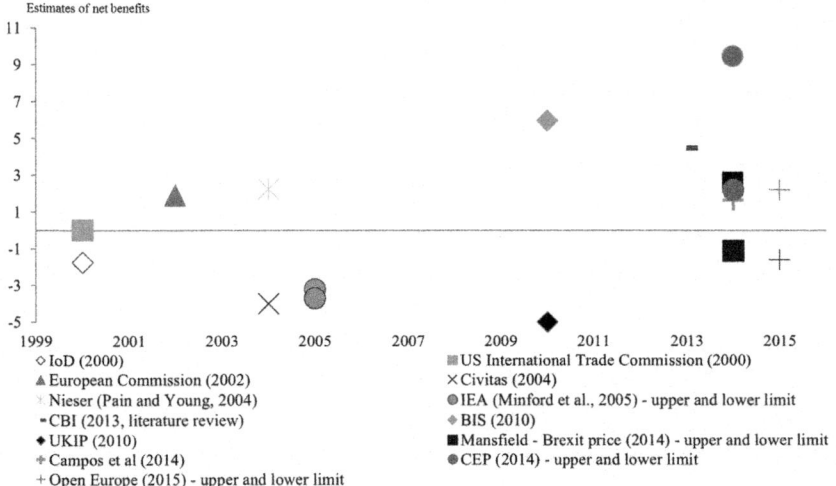

Estimates of net benefits

◇ IoD (2000)
▲ European Commission (2002)
⊤ Nieser (Pain and Young, 2004)
▪ CBI (2013, literature review)
◆ UKIP (2010)
✦ Campos et al (2014)
+ Open Europe (2015) - upper and lower limit

▦ US International Trade Commission (2000)
✕ Civitas (2004)
◉ IEA (Minford et al., 2005) - upper and lower limit
◆ BIS (2010)
■ Mansfield - Brexit price (2014) - upper and lower limit
● CEP (2014) - upper and lower limit

Fig. 7 Estimates of costs and benefits of UK's membership of the EU. *Source* Author's calculations

farming (currently receiving subsidiaries through the CAP), investment, education, and finance. In terms of budget, for instance, while the UK pays more into the EU budget than it receives from it (−0.46%), the net balance is not different from that of the Nordic EU non-euro area countries such as Denmark (−0.49%) and Sweden (−0.51%). Other countries having a negative balance are: Luxemburg and Italy (about 0.20%), Finland (∼0.30%), Austria, France, Belgium (∼0.40%), the Netherlands (−0.45%) and Germany (−0.49%) (Source: European Commission's "Financial Programming and Budget: UK").[12] Although the UK is a net contributor to the EU, certain regions receive significant support from the budget through the European Regional Development Fund and the European Social Fund. These receipts from the EU budget, for the latest year for which data behind the calculations are available, show that Wales—with a large agricultural sector—received as much as £163 per head. England received just £52 (Source: HM Consolidated statement on the use of EH fund in the UK). Such a variance in public sector receipts means that some parts of the UK (Wales and Northern Ireland) are net recipients from the EU budget while others (England and, to a lesser extent, Scotland) are net contributors. However, the net balance does not reflect the many benefits of EU membership, many of which are difficult to quantify, such as stability, security, freedom of working, living, studying and traveling within the EU. The UK government estimates that the single market brings in between GBP 31 billion and GBP 92 billion a year into the UK economy, equal to a contribution 5–15 times larger than the net UK contribution to the EU budget (Source: European Commission). The UK is also one of the top recipients of EU research funding. The UK Office of National Statistics (ONS) reports that the UK's contribution to EU research and development of €5.4 billion over the period 2007–2013. The UK received €8.8 billion in direct EU funding for research, development and innovation activities during the same period (see also The Royal Society 2016).

Finally, on the issue of finance, the current approach to a European banking union (see Macchiarelli 2016) lets foresee that the problem of funding of financial institutions will be accentuated with the UK withdrawal, having a strong impact on the extent cross-border externalities of bank failures across the EU will be addressed, particularly when they will involve guarantees to or resolution of banks which are systemic in both the euro area and the UK. While, going ahead, some of the other "outs" may make use of their option to buy-in (see also Gros and Schoenmaker 2014), provided that European resolution and deposit insurance schemes will be available, the UK's move to stay out will leave the UK and the EU in unchartered waters, given the large presence of important European banks in London. This may change going ahead.

6   Conclusion

To conclude, despite the risks that a multi-layer crisis poses to the very existence of the EU, the assumption that this could lead to less integration does not seem obvious by looking at the history of European economic and monetary integration. Being today some of the most crucial elements of integration at risk—the single market and people's ability to move freely, and the single currency itself—Europe should use awareness of its existing limits to initiate a process of reform and, hopefully, deepening. This is the spirit of the five Presidents Report. The justification of such a process of "completing" the EMU can be rationalized both under economic and political terms, being the only root to a renewed European credibility. It remains to be asked—now that the British claims as a part of the package to stay in the EU have been discarded by the exit vote—whether the space for European integration may even be larger (see also De Grauwe 2016b). This will all depend on how "low profile" the UK will accept to be in the future of Europe.

Notes

1. This is not too dissimilar to *the international relations'* trilemma: fixed exchange rates, capital flows, national policy independence.
2. For a critical discussion, see also De Grauwe (1994).
3. Nowadays, as a member of the EU (still), the UK sits the General Council of the European System of Central Banks (ESCB), comprising the President and Vice-President of the ECB, plus the governors of the national central banks of the 28 EU States.
4. Emphasis added.
5. Clearly, the idea of membership being in the "national interests" also relies on the national history linked to the traditional role of the pound and political reputation (see De Grauwe 2016a, b; Holden 2009).
6. Technically, under the provisions set by the 2009 Lisbon Treaty (Art. 50).
7. In more general terms, however, also fiscal adjustments at the euro area level (on top of flexibility) could replace the lack of monetary policy autonomy when countries face divergent patterns (i.e. like in the US; see Mundell 1973).
8. Another important recent strand highlights situations when OCA criteria are interdependent and focus on interactions between openness and mobility (Farhi and Werning 2015).
9. See Padoa-Schioppa (1999).
10. It is enough to think the used state aid measures in the form or recapitalization and asset relief measures to European banks between Oct 2008 and Dec 2012 amounted to 591.9 billion or 4.6% of EU 2012 GDP, with the highest share belonging (in the order) to Ireland,

the UK, and Germany (Source: European Commission State Aid Scoreboard 2013). Including approved aids and guarantees, this figure jumps to over 12% of the EU GDP for the period 2008–2012 only.

11. This was followed by leave (25%) and people supporting a scenario with the EU staying the same (18%). The popularity of an enhanced EU or even its evolution to a single government including the UK was the lowest (Source: British Social Attitudes Survey, 1993–2014).

12. European Commission's website "financial Programming and Budget: UK". http://ec.europa.eu/budget/mycountry/UK/index_en.cfm.

References

Alcidi, C., & Giovannini, A. (2013, April 25), The ECB dilemma—financial stability or independence? In *Reconciling governance and model: A five-fold narrative for europe*. Bruges: IED and Madariaga-College of Europe Foundation Conference at the European Parliament.

Alesina, A., & Barro, R. (2002). Currency unions. *Quarterly Journal of Economics, 117*(2), 409–436.

Angeloni, I., & Dedola, L. (1999). From the ERM to the euro: New evidence on economic and policy convergence among EU countries. *ECB Working Paper No 4.*

Baldwin, R., & Wyplosz, C. (2006). *The economics of European integration* (2nd ed.). Berkshire: McGraw-Hill Education.

Baun, M. J. (1996). The Maastricht treaty as high politics: Germany, France and the European integration. *Political Sciences Quarterly, 110*(4), 605–624.

Bayoumi, T., & Eichengreen, B. (1993). Shocking aspects of European monetary integration. In F. Torres & F. Giavazzi (Eds.), *Adjustment and growth in the European monetary union*. Cambridge: Cambridge University Press.

Bean, C. R. (1992). Economic and monetary union in Europe. *The Journal of Economic Perspectives, 6*(4), 31–52.

Begg, I. (2014). Genuine economic and monetary union. In S. Durlauf & L. Blume (Eds.), *The new Palgrave dictionary of economics*. London: Palgrave.

Begg, I., Macchiarelli, C., Bachtler, J., Mendez, C., & Wishlade, F. (2014). European economic governance and cohesion policy. *Report to the European Parliament Committee on Regional Development, European Parliament*, IP/B/REGI/IC/2013-086, Jan.

Butler, G., Jensen, M. D., & Snaith, H. (2016). "Slow change may pull us apart": Debating a British exit from the European union. *Journal of European Public Policy, 23*(9), 1278–1284.

Bordo, M. (2006). *Sudden Stops, Financial Crises and Original Sin in Emerging Countries: Déjà vu?* Paper prepared for the Conference: Global Imbalances and Risk Management. Has the Center become the Periphery? Madrid, Spain May 16–17.

Bordo, M., & James, H. (2013). The European crisis in the context of the history of previous financial crises. *Journal of Macroeconomics, 39*, 275–284.

Bordo, M. D., & Meissner, C. M. (2007). Financial crises, 1880–1913: The role of foreign currency debt. In S. Edwards, G. Esquivel & G. Márquez (Eds.), *The Decline of Latin American Economies: Growth, Institutions, and Crises.* (pp. 139–194). Chicago: University of Chicago Press.

Calmfors, L. (2001). Unemployment, labour-market reform, and monetary union. *Journal of Labor Economics, 19*(2), 265–289.

Calmfors, L., Driffill, J. (1988, April). Bargaining structure, corporatism, and macroeconomic performance. *Economic Policy, 6*, 14–61.

Campos, N., Coricelli, F., & Moretti, L. (2014). *Economic growth and political integration: Synthetic counterfactuals evidence from Europe.* mimeo.

Campos, N., Macchiarelli, C. (2016a, March 03). Brexit, 'euro-ins', and 'euro-outs'. VoxEU.org.

Campos, N., Macchiarelli, C. (2016b). Core and periphery in the European monetary union: Bayoumi-Eichengreen 25 Years Later. *Economics Letters,* in-press.

Canova, F., Ciccarelli, C., & Ortega, E. (2005). Similarities and convergence in G-7 cycles. *Journal of Monetary Economics, 54*, 85–878.

Chari, V. V., Dovis, A., & Kehoe, P. (2015). *Rethinking optimal currency areas.* Federal Reserve Bank of Minneapolis, Research Department Staff Report.

Chartered Institute of Personnel and Development. (2015, January). Employment regulation and the labour market. *Policy Report.* Available at https://www.cipd.co.uk/Images/employment-regulation-and-the-labour-market_2015_tcm18-10238.pdf.

De Grauwe, P. (1994). Towards European monetary union without the EMS. *Economic Policy, 9*(18), 149–185.

De Grauwe, P. (2016a). *Economics of Monetary Union* (11th ed.). Oxford: Oxford University Press.

De Grauwe, P. (2016b, February 24). Why the European union will benefit from brexit. *Social Europe.*

De Grauwe, P., & Mongelli, F. (2005). *Endogeneities of optimum currency areas: What brings countries sharing a single currency closer together?* (p. 0468). ECB WP: Frankfurt.

De Grauwe, P., & Ji, Y. (2013). Self-fulfilling crises in the Eurozone: An empirical test. *Journal of International Money and Finance, 34,* 15–36.

De Grauwe, P., & Ji, Y. (2015). The fragility of two monetary regimes: The European monetary system and the Eurozone. *International Journal of Finance & Economics, 20*(1), 1–15.

De la Dehesa, G. (2012). *A self-inflicted crisis? Design and management failures leading to the Eurozone crisis* (Occasional Paper No. 86). Washington DC: Group of Thirty.

De Larosière, J., Balcerowitz, L., Issing, O., Masera, R., Mc Carthy, C., Nyberg, L., Pérez, J., & Ruding, O. (2009). *The high–level group on financial supervision in the EU-de larosiere report, Brussels.*

Driffil, J. (2006). The centralization of wage bargaining revisited: What have we learnt? *Journal of Common Market Studies, 44,* 731–756.

Eichengreen, B., & Hausman, R. (1999). *Exchange rates and financial fragility.* Paper presented at Federal Reserve Bank of Kansas City symposium, New challenges for monetary policy (pp. 26–28). August, Jackson Hole, Wyoming.

Eichengreen, B., & Temin, P. (2010). Fetters of gold and paper. *Oxford Review of Economic Policy, 26*(3), 370–384.

Eichengreen B., & Wyplosz, C. (1993). *The unstable EMS* (Vol. 1993, No. 1, pp. 51–143). Brookings Papers on Economic Activities.

European Central Bank. (2010). *Recent developments in supervisory structures in the EU Member States (2007–2010),* Frankfurt, October.

European Central Bank. (2011a). *The monetary policy of the ECB.* Frankfurt: European Central Bank.

European Central Bank. (2011b, March). The reform of economic governance in the Euro Area—Essential Elements. *ECB Monthly Bulletin Article.*

Farhi, E., & Werning, I. (2015). *Labor mobility in currency unions.* MIT Mimeo.

Frankel, J., & Rose, A. (1998). The Endogeneity of the optimum currency area criteria. *Economic Journal, 108*(441), 1009–1025.

Fuest, C., & Peichl, A. (2012). European Fiscal Union: What Is It? Does It Work? And Are There Really 'No Alternatives'? *CESifo Forum 1* (special issue on European Fiscal Union), 3–9.

Gerba, E., Macchiarelli, C. (2015). *Interaction between monetary policy and bank regulation: Theory and European practice.* LSE Systemic Risk Centre, Special Paper No. 10.

Gerba, E., Macchiarelli, C. (2016, February). *Policy options and risks of an extension of the ECB's quantitative easing programme: An analysis.* Monetary Policy Dialogue, note to the European Parliament IP/A/ECON/2016-01.

Giavazzi, F., & Pagano, M. (1988). The advantage of tying one's hands: EMS discipline and central Bbank credibility. *European Economic Review, 32,* 1055–1075.

Glick, R., & Rose, A. K. (2016, August). Currency unions and trade: A post-EMU reassessment. *European Economic Review, 87,* 78–91.

Golden, M., Wallerstein, M., & Lange, P. (2006). Union centralization among advanced industrial societies: An empirical study of organisation for Economic Co-operation and Development (OECD) countries, 1950–2000. ICPSR04541-v1. *Ann Arbor, MI: Inter-University Consortium for Political and Social Research.*

Goodwin, M., Milazzo, C. (2015, December). *Britain, the European union and the referendum: What drives euroscepticism?* Europe programme briefing.

Gros, D., & Schoenmaker, D. (2014). European deposit insurance and resolution in the banking union. *Journal of Common Market Studies, 52*(3), 529–546.

Harding, D., & Pagan, A. (2006). Synchronization of cycles. *Journal of Econometrics, 132*(1), 59–79.

Holden, S. (2009). The three outsiders and the monetary union. In *SNS, EMU at ten: Should Denmark, Sweden, and the UK join? (Chapter 6).* Stockholm: SNS Förlag.

Hunt, J. (2008). The economics of German reunification. In N. Steven Durlauf & Lawrence E. Blume (Eds.), *The new Palgrave dictionary of economics,* London: Palgrave Macmillan.

International Monetary Fund. (2013). *IMF report on unconventional monetary policies—Recent experience and prospects.*

Juncker, J.-C., Tusk, D., Dijsselbloem, J., Draghi, M., & Schulz, M. (2015). *Completing Europe's economic and monetary union.* Brussels: European Commission.

Klein, M. W. (1998, March/April). European monetary union. *New England Economic Review, 3*(12).

Kontopoulos, Y., & Perotti, R. (1999). Government fragmentation and fiscal policy outcomes: Evidence from OECD countries. In J. M. Poterba &

J. Von Hagen (Eds.), *Fiscal institutions and fiscal performance (NBER conference report)* (pp. 81–102). Chicago: University of Chicago Press.

Krugman, P. R. (1993). Lessons of Massachusetts for EMU. In F. Torres & F. Giavazzi (Eds.), *Adjustment and growth in the European monetary union* (pp. 241–261). Cambridge: Cambridge University Press.

Macchiarelli, C., Sangalli, I. (2007). From EMS to EMU: An obliged passage? In *Consortium for research and continuing education in economic*. New York: Mimeo.

Macchiarelli, C. (2016). European banking union. In S. N. Durlauf & E. L. Blume (Eds.), *The new Palgrave dictionary of economics*. London: Palgrave Macmillan.

Massmann, M., & Mitchell, J. (2002). Have UK and Eurozone business cycles become more correlated? *National Institute Economic Review, 182*(1), 58–571.

Mayes, D. G. (2011). European monetary integration. In S. N. Durlauf & E. L. Blume (Eds.), *The new palgrave dictionary of economics*. Online Edition, 2011.

McKinnon, R. (1963). Optimum currency area. *American Economic Review, 53*, 717–725.

Mongelli, F. (2013). *The mutating Euro area crisis is the balance between "sceptics" and "advocates" shifting?* (p. 144). ECB WP: Frankfurt.

Moser, G., Pointner, W., & Reitschuler, G. (2004). Economic growth in Denmark, Sweden and the United Kingdom since the start of monetary union. *Monetary Policy & the Economy*, Q4/04, Oesterreichische Nationalbank.

Mundell, R. A. (1994, November 25). *The European monetary system 50 Years after bretton woods: A comparison between two systems*. Paper presented at project Europe 1985–1995. The tenth edition of the "Incontri di Rocca Salimbeni" meetings, in Siena.

Mundell, R. (1973). Uncommon arguments for common currencies. In H. G. Johnson & A. K. Swoboda (Eds.), *The economics of common currencies* (pp. 114–132). London: George Allen and Unwin Ltd.

Mundell, R. (1961). A theory of optimum currency areas. *American Economic Review, 51*, 657–665.

Nechio, F. (2011, June 13). Monetary policy when one size does not fit all. *FRBSF Economic Letter, 18*, 13.

Obstfeld, M. (2013). *Finance at center stage: Some lessons of the Euro crisis* (CEPR Discussion Paper No. DP9415).

Oliver, T. (2016). European and international views of Brexit. *Journal of European Public Policy, 23*(9), 1321–1328.

Onorante L. (2007). Monetary and fiscal policy in a monetary union. In R. Beetsma, C. Favero, A. Missale, A. Muscatelli, P. Natale, & P. Tirelli (Eds.), Monetary policy, fiscal policies and labour markets: Macroeconomic policymaking in the EMU. New York: Cambridge University Press.

Padoa-Schioppa, T. (1999, December 29). "Europas Notenbank ist einsam" ("Europe's central bank is lonely"), interview with Die Zeit.

Peersman, G., & Smets, F. (1999). The Taylor rule: A useful monetary policy benchmark for the Euro area? *International Finance, 2*(1), 85–116.

Pesaran, H., Smith, V., & Smith, R. (2007). What if the UK or Sweden had joined the Euro in 1999? An empirical evaluation using a global VAR. *International Journal of Finance & Economics, 12*(1), 55–87.

Pisani-Ferry, J. (2012). *The euro crisis and the new impossible trinity.* Brussels, Bruegel Policy Contribution 2012/01. Brussels: Bruegel.

Pisani-Ferry, J. (2013). The known unknowns and unknown unknowns of European monetary union. *Journal of International Money and Finance, 34,* 6–14.

Ramey, V. (forthcoming). Macroeconomic shocks and their propagation. In J. Taylor and H. Uhlig (eds.), *Handbook of Macroeconomics* (Vol. 2). Elsevier.

Ramiro Troitiño, D. (2016). The british position towards European integration: A different economic and political approach. *Baltic Journal of European Studies, 4*(1), 119–136.

Rodrik, D. (2007). The inescapable trilemma of the World Economy. http:// rodrik.typepad.com/dani_rodriks_weblog/2007/06/the-inescapable.html.

Salvatore, D. (1997). The common unresolved problem with the EMS and EMU. *American Economic Review, 87*(2), 224–226.

Sapir, A., Wolff, G. (2016). One market, two monies: The European union and the United Kingdom'. *Policy Brief* 2016/01. Bruegel.

Scharpf, F. W. (2011). Monetary union, fiscal crisis and the preemption of democracy. LEQS paper 36/2011.

Sinn, H.-W. (1996). International implications of German unification. *National Bureau of Economic Research (Cambridge)* (Working Paper No. 5839).

The Royal Society. (2016). *The role of the EU in international research collaboration and researcher mobility, on-line report.*

Valli V. (2002). L'Europa e l'economia mondiale. In *Trasformazioni e prospettive*, (pp. 100–128). Roma: Carocci Editore.

Velis J. O. (1995). The collapse of the EMS: Symptomatic of a doomed EMU? *International Conference of the European Community Studies Association.* Charleston (SC).

Weber, A. A. (1991). Reputation and credibility in the European monetary system. *Economic Policy, 6*(12), 58–102.

Wyplosz, C., & Kostrup, S. (2010). A common pool theory of supranational deficit ceilings. *European Economic Review, 54,* 269–278.

The UK Financial Sector and EU Integration After Brexit: The Issue of Passporting

1 Introduction

Part of London's attractiveness as international financial centre is the access to the internal market of the wider European Economic Area (EEA). By using a UK licence as European passport, foreign financial firms can offer their financial services throughout the EEA. London as financial centre is also home to the vast majority of euro-denominated trading with access to euro-settlement and clearing systems. If the UK cannot secure a 'Norway' deal and stay within EEA after Brexit, the UK will lose the passporting rights and access to the euro-settlement and clearing systems.

Analysing the impact on banking and insurance, we find that the insurance industry makes very limited use of the passport in comparison to the banking industry. Next, we analyse the impact on wholesale

D. Schoenmaker (✉)
Rotterdam School of Management, Erasmus University, Rotterdam,
The Netherlands
e-mail: dirk.schoenmaker@bruegel.org

© The Author(s) 2017
N.F. Campos and F. Coricelli (eds.), *The Economics of UK–EU Relations*,
DOI 10.1007/978-3-319-55495-2_5

banking and securities and derivatives trading. The French President, Hollande, has already announced that the City of London should no longer be able to clear euro-denominated trades after Brexit (FT 2016).

Our findings on wholesale banking and trading are indicative. The early numbers suggest that up to half of the total UK banking system relates to wholesale banking in the City of London. Wholesale banking covers the full remit of trading and derivatives activities and takes place in several currencies (US dollar, euro and pound sterling). Next, we find that, in particular, the OTC derivatives markets might be affected, as 75% of euro-denominated OTC interest rate derivatives are traded in London.

2   The Development of London's Position

London is the wholesale banking hub of the EU. Figure 1 illustrates inward banking from other EU countries and from third countries. Cross-border business from banks headquartered in other EU countries has declined from an all-time high of £2.1 trillion in 2008 to £ 1.1 trillion in 2015. While this trend is line with the general decline in cross-border banking in the EU in the aftermath of the global financial crisis, the decline is more pronounced in the UK. By contrast, cross-border banking from third countries has remained high at £2.2 trillion throughout this period.

Zooming in on inward banking from third countries, Fig. 2 shows that the vast majority of third country banking in the EU takes place in the UK. Only 20% is directed towards other EU countries. There is a slight decline of the UK's position from 83% in 2003 to 77% in 2015. Figure 2 confirms the dominant position of London as the global banking hub of Europe.

In this chapter, we review the possible impact of Brexit on the size of the UK financial sector. Haldane et al. (2010) provide an interesting discussion on the contribution of the financial sector to the economy: what is the value added of the financial sector and how to measure it.

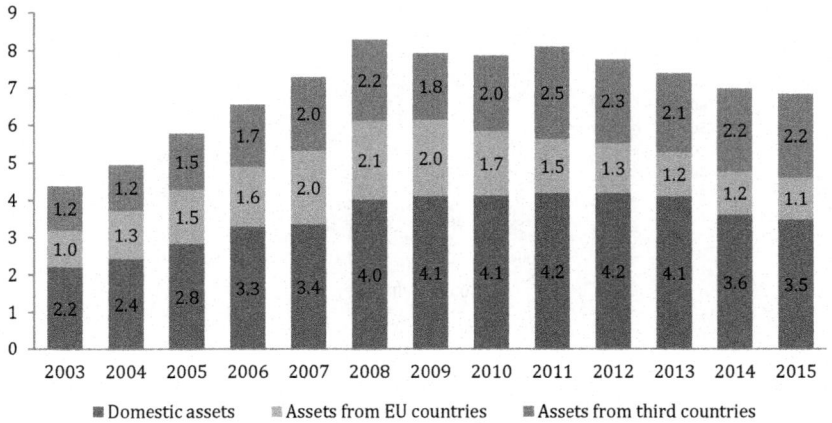

Fig. 1 Development of UK banking sector (in GBP trillions). *Source* Author calculations based on ECB (2015). *Notes* The assets of the UK banking sector are split in assets of domestic banks, assets of banks from EU countries and assets of banks from third countries

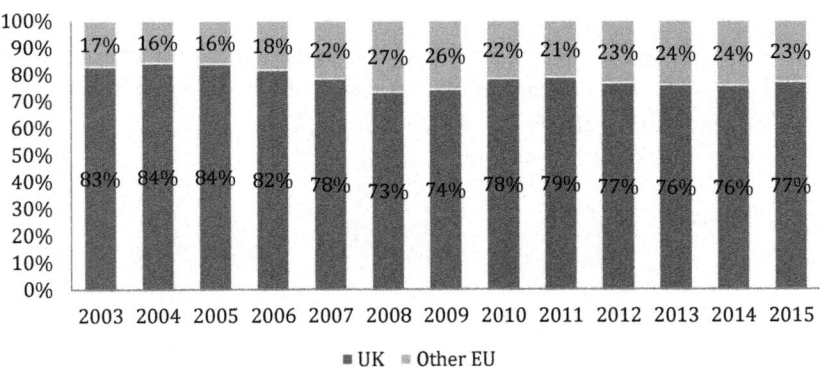

Fig. 2 Cross-border banking from third countries (share in %). *Source* Author calculations based on ECB (2015). *Notes* Total cross-border assets of banks from third countries are broken down in the UK and the rest of the EU

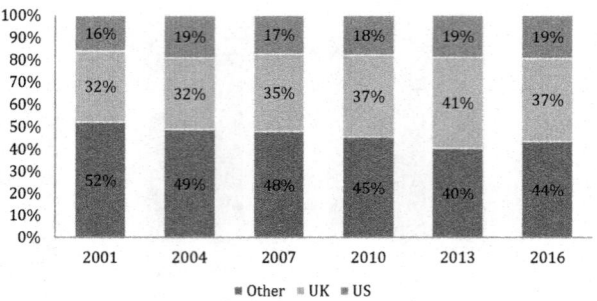

Fig. 3 Foreign exchange turnover (% share of total). *Source* 2016 Triennial Central Bank Survey of Foreign Exchange and OTC Derivatives Markets (BIS 2016)

Moving to the forex market, Fig. 3 illustrates the pre-eminent position of London in the foreign exchange (forex) market. This position has even increased from 32 to 37% over the 2003–2016 period. Forex turnover in the UK is twice as large as that in the US (19%). Figure 4 shows the OTC interest rate derivatives market. While the UK has also been the top global trading hub up to 2013, the US has overtaken the prime position in 2016. This switch mirrors the underlying shift from EUR to USD contracts. The average daily turnover of US dollar contracts rose from $639 billion in April 2013 to $1.4 trillion in April 2016.

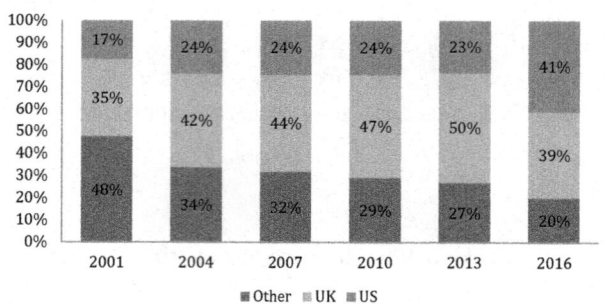

Fig. 4 OTC interest rate derivatives turnover (% share of total). *Source* 2016 Triennial Central Bank Survey of Foreign Exchange and OTC Derivatives Markets (BIS 2016)

By contrast, that of euro-denominated contracts—historically the most actively traded segment—declined from $1.1 trillion in April 2013 to $638 billion in April 2016 (BIS 2016). The UK is a major trading hub for euro-denominated contracts (see Sect. 7 below).

3 The Passport

The internal market is underpinned by a network of Directives and Regulations, which permit access to other EEA member states if a firm has a licence in one member state (the 'home' member state). The most important directives for financial services are:

- the Capital Requirements Directive (CRD IV, 2013/36/EU) for banking
- the Insurance and Reinsurance Directive (Solvency II, 2009/138/EC) for insurance
- the Markets in Financial Instruments Directive (MiFID, 2004/39/EC) for investment services
- the Alternative Investment Fund Managers Directive (AIFMD, 2011/61/EU) for hedge funds and private equity
- the Prospectus Directive (2010/73/EC) for issuing securities
- the Undertakings for the Collective Investment in Transferable Securities Directive (UCITS, 2009/65/EC) for marketing and trading investment funds

We illustrate the how the passport works legally with the Capital Requirements Directive (CRD IV), the legal framework for credit institutions (banks). The passport consist of several elements of the CRD IV:

- *Licence*: Title III of CRD IV (Articles 8–21) specifies the requirements for access to activity of credit institutions. The main element is authorisation by the home supervisor, which provides the single licence.

- *Freedom of establishment*: Title V (Articles 33–39) contains the provisions concerning the freedom of establishment and the freedom to provide services. It means that if a credit institution is authorised in one member state, it has the freedom to establish a branch in (or to provide services to) any other EEA member state without prior approval. The credit institution only needs to notify the host country supervisor.
- *Home supervision*: Title VII sets out the principles of prudential supervision, which predominantly gives powers to the home supervisor with some very limited powers for the host supervisor in the area of liquidity supervision. As these powers of liquidity supervision are related to the operations in different currencies, the new European Banking Supervision framework has decided to give up these host country powers within the euro area, which uses the single currency (Schoenmaker and Véron 2016).

This system of full access based on a single passport provided by the home-country supervisor is limited to the EEA. So if the UK were to leave the EEA, UK licenced banks (whether or not headquartered in the UK) would need to obtain an extra licence from the host supervisor in an EEA member state in order to offer financial services in that member state.

An extra licence would be necessary for all forms of cross-border services, i.e. through the establishment of a branch or subsidiary or through the direct offering of cross-border services. The UK would then become a third country, which would need to find a point of access into the EEA for business. Similarly, EEA financial institutions would need to apply for a licence to enter the UK. The passport system in the other EU financial services directives is similar to the CRD IV.

4   Banking Versus Insurance

An interesting question is whether different financial sectors are equally affected by possible changes in passporting arrangements for the financial sector. We examine the two largest financial sectors, banking and insurance. It appears that banking relies far more on the passport than insurance. We measure this by differentiating cross-border business through branches (based on the passport) and subsidiaries (new licence).

Table 1 reports the relative share of branches and subsidiaries in cross-border business. The passport (branch) is not important for insurance. The aggregate number for all EU member states is 13%, and even less for the UK at 9%. These are minor amounts. The main vehicle is through subsidiaries, because insurers want to contain 'insurance' risk in separate legal entities. At the aggregate EU level, the relative share of branches is 36% for banking.

Finally, European banks typically use their passport to enter the London wholesale market; that is for 69% of the cases. Many international banks, including the major European ones, have branches operating in London, which is an international financial centre, but actually do little business with UK clients (Burrows and Low 2015).

In summary, insurance will be far less affected than banking if and when the UK leaves the EU. Next, the major European banks would need to apply for a UK licence, if they want to keep on doing business in London. In turn, the UK banks would need to apply for a licence in the EEA (see next section).

Table 1 Cross-border business by type of entry (2014)

	Type of entry	Banking (%)	Insurance (%)
EU-wide	Branch	36	13
	Subsidiary	64	87
United Kingdom	Branch	69	9
	Subsidiary	31	91

Sources Banking entry data are from ECB (2015) and insurance entry data from Schoenmaker and Sass (2016). *Note* Banks and insurers can enter other member states by branch (no further licence and supervision) or by subsidiary (separate licence and supervision from host country). The table reports the relative share of branches and subsidiaries in cross-border business. The first rows are for all EU member states; the latter rows are for the UK

5   Wholesale Banking

What is the size of London's wholesale banking activity? Table 2 provides an overview of the total UK banking system. Most UK banking assets (£3570 billion) are held by the major UK international banks: HSBC, RBS, Barclays and Standard Chartered. While Standard Chartered operates primarily in Asia, the first three are active in Europe. HSBC and RBS have already a subsidiary (and thus a licence) on the continent: HSBC in France and RBS in the Netherlands. Barclays operates through branches, for example, in Italy and France (Schoenmaker and Véron 2016). So, only Barclays might need an extra licence to enter the EEA after Brexit. Based on the banks' annual reports, we estimate that about one third of the total assets of the major UK banks relate to their trading and derivatives books in London, amounting to £1180 billion.

The major domestic UK banks and other UK banks have most of their operations in the UK and concentrate on traditional banking business, with little or no trading or derivatives business.

Table 2 shows further that £1730 billion in assets in London is held by the major international investment banks, mainly from the US and

Table 2 The UK banking system (end-2014)

Type of Banks	Total assets (in £ billions)	Wholesale ibanking in London (in £ billions)
Major UK international banks	3570 (45%)	1180
Major UK domestic banks	1160 (15%)	–
Other UK banks	250 (3%)	–
Rest of the World Investment Banks	1730 (22%)	1730
Rest of the World Other Banks	460 (6%)	310
Branches from EEA banks	790 (10%)	530
Total UK banking system	7960 (100%)	3750

Source Total assets based on Burrows and Low (2015) and for branches from EEA banks on ECB (2015). Author estimates for wholesale banking (trading and derivatives) in London

Switzerland. These US and Swiss investment banks use London as a hub for their European operations (Goodhart and Schoenmaker 2016). Table 3 indicates that 90% of European turnover and employees of the five large US investment banks (Goldman Sachs, JP Morgan, Citigroup, Morgan Stanley, Bank of America Merrill Lynch) are located in London. These investment banks use their UK passports (both the banking licence under CRD IV and investment services licence under MiFID) to

Table 3 European operations of top five US investment banks: Turnover and Employees (end-2014)

Countries	Panel A: Turnover by Country (EUR–millions)	
United Kingdom	22,744	92%
Germany	513	2%
France	361	1%
Italy	193	1%
Ireland	201	1%
Luxembourg	276	1%
Other EU	438	2%
Total	24,727	100%
Countries	Panel B: Number of Employees by Country	
United Kingdom	26,629	89%
Germany	794	3%
France	293	1%
Italy	326	1%
Ireland	1011	3%
Luxembourg	491	2%
Other EU	365	1%
Total	29,909	100%

Source Goodhart and Schoenmaker (2016)
Note The data refer to the five US investment banks' investment banking activities in Europe. Goodhart and Schoenmaker (2016) provide a breakbown for each bank

conduct business throughout the EEA. These investment banks are currently looking for a new passport in the EEA.

At this stage, it is guesswork how much of their derivatives and securities trading and corporate finance business US investment banks might move to continental Europe. Early estimates indicate a minimum of 20%. At some point, the liquidity in certain markets might move to the continent, in which case part of the trading floor will also move (OTC derivatives are a case in point; see next section).

If the US investment banks relocate part of their operations to the euro area, the ECB will become their supervisor if their assets are greater than €30 billion. While it is appropriate that a large supervisor like the ECB would be responsible, rather than smaller national supervisors, the ECB will need to beef up its markets (derivatives and securities trading and corporate finance) expertise to do the job (Danielsson et al. 2016).

Next, the category 'rest of the world other banks' includes subsidiaries of overseas banks operating in the United Kingdom. Many international banks, including the major European ones, also have substantial branches in London, including Deutsche Bank, BNP Paribas, Societe Generale, ING and UniCredit. Deutsche Bank with total assets of €1.629 billion receives, for example, 19% of its net revenues from its UK branch (Deutsche Bank, Annual Report 2015). Most of these foreign subsidiaries and branches actually do little business with UK clients. Our conservative estimate is that two thirds of their UK business are related to wholesale banking.

In sum, Table 2 estimates that close to half (£3750 billion) of the total UK banking system is related to wholesale banking in London. In the next section, we provide a breakdown of wholesale business by category (securities and derivatives) and currency (sterling, dollar and euro).

6   Infrastructure

Given the amount of euro-denominated finance carried out in the UK, it is important that London, within the EEA, has direct access to the infrastructure for wholesale payments (TARGET2) and clearing

(LCH-Clearnet) in euros. TARGET2, the payments system for the euro area, permits national central banks, banks and designated financial institutions within the EEA to join even if they are outside the euro area (Armstrong 2016). UK banks and other designated financial institutions are permitted to be direct participants in TARGET2 even though the Bank of England does not participate.

Armstrong (2016) argues that if the UK were to leave the EU and not join the EEA, then banks in the UK could no longer be direct members of TARGET2. They would have to operate through subsidiaries (or perhaps branches assuming the UK is deemed 'equivalent' in terms of regulation) within the EEA. This would make euro banking via the UK more expensive. It would also erode the attraction of London as a destination for non-EEA banks to establish their EU headquarters.

Moving to clearing, central counterparties (CCPs) are important for the settlement of securities and derivatives transactions. There are three clearing houses operating in the UK which are recognised by both the UK and the EU: CME Europe, a derivatives exchange and wholly owned subsidiary of US-based CME group, LCH.Clearnet Group Ltd, majority owned and operated by the London Stock Exchange Group and the London Metal Exchange Limited. Of the three clearing houses, LCH has by far the biggest share of euro-denominated clearing in the UK (Batsaikhan 2016).

The European Central Bank initially exempted the UK entity of LCH from TARGET2 as part of its 'location requirement', but the Court of Justice of the EU (ECJ) subsequently decided that the ECB has no competence under the Treaty on the Functioning of the European Union (TFEU) to impose such requirements on the clearing houses. Furthermore, by imposing location requirements, the ECB violated the freedom of establishment, freedom to provide services and freedom of movement of capital in the single market (Batsaikhan 2016; Armstrong 2016). But outside the EEA, the UK would no longer have the protection of the TFEU and the ECJ. This is no problem for LCH.Clearnet Group itself, as it has major entities in New York, London and France (see Table 2). If needed, LCH can thus move its euro-denominated clearing business to Paris (Table 4).

Table 4 LCH Clearing—overview

LCH.Clearnet Group			
Subsidiary	LCH.Clearnet Limited	LCH.Clearnet SA	LCH Clearnet LLC
Location	London, UK	Paris, France	New York, US
Products	OTC Swaps, Forex, Derivatives, Equities and Bonds, Repos	Derivatives, Equities and Bonds, Credit default swaps, Repos	OTC Swaps
Profit after tax (mln. Euros), 2015	63.8	28.2	10.2
Headcount, 2015	452	168	12

Source LCH Annual Report 2015

7   Trading

The final step for the assessment of the impact of Brexit on the City of London is an estimation of euro-denominated trading. At the outset, we stress that our calculations provide a preliminary assessment of the main market segments and should be interpreted with some caution. The main purpose of our preliminary calculations is to get an idea of the possible impact.

The main wholesale financial markets in London cover:

- Derivatives
- Foreign exchange trading
- Private and public bond trading
- Equity trading
- Commodities trading

If access to euro clearing and settlement in London ceases, we expect the greatest impact to be on the bond and derivatives markets. Forex is an international market, in which London has a prime position. Settlement of FX transactions happens through CLS (originally Continous Linked Settlement), the largest multicurrency cash settlement system to mitigate settlement risk for the FX transactions of its member banks, and is thus not dependent on London's access to TARGET2. That would therefore not need to change should access to TARGET2 be stopped. Next, the settlement of equity trades is closely linked to the respective stock exchanges, on which the equity trades are executed. Finally, commodities (e.g. crude oil and metals) trading is largely a dollar-denominated business.

The BIS Triennial Central Bank Survey of foreign exchange and derivatives market activity is the largest survey in its field (BIS 2016). Table 5 provides figures for the OTC single currency interest rate derivatives, which counts for the majority (79%) of the global OTC derivatives market. It shows that London accounts for about 75% of euro-denominated trades and New York for 78% of the US dollar trades in 2016 (Panel B of Table 5). These large shares are no surprise, because these two markets are the most liquid interest rate derivatives markets in euros and dollars, respectively, and thus attract the majority of trading in the respective currencies. While 50% of the global OTC interest rate derivatives market related to euro-denominated derivatives in 2013, this position was taken over by dollar-denominated derivatives in 2016.

What do these statistics tell us? First, the City of London is currently home to the main market in euro-denominated interest rate derivatives (with 75% of euro-denominated trading). Second, the potential impact for the City of London is that up to 49% (=$573.7 billion/$1180.2 billion) of its interest rate derivatives market could move to continental Europe after Brexit. Third, France is emerging as the dominant player on the continent. France improved its share of euro-denominated derivatives from 10.6% in 2013 to 13.2% in 2016, while Germany dropped from 6.6 to 2.2% over the same period.

Bond trading is less centralised and done through different platforms, each of which has its own clearing and settlement arrangements. Therefore, we cannot speak of a central market place(s). Nevertheless, we try to give a picture of activity using two indicators: amounts outstanding and cleared trades. Table 6 provides an overview of the amount of outstanding private debt securities in the major countries: France, Germany, the UK and the US. The amounts are broken down by type of bond (bank, other financial or corporate) and currency (euro and US dollar). The relative share of outstanding securities is a good proxy for the relative

Table 5 Global OTC single currency interest rate derivatives turnover in April 2013 and 2016 (Daily averages in millions of USD)

Panel A	France		Germany		United Kingdom		United States		Total
April 2013	Amount	Share of total (%)	Amount	Share of total (%)	Amount	Share of total (%)	Amount	Share of total (%)	Amount
Euro	141,245	10.6	88,125	6.6	927,840	69.4	27,090	2.0	1336,075
Pound sterling	4746	2.3	4728	2.3	189,802	91.9	3162	1.5	206,643
US dollar	52,080	6.7	6205	0.8	110,235	14.2	546,268	70.4	776,268
TOTAL	202,210	7.3	101,347	3.7	1,347,749	48.9	628,153	22.8	2,758,583

Panel B	France		Germany		United Kingdom		United States		Total
April 2016	Amount	Share of total (%)	Amount	Share of total (%)	Amount	Share of total (%)	Amount	Share of total (%)	Amount
Euro	100,648	13.2	16,562	2.2	573,664	75.2	6832	0.9	762,494
Pound sterling	6648	2.5	509	0.2	247,489	94.8	2333	0.9	261,113
US dollar	26,833	1.8	2455	0.2	215,157	14.4	1167,958	78.0	1497,627
TOTAL	141,215	4.7	31,311	1.0	1,180,246	39.0	1,240,774	41.0	3,028,031

Source BIS Triennial Central Bank Survey of foreign exchange and derivatives markets activity (BIS 2015, 2016)

Table 6 Private debt securities outstanding, Q1 2016 (in billion USD)

	France		Germany		United Kingdom		United States		TOTAL
	Amount	Share of total (%)	Amount	Share of total (%)	Amount	Share of total (%)	Amount	Share of total (%)	Amount
Euro	2029.6	21.2	1373.1	14.4	1568.3	16.4	1084.1	11.3	9555.2
– banks	900.1	20.3	368.2	8.3	795	17.9	384.6	8.7	4436.6
– other financials	467.1	17.9	460.8	17.6	505.1	19.3	259.3	9.9	2616.1
– corporates	662.4	26.5	544.1	21.7	268.2	10.7	440.2	17.6	2502.5
US dollar	614.9	4.3	934.2	6.5	1678.6	11.8	3929.1	27.5	14267.2
– banks	225.4	4.5	386.2	7.8	821.1	16.5	720.5	14.5	4973.4
– other financials	225.2	4.0	450.4	8.0	522.1	9.3	2514.9	44.8	5618.2
– corporates	164.3	4.5	97.6	2.7	335.4	9.1	693.7	18.9	3675.6
TOTAL	5289		4614.6		6493.8		10,026.4		47,644.8

Source BIS Triennial Central Bank Survey of foreign exchange and derivatives markets activity (BIS 2015 and 2016), Debt securities issues and amounts outstanding (Table C3). *Note* Amount of issue for each country is the sum of resident issuers and national issuers. Total amount is the total for all countries share of trading. London has a less dominant position in the private bond market than in the derivatives market. The UK market share of euro-denominated private bonds is about 16%, while Germany and France have 21 and 14% respectively. Moreover, in the corporate bond segment, Germany (27%) and France (22%) have larger market shares than the UK (11%).

Moving to government bond trading, Fig. 5 shows the monthly amount of cleared government bond trades (both cash bond and repo trades) executed by LCH.Clearnet. The UK entity clears trades for the following markets: Austrian, Belgian, Dutch, German, Irish, Finnish, Portuguese, Slovakian, Slovenian and UK government bonds. The French entity processes the cash trades and reports for Italian, French and Spanish government securities. LCH.Clearnet thus serves the major markets for euro-area government bonds. It is interesting to see that French entity has recently overtaken the UK entity, partly because of the increased trade in euro government bonds from the south of Europe.

The trading and clearing of the bonds of the nine euro-area governments, which now done in the UK, could be easily transferred to the French entity, if the UK entity can no longer clear euro-denominated trades. Figure 5 shows that monthly government bond trading amounts to €6 trillion, both in the UK and France.

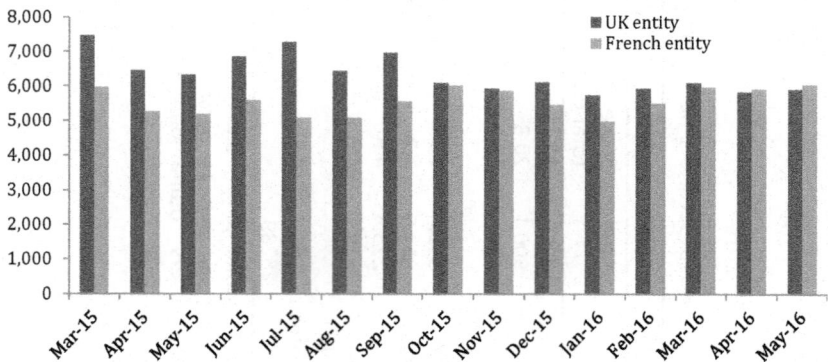

Fig. 5 Monthly amount of cleared government bond trades by LCH (in EUR billions). *Source* LCH Group (2016), http://www.lch.com/asset-classes/repoclear/volumes

It should be noted that LCH.Clearnet shows only a partial picture of euro government bond clearing. Euroclear in Brussels and Clearstream in Frankfurt also clear a large amount of euro-area government bonds.

In summary, the City of London has a dominant position in the euro-denominated OTC derivatives markets, which it might lose after Brexit. Its position in bond trading is more on par with France and Germany.

8 Concluding Remarks and Future Relationship with the EU

Negotiations about the future relationship between the UK and the EU have still to start at the time of writing (September 2016). Pisani-Ferry et al. (2016) give an overview of the different models for market access provided by the EU to financial sectors in non-EU member states (i.e. Norway model, Switzerland model, Turkey model, Canada model and the WTO model). A key issue is whether the UK wants to remain in the internal market. An important requirement for staying within the internal market is the acceptance of the supranational institutions (the European Commission and the European Court of Justice), which uphold the appropriate functioning of the internal market. Pisani-Ferry et al. (2016) have made a proposal for a continental partnership, whereby the UK would have a say on EU policies but the ultimate formal authority would remain with the EU. This partnership could keep the UK in the internal market.

If the UK were not to remain in the internal market, it would become a third country. The EU applies an equivalence regime, which allows access to an EU country from third countries if the EU (the European Commission and/or relevant supervisors) deem the supervision of the third country equivalent (Goodhart and Schoenmaker 2016). Nevertheless, the relevant supervisor(s) in the EU country can still impose regulatory and supervisory requirements. Moreover, the third country licence does not provide the passport to do business across the EU.

Whatever model is chosen, there is a need for transitional arrangements to provide certainty to financial services and markets in the period between the UK's withdrawal and its future relationship with the EU (Schoenmaker 2016). A key element in the transition is grandfather clauses and a sufficiently long grace period. Grandfathering allows a smooth transition from the old to the new regime. It means that a licence received under the old regime remains valid under the new regime (i.e. is grandfathered). Another element is the legal form of the partnership between the EU and the UK. The more this relationship is hard-wired in a Treaty, the less scope there is for changing parts of the relationship in the future. This provides more certainty for financial services providers. Nevertheless, it will be difficult to address the uncertainty on the outcome during the negotiations. A clear and joint vision on the desired outcome from the outset and a relatively speedily negotiation are helpful to keep this uncertainty to a minimum.

The UK government faces for its financial services sector a fundamental choice between global and EU business. On the one hand, London can position itself as an international financial centre with light-touch regulation and supervision to try to gain extra global business. But under that model, the equivalence of UK regulation and supervision will come under pressure, which makes access to the EU more difficult and cumbersome (extra regulatory and supervisory requirements from the EU). On the other hand, the UK can choose to remain close (i.e. equivalent) to EU legislation and thus favour its regional business in the EU. Under this model, London can still attract global business, as it does currently.

Acknowledgement The paper draws on two blogposts 'Losing "EU passport" would damage City of London' and "Lost passports: a guide to the Brexit fallout for the City of London" published in June 2016 at Bruegel. The author would like to thank Uuree Batsaikhan and Elena Vaccarino for excellent research assistance.

References

Armstrong, A. (2016). EU membership, financial services and stability. *National Institute Economic Review, 236,* 31–38.

Bank for International Settlements. (2015). *Triennial Central Bank survey of foreign exchange and derivatives market activity in 2013.* Basel: Bank for International Settlements.

Bank for International Settlements. (2016). *2016 Triennial Central Bank survey of Foreign exchange and OTC derivatives markets.* Basel: Bank for International Settlements.

Batsaikhan, U. (2016, June 7). Brexit and the UK's Euro-denominated market: The role of clearing houses. Blogpost, Bruegel.

Burrows, O., & Low, K. (2015). Mapping the UK financial system. *Bank of England Quarterly Bulletin 2015 Q2,* Bank of England.

Danielsson, Macrae, & Zigrand. (2016, June 7). On the financial market consequences of Brexit, *Voxeu.*

ECB. (2015). *EU structural financial indicators 2014.* Frankfurt: ECB.

FT. (2016, June 29). François Hollande rules out city's euro clearing role.

Goodhart, C., & Schoenmaker, D. (2016). The global investment banks are now all becoming American: Does that matter for Europeans? *Journal of Financial Regulation, 2,* 163–181.

Haldane, A., Brennan, S., & Madouros, V. (2010). What is the contribution of the financial sector: Miracle or mirage? In A. Turner et al. (Eds.), *The future of finance: The LSE Report.* London: LSE.

Pisani-Ferry, J., Röttgen, N., Sapir, A., Tucker, P., & Wolff, G. (2016, August 29). Europe after Brexit: A proposal for a continental partnership. Brussels: Bruegel.

Schoenmaker, D. (2016, September). *Written evidence for the house of lords EU sub-committee on financial affairs chaired by Baroness Falkner of Margravine on the future of financial services in the UK following the vote to leave the European union',* Bruegel. Available at http://bruegel.org/2016/09/the-future-of-financial-services-in-the-uk-following-the-brexit-vote/.

Schoenmaker, D., & Sass, J. (2016). Cross-border insurance in Europe: Challenges for supervision. *The Geneva Papers on Risk and Insurance, 41,* 351–377.

Schoenmaker, D., & Véron, N. (2016) (Eds.). *European banking supervision: The first eighteen months.* Blueprint 25. Bruegel. Available at http://bruegel.org/2016/06/blueprint-european-bankingsupervisionthe-first-eighteen-months/.

Author Biography

Dirk Schoenmaker is a Professor of Banking and Finance at the Rotterdam School of Management, Erasmus University, and a Senior Fellow at the Brussels-based think tank Bruegel. He is also a Research Fellow at the CEPR and a member of the Advisory Scientific Committee of the European Systemic Risk Board at the ECB.

Foreign Direct Investment and the Relationship Between the United Kingdom and the European Union

Randolph L. Bruno, Nauro F. Campos, Saul Estrin and Meng Tian

1 Introduction

Economic integration is often considered to be a conduit for international trade, but recent developments have shown it also to be a powerful force in FDI terms (Anderson and van Wincoop 2003, 2004). At the same time, the gravity model, one of the most successful empirical models in economics (Anderson 2011) and a staple of international economics, explains remarkably well the observed variation in economic interactions in trade and factor movements, notably FDI. It analyses bilateral cross-border flows (trade, migration, investment, etc.) in terms of the

Prepared for Campos, N. and F. Coricelli (eds) *The Economics of the EU–UK Relationship: From the Treaty of Rome to the Vote for Brexit*, Palgrave Macmillan, forthcoming.

R.L. Bruno (✉)
University College London, London, UK
e-mail: randolph.bruno@ucl.ac.uk

N.F. Campos
Brunel University London, London, UK
e-mail: nauro.campos@brunel.ac.uk

© The Author(s) 2017
N.F. Campos and F. Coricelli (eds.), *The Economics of UK–EU Relations*,
DOI 10.1007/978-3-319-55495-2_6

139

relative size and distance between countries/regions (see Head and Mayer 2014, for an authoritative review). A country's economic size is expected to have a positive effect on bilateral flows while distance is expected to have a negative effect. In fact, distance is often taken to reflect a whole range of trade costs including language, bureaucracy, culture, etc. The gravity model therefore highlights the potential for trade and FDI between relatively large economies that are close together geographically. This could be an important economic phenomenon because inward FDI has been found to be a major contributor to the diffusion of managerial best practices (Bloom et al. 2012). It increases competition and shores up technological innovation and it is believed to do so in a deeper and more resilient fashion than other international capital flows.

By reducing 'distance', the gravity model leads one to expect a significant positive impact on the level of FDI from institutionally embedded political and economic ties, such as the European Union, especially between spatially close and relatively large economies. However, although the benefits of FDI are well established in the economic literature,[1] there is a dearth of analysis of the impact of the European integration experience on the scale of FDI, not to mention a complete absence of literature concerning the impact of European disintegration. In the light of this, this paper offers more contemporary and rigorous estimates of the effect of membership of the European Union (EU) on inflows of foreign direct investment, which also provide an indication of the likely effect of EU exit. Given the recent vote by the UK to leave the European Union, we undertake additional empirical work with a special focus on United Kingdom. Despite the obvious importance of the subject, the literature focusing on potential reasons for foreign investors to choose the UK vis-à-vis say Germany, Poland or Switzerland remains scarce.

S. Estrin
London School of Economics, London, UK
e-mail: s.estrin@lse.ac.uk

M. Tian
Peking University & London School of Economics, Beijing, China
e-mail: caroltianmeng@gmail.com

We are also interested in the potential value of an indirect comparison between the trade effects of the EU and the FDI effects of currency unions such as the Euro, and the implications of recent methodological developments. For example, Glick and Rose (2016) find that their earlier estimates (Glick and Rose 2002) on the impact of currency unions were statistically fragile when subjected to a wide range of modern and sophisticated econometric techniques. We therefore parallel Glick and Rose in asking whether the use of modern econometric techniques eliminates the effects of the EU on FDI. *We find that it does not.* Using best available econometric methods, we find that EU membership always significantly increases FDI inflows, by around 28% depending on the precise choice of econometric technique and we posit this to be a lower bound. This result implies that for a country like the UK, leaving the EU would reduce FDI inflows by around 22%. We show that this finding is consistent with alternative methodologies that look specifically at the UK experience of FDI compared to other countries.

We first summarize recent conceptual and methodological developments in Sect. 2 before outlining the interpretation of some graphical analyses on FDI dynamics in Sect. 3. The data and empirical strategy are discussed in Sect. 4 while Sect. 5 reports the main new empirical findings about the significant positive effects of being in the EU, from a gravity model of bilateral FDI flows with a special focus on the United Kingdom. Section 6 concludes.

2 Background on FDI, Trade and the European Union: Recent Developments

The objective of this section is to put forward a conceptual framework that helps us to understand the effect of economic integration on FDI inflows. The distinction between shallow and deep integration is useful in this case: shallow integration is epitomized by the free trade area model and is restricted to economic integration, while deep integration combines economic and political aspects (Campos et al. 2015). An important case of deep integration is the customs union model in which economic ties are supported by the creation of common institutions to manage conflict, which may emerge, for instance, regarding the common external tariff. The European Union is the most sophisticated example of deep integration and it is quite remarkable to realize that considerable lacunae remain with respect to our understanding of whether and how EU integration has affected FDI inflows (Campos and Coricelli 2015).

2.1 The Impact of FDI

The changing nature of international trade (Baldwin 2016) is worthy of note for our understanding of FDI and the European Union. Traditionally, international trade has focused on final goods and was driven by the exploitation of mutual comparative advantage. In the last two or three decades, international trade has increasingly focused on trade in parts and components (instead of final goods) and has been increasingly driven by domestic absorptive capacity. Deep integration has contributed to the emergence of global value chains (Amador and di Mauro 2015) in which production is spread across various countries or, to put it differently, to a larger role for intra-industry trade. UNCTAD (WIR 2016) estimates that 60% of global trade is in intermediate goods and services.

There is an enormous literature on the impact of FDI on the host economy (see Bruno et al. 2017), which attests to the importance of these factor flows for national economic performance. As we have noted, FDI matters because the entry of foreign firms in the domestic market increases competition and shores up technological innovation both in terms of product and process (Alfaro et al. 2004). It also puts pressure simultaneously on their direct domestic competitors in the host economy, as well as on upstream and downstream firms (Javorcic 2004; Mastromarco and Simar 2015). Importantly, FDI entails the diffusion of frontier management practices (Bloom et al. 2012). FDI is often conceived as being more resilient than other international capital flows (portfolio investment, for instance) and may exhibit important complementarity patterns not only with respect to international trade, but also with other elements of financial globalization.

To understand the nature of the phenomenon and how institutions of economic integration might influence FDI, it is useful to distinguish between horizontal and vertical effects of FDI.[2] The former refers to spillovers from the foreign firm to its domestic competitors, while the latter refers to spillovers to suppliers and customers; as noted above the latter is an increasing important element in global trade. Havránek and Iršová have authored two important surveys of the large literatures on horizontal and vertical spillovers. Havránek and Iršová (2011) focus on the latter. They estimate that spillovers from FDI to suppliers tend to be economically larger (and statistically significant) than spillover to buyers. Interestingly, they also find that these spillovers tend to be larger in countries with underdeveloped financial systems, that are more open to international trade, and that are generated by investors who have only a slight technological edge over local firms. This somewhat surprising pattern points to the importance of absorptive capacity and diffusion mechanisms.

Iršová and Havránek (2013) review the evidence on horizontal spillovers. They present a quantitative review of the econometric evidence using meta-regression analysis tools. In contrast to the findings about vertical spillovers, they conclude that horizontal spillovers are on average zero, but their sign and magnitude depend systematically on the characteristics of domestic and foreign firms' investors, with the size of the technological gap between them and ownership structure playing major roles. They find that joint ventures between domestic and foreign firms are the structure that delivers the largest benefits. Similar to the case of vertical spillovers, they find that the positive effects from FDI are substantially larger when the technological gap between domestic and foreign firms is small. Thus the evidence about the impact of FDI is consistent with that about its pattern, with increasing importance of global value chains and vertical spillover effects.

2.2 Methodological Developments in the FDI Literature

We saw in the 'Introduction' that the gravity model was originally developed for international trade flows but as Anderson (2011) has pointed out, the theoretical underpinnings apply with equal force to output and factor input flows. The last two decades have witnessed enormous progress in this area. Among many influential pieces, Anderson and van Wincoop (2003) and Santos Silva and Tenreyro (2006) are the crucial ones for our purposes. This new structural gravity approach (Fally 2015) provides needed theoretical underpinnings as well as strong support for the econometric estimation of gravity models. But these advances in method have brought into question long-established findings. For example, focusing exclusively on trade, Glick and Rose (2016) find that earlier significant estimates of the effect of currency union membership are not robust to the application of newer and more sophisticated econometric techniques, specifically the Poisson estimator. Most of these techniques became standard after they published their original paper (Glick and Rose 2002).

The seminal paper in the econometric evaluation of free trade area agreements is by Baier and Bergstrand (2007). This paper is one of the first to make the point that moving away from a cross-section design to one based on panel data was necessary in order to deal with serious concerns about endogeneity bias (see also Baier et al. 2008; Egger and Pfaffermayr 2004). Moreover, this literature generates a number of valuable estimates of the economic benefits of deep vis-à-vis shallow integration. For instance, Baier et al. (2008) estimate that membership in the European Union leads to increases in bilateral international trade of the order of between 127 and 146% 10–15 years after joining. This compares very favourably with equivalently estimated benefits from shallow integration: for instance, they also find that membership in the European Free Trade Association (EFTA) generates increases in bilateral trade that are of about one quarter of the size of those generated from deep integration agreements [such as the EU and the European Economic Area (EEA)]. The latter show increases of only about 35% over the 10–15-years period following the start of membership.

There has also been important research on individual aspects of deep integration on FDI inflows. Of particular interest in our case is the role of deepening monetary integration (for instance, by using a single currency) in affecting trade and FDI inflows. De Sousa and Lochard's paper (2011) is especially relevant in this respect because it investigates whether the creation of the euro (in the context of the European Monetary Union, EMU) in 1999 explains the sharp increase in intra-European investment flows. They tackle these questions using a gravity model for bilateral foreign direct investment. Their main finding is that the euro increased intra-EMU FDI stocks by around 30%. More importantly, they find evidence that this effect varies over time and across EMU members: it is significantly larger for outward investments of those less-developed EMU members.

There has also been an important stream of recent studies about FDI from a regional economics perspective, of which a good example is that of Basile et al. (2008). This paper uses panel firm-level data over the period 1991–1999 covering more than 5500 foreign subsidiaries in 50 regions of eight different 8 EU countries. The methodology they use is the mixed-logit location choice model, which allows the investigation of the effects of EU regional policy (Structural Funds) on the location choice of foreign subsidiaries. Their main conclusion is that accounting for agglomeration economies and various regional and country-level characteristics, these regional policy instruments are found to be an effective factor in explaining FDI location. Although the eligibility criteria for EU regional assistance funds are restrictive—regions with per capita income below 70% of the EU average qualify—evidence of this positive effect provides an additional reason why we should expect an FDI premium from EU membership, especially in poorer countries or countries containing poorer regions, such as the UK.

One additional issue to consider is the complex relationship between international trade and FDI inflows. This has been traditionally framed in terms of tariff-jumping FDI decisions [see Motta (1992) for a classic treatment] and has gained further impetus with recent work on heterogeneous firms. Helpman et al. (2004) is the seminal piece in this respect. They put forward a multi-country, multi-sector general equilibrium model that highlights the decision of heterogeneous firms to sell in foreign markets either through exports or through a local subsidiary (FDI). Econometric evidence for the model is presented focusing on US affiliate sales and US exports in 38 countries and 52 sectors. Two particularly important findings for our purposes are (1) strong negative effects on export sales relative to FDI from sector and country-specific transport costs and tariffs, providing micro-foundations for distance effects within the gravity model, and (2) strong positive support for the effects of firm-level heterogeneity on the relative export and FDI sales (with greater firm heterogeneity found to lead to significantly more FDI sales relative to export sales.)

A more recent take on this issue is that of Conconi et al. (2015) which looks at how uncertainty affects firms' internationalization choices in terms of the trade-off between exports and foreign direct investment. The theoretical framework they put forward is centred on the notion that firms are uncertain about their profitability in a foreign market and thus experiment via exports before engaging in FDI. The main novel idea is therefore that firms first choose to export in order to learn about the market and the country and, once learning has taken place, go on to substitute these exports by directly investing. If firms export before investing in foreign markets, the trade-off is not rigid and may be subject to change over time. Conconi et al. (2015) find support for this prediction in that the probability that a firm starts investing in a foreign country significantly increases with its export experience in that country.

2.3 The Gravity Model

Although the gravity model was initially developed as a purely empirical model, in the last decade or so it has been given solid theoretical foundations in the trade literature. Maybe the simplest way to derive theoretically the gravity equation is to impose a market-clearing condition on an expenditure equation. We follow Baldwin and Taglioni (2007) (Head and Mayer 2014, provide a useful discussion of the main choices involved) and, using CES preferences for differentiated varieties, write the expenditure equation as

$$\vartheta_{od} \equiv \left(\frac{p_{od}}{p_d}\right)^{1-\sigma} E_d \qquad (1)$$

where the left-hand side represents total spending in country d on a variety produced in country o (d for destination, o for origin), p_{od} is the consumer price in country d of a variety produced in country o, p_d is the price index of all varieties in country d, σ is the elasticity of substitution among varieties (assumed >1) and E_d is the total consumer expenditure in the destination country.

Profit maximization by producers in country o yields $p_{od} = \mu_{od} m_o \tau_{od}$ where μ_{od} is the optimal mark-up, m_o is the marginal cost and τ_{od} represents bilateral trade costs. Assuming monopolistic or perfect competition, the mark-up is identical for all destinations. For the case of Dixit–Stiglitz monopolistic competition, the mark-up is $\sigma/(\sigma-1)$ which means that consumer prices in country i are $p_{oo} = (\sigma/(\sigma-1)) \, m_o \tau_{oo}$ and $\tau_{oo} = 1$ if we assume there are no internal/domestic barriers. Assuming symmetry of varieties for convenience and summing over all varieties yields

$$V_{od} = n_o p_{oo}^{1-\sigma} \frac{\tau_{od}^{1-\sigma}}{p_d^{1-\sigma}} E_d \qquad (2)$$

where V_{od} is the aggregate value of the bilateral trade flow from origin to destination and n_o is the number of varieties produced in origin and sold in destination.

The market-clearing condition requires that supply and demand match: hence summing Eq. (2) over all destinations (including own sales) is set equal to the country total output (Y_o). The condition can then be stated as

$$Y_o = n_o p_{oo}^{1-\sigma} \sum_d \tau_{od}^{1-\sigma} p_d^{1-\sigma} E_d \qquad (3)$$

and solving it yields $n_o p_{oo}^{1-\sigma} = Y_o/\Omega_o$ where Ω_o is an index of market-potential. Substituting this market-clearing condition on the expenditure function yields the gravity equation:

$$V_{od} = \tau_{od}^{1-\sigma} \frac{E_d Y_o}{p_d^{1-\sigma} \Omega_o} \qquad (4)$$

For the econometric implementation of Eq. (4), E_d is proxied by the destination country's GDP, Y_o is proxied by the origin country's GDP,

$p_d^{1-\sigma}\Omega_o$ is the multilateral trade resistance term, and τ is proxied by bilateral distance. The intuitive interpretation of the model is easy to visualize: bilateral trade is a positive function of the size of the trade partners and it is a negative function of the distance between them. Anderson (2011) explains how this framework can be extended for factor flows such as FDI.

3   FDI in European Union and the United Kingdom

This section aims to provide descriptive evidence to motivate our empirical analysis, explaining the trends and development of foreign direct investment in European Union, with a special focus on major economies such as France, Germany, Holland, and the UK. The UK is then further analysed as a major FDI recipient country which is now intending to leave the European Union.

3.1   The Performance of FDI Inflows Between and into EU Countries

Despite of the recent burst of FDI growth among emerging markets, the EU has maintained a stable growth of FDI at a level consistent with the remainder of the world economy and remaining as the largest investor and recipient of FDI globally. We focus our attention in this chapter on the impact of EU membership on FDI inflows in the context of OECD countries, as these economies share similar levels of development to most of EU member countries. Moreover, consistent bilateral FDI data over time, which is critical for the application of the gravity framework, is rarely available except within the OECD.

In Fig. 1 below, we report the dynamic of FDI inflows between OECD countries categorised into four types: inflows from EU to EU; from non-EU to non-EU; from non-EU to EU; and finally from EU to non-EU. The figure provides a clear indication that intra-EU inflows (from EU to EU) outperform all the other categories of foreign investment, indicating

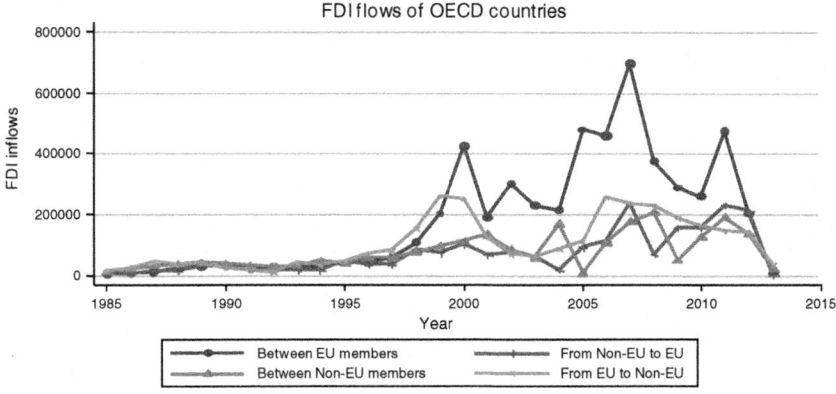

Fig. 1   FDI net inflows in OECD countries: 1985–2013. *Source* Authors' calculations

how, within the OECD context, the EU can be seen as a powerful institutional device for integration through fixed capital flows.

The Figure also provides evidence that the EU has significant advantages among OECD countries in being able to attract FDI from non-OECD economies. This leads us to investigate how each member country has benefited from being in the union. Figure 2 presents FDI inflows as against GDP per capita for EU and non-EU members in 3 years, 1985, 2000 and 2015. We can take away three main messages. First, the FDI phenomenon has exploded only in recent years. If we compare 1985 with 2000 there has clearly been a major expansion in FDI inflows in the last decade of twentieth century. Second, in addition to the USA (which always been a major FDI host economy) there are three EU countries that stand out as major recipients of FDI in absolute terms in 2003: Germany, UK and Holland, though inflows are also high in France and Spain. Thirdly and particularly important for our analysis, subsequent to the 2008 crisis there has been a sort of re-convergence effect of FDI in absolute values in 2015.

More specifically, we take a closer look at the recent performance of four of the largest FDI recipient countries in the EU, the UK, Holland, France, and Germany in Fig. 3. We find that the volumes that went to France and Germany were relatively stable during the examined period. However, the UK enjoyed more growth between 2004–2008, and Netherlands experienced even higher growth for that period and after 2010.

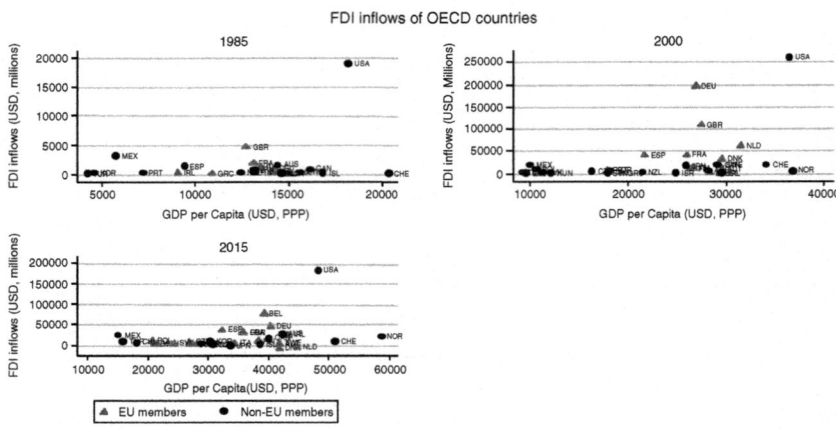

Fig. 2 FDI net inflows and GDP per capita: a snapshot in 1985, 2000 and 2015.[3]
Source Authors' calculations

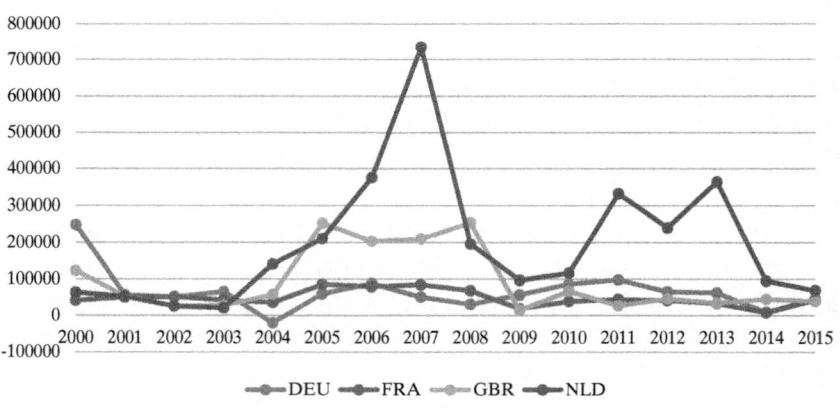

Fig. 3 FDI inflows into UK, Holland, France and Germany, 2000–2015 (millions of USD). *Source* Authors' calculations

3.2   UK as the Main FDI Recipient Within EU

In fact, the United Kingdom has long been one of the main FDI recipients in Europe. If we consider FDI stocks, in 2015 these represented 55% of GDP in the UK as against 42% in Germany (OECD 2016a, b). Stocks reached 71% of GDP in 2009, compared with only

48% across the European Union in that year. Turning to flows (Fig. 4), in line with global FDI flows, net FDI inflows to the UK were small in absolute terms until the mid-1990s. In the subsequent period they exhibited two periods of rapid expansion, one in the second half of the 1990s and the other before the financial crisis up to 2008. The 2008 financial crisis generated a substantial 'sudden stop' in UK FDI inflows.

Figure 4 presents the FDI inflows into the UK by source regions: EU member countries, non-EU OECD members, and the rest of world. As exhibited in the figure, the EU has been the most important source of FDI to the UK, and the volume also grows with the same pattern as the total FDI inflows into the UK. Even though with the expansion of emerging markets, UK begun to receive more investments from other parts of the world, the importance of EU is not diminishing. Being a member of the EU is often regarded as one of the major attractions of the UK to bring in foreign investors. UK firms have long enjoyed the benefits of unrestricted access to the huge European Single Market.

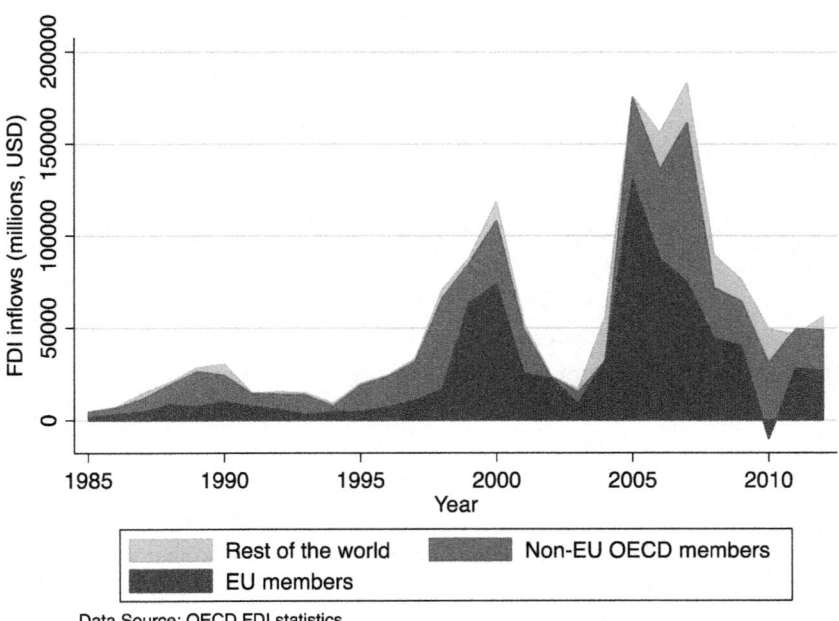

Data Source: OECD FDI statistics

Fig. 4 Inward foreign direct investment flows to the UK by source region: 1985–2014

One important final consideration regards the sectoral distribution of FDI inflows into the UK. Not only a huge share of it goes into services (which includes financial intermediation) but more importantly this percentage has been rising over time. In 2011, the share of FDI stock in the service sector crossed the mark of 70% of the total. This represents a substantial increase from similar figures of around 60% in the late 1990s (Driffield et al. 2013). The comparable share for manufacturing moves down from 27% in late 1990s to <20% recently. This has significant and still under-appreciated consequences in light of the decision to leave the EU. The type of FDI the UK has been attracting the most is the most mobile type, that is, FDI that can change location quickly and at relatively little cost.

4   Data and Empirical Strategy

Our objective is to estimate the impact of EU membership on FDI, with particular reference to the UK. To achieve this, we first use the synthetic control method (SCM) to investigate the impact of the UK joining the European Single Market in 1986 using data from the World Bank's World Development Indicators. The main part of our study is based on the estimation of a gravity model, and for this we collected the most recently available data on bilateral FDI flows, GDP and GDP per capita (sender and target, i.e. origin and destination), bilateral distance and the shares of manufacturing output, exports and imports in total GDP which covers 34 OECD countries between 1985 and 2013.[4] The OECD is the only systematic source of bilateral FDI flows, which are required for the estimation of gravity FDI models, and hence the only feasible data to estimate our models. Even so, our data still represent more than 70% of global FDI inflows. Moreover, the countries being all OECD members, implies that the data are likely of reasonable quality and collected in a homogenous manner. The disadvantage of our data is that of necessity they exclude most developing countries, including China and India, and they have become increasingly significant for FDI in recent years, though not historically over the whole sample period. Notice that a by-product of this drawback is that we are limited in the currency unions we can study (for example, vis-à-vis Glick and Rose 2016).

Our first exercise is to explore the impact of EU membership on UK FDI by using the *'synthetic control methods for causal inference in comparative case studies'* or, in short, synthetic counterfactuals, which was initially proposed in Abadie and Gardeazabal (2003). The method has since become extremely widely used. Imbens and Wooldridge (2009) discuss the synthetic counterfactuals method among other recent developments in the econometrics of programme evaluation and Athey and Imbens describe it as 'one of the most important developments in programme evaluation in the last decade' (Athey and Imbens 2016, p. 5). The synthetic control method estimates the effect of a given intervention by comparing the evolution of an aggregate outcome variable for a country affected by the intervention vis-à-vis the evolution of the same aggregate outcome for a synthetic control group.

The synthetic counterfactual method therefore exploits the construction of a 'synthetic control group', or in the words of Imbens and Wooldridge, of an 'artificial control group' (2009, p. 72). It does so by searching for a weighted combination of other units (in this case, control countries), which are chosen to match as close as possible the country affected by the intervention, before the intervention or treatment occurs, for a set of predictors of the outcome variable. The evolution of the outcome for the synthetic control group is an estimate of the counterfactual. It shows what the behaviour of the outcome variable, in our case FDI inflows, would have been for the affected country if the intervention (the creation of the Single European Market) had (not) happened in the same way as in the control group.

Our other modelling strategy follows the standard structural gravity approach recently developed in the literature: a similar specification is used by Baier and Bergstrand (2007, e.g. see Eqs. (9) and (10)). Gravity has gravitas. The original gravity study was authored by Jan Tinbergen, the first winner of the Nobel Prize in Economics. These original estimations used pooled OLS methods without time or country fixed-effects. The inclusion of fixed effects has (justifiably) become a standard estimation feature, usually by adding 'dyadic fixed effects', that is, a dummy variable for each 'unordered' pair of countries involved in a bilateral flow.

These dummies control for any *time-invariant* characteristic common to every pair of trading partners. A number of theoretically important determinants of FDI fall into this category of fixed effects, particularly the distance between countries—a key element of the gravity framework—and whether countries share a common culture, language or border. The subsequent step in the evolution of gravity modelling was the use of time-varying country as well as dyadic fixed effects, to further control for time-specific factors across countries, such as the dynamic of common macroeconomic shocks. The current stage in the evolution of modelling gravity is the use of the Poisson estimator (Santos Silva and Tenreyro 2006), which takes account of the fact that FDI from each source economy tends to arrive independently of FDI from every other economy.

Baldwin (2006) and Baldwin and Taglioni (2007) provide important insights for the application of the gravity model in the empirical analysis. They derive the basic gravity estimating equation for trade that we use for FDI:

$$ln\left(bilateral\,flow\,of\,FDI_{o,d,t}\right) = \alpha_0 + \alpha_1 lnX_{o,t} + \alpha_2 lnX_{d,t} + \alpha_3 Z_{o,d,t}$$
$$+ \eta_{o,d} + T_t + u_{o,d,t}$$

$$(5)$$

where $ln(.)$ stands for a natural logarithm and the $X_{o,t}$ is a vector of characteristics of the origin country, o, in year t. This can be derived from Eq. (4) above (Anderson 2011) and will include measures of the size (GDP) and wealth (GDP per capita) of the country. Similarly $X_{d,t}$ is a vector of destination nation's characteristics. The $Z_{o,d,t}$ is a vector of time-varying characteristics specific to a country pair. Being a member of the EU will be one of the time-varying observable characteristics of a country that enter the $X_{o,t}$ and $X_{d,t.}$ vectors. It is hard to control adequately for the wide variety of FDI-relevant characteristics using observable variables. To deal with this potential major source of unobserved heterogeneity, a dyadic fixed effect $(\eta_{o,d})$ is therefore included in the equation, i.e. a dummy variable for each unordered pair of countries —around 630 fixed effects. It will include things like geographical distance (a proxy for trade costs) and cultural distance (colonial history, common language, etc.) since geography is time invariant over our sample period and cultural factors do not change greatly over time. Hence the coefficients of interest are identified from the impact of changes in trading relationships (and other economic variables) over time on the change in FDI flows over time. We also include a full set of time dummies T_t to control for global macroeconomic shocks.

Dyadic fixed effects and time dummies are important for this analysis. The inclusion of bilateral fixed effects helps to minimize the impact of the exclusion of many of the usual suspects in explaining FDI flows, i.e. pair unobserved heterogeneity such as cultural distance, bilateral regulatory agreements, etc. In other words, the model mitigates the usual concern regarding 'omitted variable bias' in these types of empirical analyses. Year fixed effects are also important. They reflect the macro phenomena that are common across all country-pairs. The $u_{o,d,t}$ is an error term. The standard errors are clustered by dyadic pair to allow for serial correlation of the errors.

Our specification follows a threefold estimation strategy. First, we estimate a baseline model using the natural logarithm of bilateral FDI flows as dependent variable; second, we estimate a Poisson model; and finally, we estimate a Heckman model that takes into account the zero flows bilateral trade and as such has a larger number of observations. Let us outline them in order.

The first is the baseline model against which we compare our results. The second is our preferred estimation model given the state of the art of the literature (see Glick and Rose 2016) and the final model allows us to address the selection problem caused by the large number of countries for which there is no observation on bilateral FDI flows. The OLS and Poisson regression may be biased by the inclusion of 'positive only' data of bilateral FDI flows since 41% of the observations are zero. The OLS model deals with this by giving a value of $1 of FDI to the missing value that allows us to take logarithms. But this is rather arbitrary and the fact that there are no bilateral trade flows between two countries may be telling us more about the costs of doing business between the pair of countries. We address this issue via a Heckman selection model in which we first estimate a selection equation. The likelihood of non-zero flows is modelled as a function of manufacturing, exports and import shares as well as the per capita GDP of the destination country.

5   Econometric Results

This section presents three sets of econometric results. The first uses the synthetic control method to investigate by how much FDI inflows into the UK would differ under the counterfactual scenario of the UK not having joined the European Single Market in 1986. We then go on to present the results from our gravity equation estimates. We use the findings to calculate the 'FDI premium' from EU membership. Finally, we go on the present a hypothetical 'EU without the UK' empirical exercise, in other words an UK outside the EU counterfactual via an empirical regression model instead, to gauge the statistically significance of such an event. In order to assess the role of EU for the UK vis-à-vis other countries, we perform the same exercise for Germany, France and Italy.

5.1   Synthetic Counterfactuals Method

Our first step is to estimate counterfactual scenarios illustrating what would be the levels of FDI inflows if the UK had never been a full-fledged member of the European Union using the synthetic counterfactuals methodology. We estimate the effect of the onset of the European Single Market Programme by comparing the evolution of FDI inflows for a country affected by the intervention vis-à-vis the evolution of FDI for a synthetic control group. The synthetic control method answers questions such as 'what would have been the level of FDI inflows in the UK after 1986 if the UK had not had full access to the ESM?'

In Fig. 5, the dashed red line shows their 'synthetic counterfactual' estimates, showing what would have been FDI net inflows after 1986 if the UK had decided *not* to join the Single Market. They are based on a simple model focusing on per capita GDP, GDP growth rates, the share of manufacturing value added in GDP, the share of government consumption in GDP, investment, and trade openness as determinants of

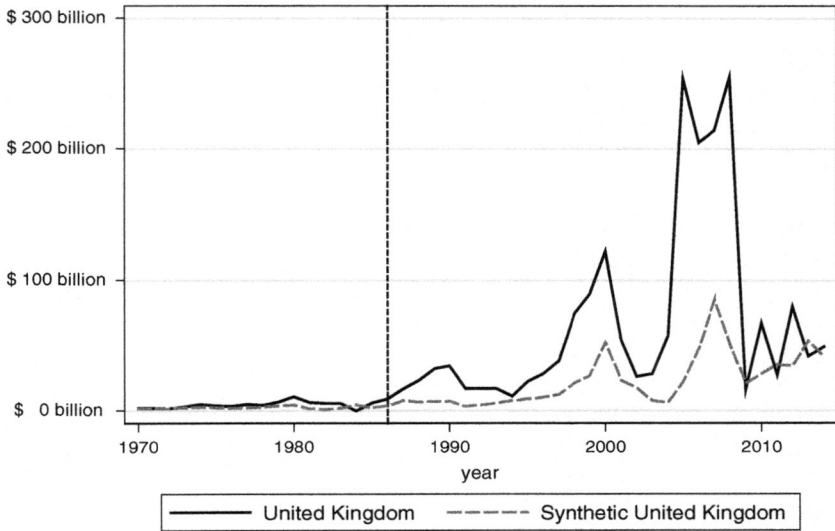

Fig. 5 What would UK FDI net inflows be if the UK had not been in the EU Single Market? *Source* Authors' calculations. *Notes* FDI is measured in nominal US$. The actual FDI flows for the UK (*solid black line*) are compared to a counterfactual (*dashed line*) of a "synthetic UK" made up of a weighted basket of basically three other countries (mostly Canada and New Zealand, but also United States). *Vertical line marks* year 1986 and onset of the EU Single Market

FDI location choice. The following estimated weights were obtained: Canada (approximately 60%), New Zealand (approximately 30%) and the United States (approximately 5%) with other countries having smaller weights.

The results suggest that the Single Market played a key role in mobilizing FDI to and from the UK. Interestingly, they show that the bulk of these benefits (indicated by comparison with the FDI would have received in the circumstance when the UK had chosen to opt out of the Single European market) occurred post-Euro (Sanso-Navarro 2011; Christodoulakis and Sarantides 2016), between the dot-com bubble and the financial crisis. In other words, these results suggest that for the whole period of 1986–2014, the UK would have received on average about 30% less FDI had it not been in the EU, but that this average conceals large variations over time that deserve further study; the bulk of the 'loss' was from the mid-1990s. Here we use these estimates simply to motivate and gauge those from the gravity framework that follows so future research will benefit from taking a closer look at this issue using the synthetic control method.

5.2 The Gravity Model Estimates

We now turn to our gravity equation estimates. Table 1 reports our main results with the dependent variable being the bilateral FDI flows and the independent variables being the GDP and the GDP per capita for both sender and receiver country (all in logs). How can one assess the impact of EU membership? We use the country-specific step dummies (zero prior to membership, unity post-membership) to capture the *membership treatment effect* for both the target and the sender country though our discussion will focus on the interpretation of the former, i.e. the effect of membership on FDI inflows.[5]

As can be seen in Table 1, the regressors in all three specifications, i.e. OLS, Poisson and Heckman, carry the expected signs. As predicted by the gravity model, the impact of the size (measured by GDP) of country pair engaging in FDI is positive and has a coefficient close to one while the level of development (GDP per capita) of the sender also exerts a positive effect on FDI inflows. Turning to the Heckman methodology in columns (3) and (4) of Table 1, the selection equation generates some interesting lessons: a higher likelihood of positive FDI flows is related to lower per capita GDP in the destination country (FDI goes to countries where the return to capital is higher), higher industry shares (better integration in the value chain), lower export shares (substitution effect between FDI and trade) and higher import shares of the target.

The main variable of interest for this study is the one capturing the effect of EU membership on FDI *inflows*, for which there are estimates for all three methodologies in columns (1) to (3) respectively. The estimated coefficients for the EU target dummy for the host economy ranges between 14 and 38% depending on the estimator. This coefficient is always statistically significant. On the baseline OLS estimate of column (1), the effect is 33% ($=e^{0.285} - 1$). In the Poisson model of column (2),

Table 1 Panel estimates of the effects of EU membership on FDI inflows

Dependent variable	(1) Ln (1 + FDI)	(2) FDI	(3) Ln (FDI)	(4) Dummy 1 (FDI > 0)
EU member (target)	0.285***	0.320*	0.132***	
	(0.077)	(0.163)	(0.050)	
EU member (sender)	−0.010	0.828***	0.199***	
	(0.079)	(0.191)	(0.050)	
Ln (GDP, target)	0.473***	3.799***	0.686***	
	(0.056)	(1.432)	(0.226)	
Ln (GDP, sender)	0.500***	3.903***	0.766***	
	(0.154)	(1.462)	(0.226)	
Ln (GDP per capita, target)	0.180	−1.489	−0.010	0.230***
	(0.158)	(1.513)	(0.255)	(0.017)
Ln (GDP per capita, sender)	1.450***	−1.125	1.655***	
	(0.154)	(1.623)	(0.254)	
Manufacturing value added/GDP (target)				0.005***
				(0.002)
Exports/GDP (target)				−0.013***
				(0.001)
Imports/GDP (target)				0.011***
				(0.002)
Mills' Ratio			1.043***	
			(0.164)	
Observations	33,524	33,147	33,524	33,524

Notes *** indicates significance at the 1% level, ** at the 5% level and * at the 10% level. Coefficients with standard errors (clustered by 630 bilateral country pair in first two columns) in brackets. All regressions include fixed effects for years and dyadic pair. Column (1) is estimated by OLS. Column (2) is estimated by Poisson PML. Columns (3) and (4) are a two-part Heckman selection equation. The dependent variable in column (4) is a dummy equal to 1 if there are any FDI inflows and zero otherwise. The Mills' ratio is constructed from this column and included in column (3). The 34 OECD countries included are Austria, Australia, Belgium, Canada, Chile, Czech Republic, Denmark, Estonia, Finland, France, Germany, Greece, Hungary, Iceland, Ireland, Israel, Italy, Japan, Korea, Luxembourg, Mexico, Netherlands, Norway, New Zealand, Poland, Portugal, Slovakia, Slovenia, Spain, Sweden, Switzerland, Turkey, UK and the US. "Target" indicates the country which is the recipient of the FDI and "sender" indicates the country is the sender of the FDI

it is 38% (=$e^{0.32}$ − 1). In column (3), which tries to control for selection on the zeros, the effect is 14% (=$e^{0.13}$ − 1). A simple average of these three estimates would be 28% and we consider this as the 'baseline case'.

This suggests that EU membership increases FDI inflows to each member country by about 30%, and that this can be applied in particular to the UK.

In terms of considering the impact of Brexit, one would be running the same experiment in reverse (with a country leaving rather than joining the EU) so the proportionate effect would be smaller. For example, if joining the EU increases FDI in a country by 28%, we would predict that the same country's leaving the EU would reduce FDI by 22% (28% = 0.22/(1 + 0.22)). Similarly, the three estimates of 14, 33 and 38% translate to average exit-induced falls of FDI of 12, 25 and 28%, respectively. These estimates would apply to any country considering exit, including the UK.

Can one use these estimates of the past effects of the EU on FDI as a guide to the future, with reference to calculating the effect of Brexit? It is true that the effects going forward of EU membership could be smaller than in the past. But it is equally possible they may be larger. These results are the best estimates at present on the basis of current evidence. A baseline case that things will be similar to what has occurred in the past, unless there is a strong reason to think otherwise, seems a reasonable starting point for discussion.[6]

5.3 Robustness Checks

We have subjected our estimates to a wide range of robustness checks. First, we are implicitly treating the counterfactual to EU membership as being a member of the World Trade Organization (WTO), the reason being that the omitted category is non-EU that broadly speaking is identified with WTO members (as OECD countries are). In fact, when we think specifically of Brexit, we may believe that membership of the European Free Trade Association (EFTA) or the European Economic Area (EEA) would be a more likely alternative for the UK after leaving the EU (Dhingra et al. 2016). This is what is reported in Table 2. If we add two dummy variables for being an EFTA sender or target to column (1) and (2) OLS and PPML, respectively, both coefficients are statistically insignificant and the EU recipient dummy remains positive and

Table 2 Panel estimates of the effects of EU, EFTA and NAFTA membership

Dependent variable	(1) OLS Ln(1+FDI)	(2) PPML FDI	(3) OLS Ln(1 + FDI)	(4) PPML FDI
EU member (target)	0.32495***	0.38476***	0.28616***	0.49704***
	(0.10146)	(0.12344)	(0.076)	(0.158)
EU member (sender)	0.02813	0.31516	−0.02331	0.67110***
	(0.09968)	(0.20758)	(0.076)	(0.18)
EFTA member (target)	−0.06782	−0.49005		
	(0.14473)	(0.31264)		
EFTA member (sender)	0.12395	0.87104**		
	(0.15167)	(0.35417)		
NAFTA member (target)			−0.17292	−0.37798
			(0.141)	(0.266)
NAFTA member (sender)			−0.23923	−1.12852***
			(0.147)	(0.308)
Ln (GDP, target)	0.40517***	3.85951***	0.42154***	5.19508***
	(0.05226)	(1.45283)	(0.053)	(1.58)
Ln (GDP, sender)	0.45067***	4.04238***	0.45750***	5.38103***
	(0.05418)	(1.48331)	(−0.054)	(−1.611)
Ln (GDP per capita, target)	−0.46443***	−1.56296	−0.44021***	−3.15931**
	(0.14305)	(1.47634)	(0.135)	(1.61)
Ln (GDP per capita, sender)	0.80930***	−1.15654	0.89843***	−2.5781
	(0.14116)	(1.55632)	(0.133)	(1.709)
Observations	31779	29785	32,538	30,535

Notes *** indicates significance at the 1% level, ** at the 5% level and * at the 10% level. Coefficients with standard errors (clustered by 630 bilateral country pair in first two columns) in brackets. All regressions include fixed effects for years and dyadic pair. Column (1) and (3) are estimated by OLS. Column (2) and (4) are estimated by Poisson PML

significant (in the 0.32–0.38 range and highly significant). This suggests that it is being in the EU that matters. Further, the point estimate on being an EFTA recipient is actually negative. This implies that there may be some diversion from EFTA members like Switzerland to EU members (for example, because Switzerland is not in the single market for financial services). In columns (3) and (4), we repeat the same exercise by looking at NAFTA instead. Similar conclusions unfold: the EU membership dummy remains highly significant and positive and no premium seems to be associated with NAFTA as far as FDI inflows (i.e. looking at the target dummy) are concerned.

Second, our approach has focused on modelling FDI inflows, but an alternative would be to use FDI *stocks*. Our robustness checks show that doing so yields qualitatively similar results.[7] With stocks rather than flows as the dependent variable, the EU membership recipient dummy always attracts a positive coefficient in the three specifications.

How do these results compare with other estimates in the literature? As noted in Sect. 2, the synthetic cohort approach generates EU membership effects of 25–30% for the United Kingdom, which are very much in the same ballpark. Straathof et al. (2008) also use a gravity model to look at bilateral FDI stocks. One of their specifications uses dyadic fixed effects but a somewhat different set of controls on earlier data (1981–2005). They find that if a country is a member of the EU, it enjoys a 28% increase in its inward FDI stocks from other EU countries and a 14% increase from non-EU countries.

We can also look at the bilateral trade flows literature for a comparison, but we need to bear in mind that we focus on bilateral FDI flows in our model. Baier and Bergstrand (2007) find that free trade areas (FTAs) increase trade by about 100% after 10 years. We find instead that EU membership increases FDI inflows by about 28% over the medium to long run in a country that is a member of the EU. The difference in the size of the coefficient may be caused by the fact that trade is easier to adjust than FDI flows.

5.4   UK Specific Effects

Thus far, our results represent an average effect for all EU economies applied to the case of the UK. We next analyse whether the EU premium is country specific, in particular how the UK stands in this regard in comparison with the three other major EU economies, namely Germany, France and Italy.

The exercise we now run is the following: suppose we create a new purely theoretical EU variable that excludes—in turn—the United Kingdom, Germany, Italy and France from the step dummy coding of the EU membership variable upon which our analysis so far has been based. These four countries are the largest and politically the most important ones in the

European Union. As an example, consider the following regressions: the EU membership target variable is constructed as the all EU members in the OECD database except UK, Germany, Italy and France, respectively, which will be codified as a separate target (d) country dummy:

$$\ln\left(\textit{Bilateral Inflow of FDI}_{o,d,t}\right) = \alpha_0 + \alpha_1 \ln X_{o,t} + \alpha_2 \ln X_{d,t} + \alpha_3 Z_{o,d,t}$$
$$+ \alpha_4 EU_{d,t}^{(\text{but}-\text{UK})} + \alpha_5 UK_{d,t} + \eta_{o,d}$$
$$+ T_t + u_{o,d,t}$$

$$(6)$$

$$\ln\left(\textit{Bilateral Inflow of FDI}_{o,d,t}\right) = \alpha_0 + \alpha_1 \ln X_{o,t} + \alpha_2 \ln X_{d,t} + \alpha_3 Z_{o,d,t}$$
$$+ \alpha_4 EU_{d,t}^{(\text{but}-\text{Germany})} + \alpha_5 Germany_{d,t}$$
$$+ \eta_{o,d} + T_t + u_{o,d,t}$$

$$(7)$$

$$\ln\left(\textit{Bilateral Inflow of FDI}_{o,d,t}\right) = \alpha_0 + \alpha_1 \ln X_{o,t} + \alpha_2 \ln X_{d,t} + \alpha_3 Z_{o,d,t}$$
$$+ \alpha_4 EU_{d,t}^{(\text{but}-\text{France})} + \alpha_5 France_{d,t}$$
$$+ \eta_{o,d} + T_t + u_{o,d,t}$$

$$(8)$$

$$\ln\left(\textit{Bilateral Inflow of FDI}_{o,d,t}\right) = \alpha_0 + \alpha_1 \ln X_{o,t} + \alpha_2 \ln X_{d,t} + \alpha_3 Z_{o,d,t}$$
$$+ \alpha_4 EU_{d,t}^{(\text{but}-\text{Italy})} + \alpha_5 Italy_{d,t} + \eta_{o,d}$$
$$+ T_t + u_{o,d,t}$$

$$(9)$$

Taking Eq. (6) as an illustration of the method, the interpretation of the two separate dummies (step for EU and country for UK)[8] is as follow: taking the excluded country—UK—as the reference country and assuming it has not joined the EU in the 1985–2013 time span, we measure its '*independent*' effect on FDI inflows vis-à-vis the *restricted* EU (but-UK). Any significant positive sign on the UK dummy will support the hypothesis that FDI had flowed to UK due to *its* national own specificities, i.e. a benefit in FDI inflows *regardless* of the EU membership, whereas a significant sign on the EU dummy would signal a genuine membership effect, i.e. a benefit in FDI inflows *independent* of the characteristics of the UK.

In order to corroborate our empirical strategy, we perform the same exercise for four major economies in the all-EU compact,[9] as mentioned these being the United Kingdom, Germany, Italy and France. We summarize the four separate hypotheses in Table 3.

The EU membership target variable excludes one country at the time and the specific country-target dummy is reported separately to disentangle the country/EU membership effect (see Table 4). In all four columns of Table 4, we use our preferred empirical gravity model from

Table 3 Comparing UK, Germany, France and Italy in separate empirical models

	Empirical model	Specification	Hypothesis tested
United Kingdom	Separate UK effect from the EU compact	EU-but-UK step dummy for target UK country Dummy for target	Genuine UK benefits in terms of FDI inflows due to country's characteristics VS. genuine EU membership effect (where UK is excluded)
Germany	Separate Germany effect from the EU compact	EU-but-Germany step dummy for target Germany country Dummy for target	Genuine Germany benefit in terms of FDI inflows due to country's characteristics VS. genuine EU membership effect (where Germany is excluded)
France	Separate France effect from the EU compact	EU-but-France step dummy for target France country Dummy for target	Genuine France benefit in terms of FDI inflows due to country's characteristics VS. genuine EU membership effect (where France is excluded)
Italy	Separate Italy effect from the EU compact	EU-but-Italy step dummy for target Italy country Dummy for target	Genuine Italy benefit in terms of FDI inflows due to country's characteristics VS. genuine EU membership effect (where Italy is excluded)

Table 4 Regressions of the effects of EU membership vis-à-vis the four major economies on FDI inflows (target): PPML

	UK versus. EU	Germany versus. EU	France versus. EU	Italy versus. EU
EU member (target, excl. UK)	0.35245**			
	(0.16365)			
UK_d (target)	0.16054			
	(0.27549)			
EU member (target, excl. Germany)		0.32590**		
		(0.15980)		
$Germany_d$ (target)		0.31293		
		(0.29246)		
EU member (target, excl. France)			0.33197**	
			(0.15695)	
$France_d$ (target)			0.21474	
			(0.25393)	
EU member (target, excl. Italy)				0.31978**
				(0.15815)
$Italy_d$ (target)				0.55976
				(0.34456)
EU member (sender)	0.79253***	0.83222***	0.82450***	0.83746***
	(0.18803)	(0.18330)	(0.18732)	(0.18420)
lnGDP (sender)	3.90119***	3.90185***	3.90123***	3.90514***
	(1.44654)	(1.44691)	(1.44765)	(1.44699)
lnGDP (target)	3.80584***	3.79836***	3.79991***	3.79866***
	(1.41892)	(1.41876)	(1.41804)	(1.41835)
lnGDPPC (sender)	−0.95913	−0.96771	−0.96296	−0.97089
	(1.52164)	(1.52344)	(1.52568)	(1.52303)
lnGDPPC (target)	−1.34307	−1.32519	−1.32951	−1.3243
	(1.42114)	(1.42103)	(1.41940)	(1.42098)
Observations	30,535	30,535	30,535	30,535
R-squared	0.4354	0.43451	0.43436	0.43508
Year FE	Yes	Yes	Yes	Yes
Bilateral FE	Yes	Yes	Yes	Yes
Clustered	Dyadic pair	Dyadic pair	Dyadic pair	Dyadic pair

Notes *** indicates significance at the 1% level, ** at the 5% level and * at the 10% level. Coefficients with standard errors (clustered by 630 bilateral country pair in first two columns) in brackets

Table 5 The effects of EU membership vis-à-vis the four major economies on FDI inflows, an interpretation

	Empirical question	Four possible outcomes in Eqs. 6–9	Summary of results from Table 3
United Kingdom	Is there a genuine benefits in terms of FDI inflows due to country's effect?	1. α_4 & α_5 insignificant => no membership nor country effect	EU effect (α_4 significant), no country effect (α_5 significant)
Germany	Alternatively are those benefits due to the European Union membership?	2. α_4 & α_5 significant => both membership and country effect	EU effect (α_4 significant), no country effect (α_5 significant)
France		3. Only α_4 significant => no independent country effect	EU effect (α_4 significant), no country effect (α_5 significant)
Italy		4. Only α_5 significant => independent country effect	EU effect (α_4 significant), no country effect (α_5 significant)

Table 1, the PPML estimation regression. The results are clear-cut: the EU membership target dummy (premium of EU) remains always highly significant and the individual country dummies (Germany, France, Italy and United Kingdom)[10] are never statistically significant. This means that the impact of individual country factors in terms of FDI inflows is not independent from that of EU membership for all four major economies. Hence all four countries would have performed much worse in terms of FDI inflows had they stayed outside the EU in the 1985–2013 time span.

In order to develop our understanding of the relationship between EU membership and FDI, let us look at the taxonomy presented in Table 5 for the four regressions testing the same hypothesis for each country separately. We can conclude that United Kingdom, Germany, France and Italy do not appear to experience a benefit in term of FDI inflows due to an independent country effect. On the contrary, they all have benefitted from EU membership. We posit that these results corroborate our synthetic counterfactual results: had UK been outside ESM, it would have lost in terms of FDI in the last three decades.

Finally, we report the impact of EU membership on FDI for sub-samples excluding one country at the time. In Fig. 6, the vertical bars for each country reports the effect of EU membership if one country at the time is excluded from the regression sample when estimating our baseline model from Eq. (5) in Sect. 4 'Data and Empirical Strategy'. What we can note is the remarkable stability of the regressions results for each subsample, meaning that there is no a single country that, if excluded from the EU, would massively affect the EU membership impact on FDI inflows. We posit that this finding would carry some weight in future studies of the impact of UK Brexit *on* the EU itself. We leave this point for further research.

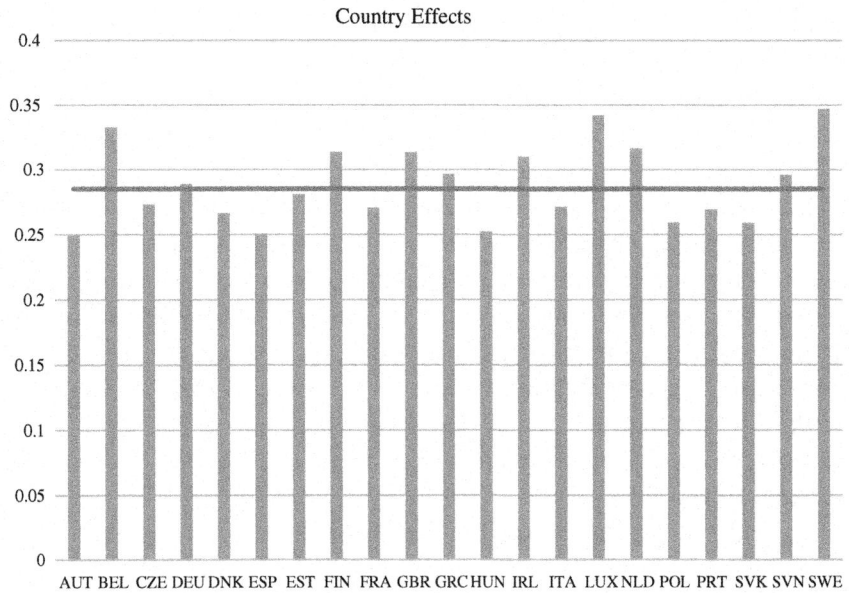

Fig. 6 The EU membership impact on FDI target for a sub-samples excluding one country at the time

6   Conclusions

The relationship between the United Kingdom and the European Union was never straightforward and has become increasingly complex as the mode of integration has deepened over time, in particular after the launch of the European Single Market in the mid-1980s. Foreign direct investment is one avenue that was not acutely important when the UK joined back in 1973, but has become absolutely central to comprehend the UK–EU relationship today. Despite wide agreement about the central relevance of FDI, at least since the mid-1990s, there remains a surprising dearth in terms of the empirical evidence about main drivers of FDI flows within the EU in general and especially for the UK case. This is remarkable given the fact that the UK is one of the top sources as well as destinations of FDI in the world. The objective of this chapter was to contribute to closing this gap in knowledge.

In this chapter, we investigated how much additional FDI inflows a country receives as a direct consequence of it being a member of a trading bloc, in our case, a member of the European Union. Specifically, the question we addressed was: is there substantive evidence that EU membership, in general, increased the inflows on FDI into the United Kingdom?

This chapter presents novel econometric evidence from two very different econometric methods, namely the synthetic control method and the gravity model, of the direct effect of EU membership on FDI inflows. The two methods also use very different types of data which of course help us to assess the robustness of our results. The synthetic control method employs annual macroeconomic data series and focuses on constructing a counterfactual scenario in which we estimate FDI inflows to the UK if it had not joined the Single Market in 1986. The gravity framework uses bilateral (dyadic) FDI data from 34 OECD countries between 1985–2013.

We find it to be very reassuring that our two main sets of results turn out to be quite similar (especially given the different methods, data type, data series, sample of countries and time window). All our results indicate that EU membership in general (and Single Market access specifically) increases FDI inflows by about 30%. This implies that a country leaving the EU would face a reduction in FDI inflows of around 22%. Our three main estimates range between 14 and 38% depending on the choice of econometric technique. The impact of EU membership on FDI to the UK are comparable to other major economies within the EU, like Germany, France and Italy, and for all of them, national characteristics seem less important than EU membership. In a nutshell, we find that the effect of EU membership has been robustly to increase FDI inflows.

There are various directions for future research one can discuss but we shall focus on three. One important issue to be further investigated in this context regards the potential lessons from further disaggregation of the data. Sectoral analysis is particularly important in this case in light of the rapidly increasing share of financial services in overall FDI inflows since the early 1990s. Further disaggregation in terms of different regions of the UK, especially in light of the Brexit vote, also seems to be a rather fruitful avenue to better understand the extent to which EU membership effects are heterogeneous within a given country.

A second direction we believe should be pursued more attentively is to examine more deeply the macroeconomic effects of FDI, especially whether there are important differences between its effects on gross output vis-à-vis total factor productivity. This type of analysis could also easily be combined with the previous suggestion in order to give us a firmer grip on the issue of potential endogeneity.

The third and final direction for further research involves trying to go deeper in terms of the political economy determinants of FDI and how they strategically complement or substitute for the more traditional drivers. The idea here would be to try to bring together as many as possible of the potential channels between deep integration and FDI and to examine more closely how these determinants, as a whole, affect the direction and dynamics of FDI inflows.

Notes

1. For example, see Alfaro et al. (2004) on international macro data or Haskel et al. (2007) on UK micro-data.
2. For an overview of the FDI literature, see Faeth (2009) for a survey organized in terms of the main theoretical models, Yeaple (2013) for a

survey with emphasis on industrial organization literature, Harrison and Rodriguez-Clare (2010) for a survey that tried to give equal weight to both developing and developed countries as well as to trade and FDI linkages among these countries, and Aggarwal (1980) and Saggi (2002) for surveys of the earlier (pre-globalization) literature.

3. The 2015 figure reports a much less stark increase vis-à-vis 1985 due to the post financial crises drop in FDI in Western countries.

4. The maximum theoretical number of observations is 34 * 33 * 29 = 32,538. For many countries, especially before the 1980s, bilateral FDI flows are in fact zero. The missing values for FDI in the data reflect these zeros (and a few near zero). Missing observations are assigned zeros (which explains the different number of observations in Tables 2 and 3). We used the Heckman selection model below to address whether we should treat these zeros in FDI in a special way.

5. For some countries in the 1985–2013 sample the dummy will be always 0 (e.g. USA), for other always 1 (e.g. Italy) and for others a step dummies (e.g. Estonia). No country yet has a switch from 1 to 0; Brexit represents the first occurrence of this type. Future research will always exploit this type of variation. What qualifies the switch of the step dummy from 0 to 1 is membership of the EU not the OECD.

6. PWC (2016) find that Brexit will induce a fall of UK FDI by 25% by 2020, a very similar magnitude to our own.

7. Available upon request.

8. And likewise for Germany, France and Italy in Eqs. (7), (8) and (9), respectively.

9. We could check the results of the regression for each and every EU member ideally, but we would indeed not expect that minor countries (e.g. Estonia) would be responsible for the overall EU membership effect.

10. We cannot exclude that, for other smaller EU economies, the impact might be different.

Acknowledgments We would like to thank, without implicating, Fabrizio Coricelli, Nicholas Crafts, Swati Dhingra, Peter Egger, Jan Fidrmuc, Michele Ruta, John Springford, John Van Reenen and seminar participants at Brunel University London, DIW, ECB, LSE, NIESR and World Bank for valuable comments on previous versions.

References

Abadie, A., & Gardeazabal, J. (2003). The economic costs of conflict: A case study of the Basque Country. *American Economic Review, 93*(1), 113–132.

Aggarwal, J. (1980). Determinants of foreign direct investment: A survey. *Weltwirtschaftliches Archiv, 116*(4), 739–773.

Alfaro, L., Chanda, A., Kalemli-Ozcan, S., & Sayek, S. (2004). FDI and economic growth: The role of local financial markets. *Journal of International Economics, 64*(1), 89–112.

Amador, J., & di Mauro, F. (Eds.). (2015). *The age of global value chains: Maps and policy issues.* London: CEPR.

Anderson, J. (2011). The gravity model. *Annual Review of Economics, 3*(3), 133–160.

Anderson, J., & van Wincoop, E. (2003). Gravity and gravitas: A solution to the Border puzzle. *American Economic Review, 93*(1), 170–192.

Anderson, James E., & van Wincoop, Eric. (2004). Trade costs. *Journal of Economic Literature, 42*, 691–751.

Athey, S., & Imbens, G. (2016, July). *The state of applied econometrics: Causality and policy evaluation.* Stanford University, Mimeo.

Baier, S. L., & Bergstrand, J. H. (2007). Do free trade agreements actually increase members' International trade? *Journal of International Economics, 71*, 72–95.

Baier, S. L., Bergstrand, J. H., Egger, P., & McLughlin, P. A. (2008). Do economic integration agreements actually work? Issues in understanding the causes and consequences of the growth of regionalism. *The World Economy*, 461–497.

Baldwin, R. (2006). Multilateralising regionalism: Spaghetti bowls as building blocs on the path to global free trade. *The World Economy, 29*(11), 1451–1518.

Baldwin, R. (2016). The World Trade Organisation and the future of multilateralism. *Journal of Economic Perspectives, 30*(1), 95–116.

Baldwin, R., & Taglioni, D. (2007). *Gravity for dummies and dummies for gravity equations* (NBER Working Paper No. 12516).

Basile, R., Castellani, D., & Zanfei, A. (2008). Location choices of multinational firms in Europe: The role of EU cohesion policy. *Journal of International Economics, 74*(2), 328–340.

Bloom, N., Sadun, R., & Van Reenen, J. (2012). Americans do IT better: US multinationals and the productivity miracle. *American Economic Review, 102*(1), 167–201.

Bruno, R. L., Campos, N., & Estrin, S. (2017). The Benefits from Foreign Direct Investment in a Cross-Country Context: A Meta-Analysis, London CEPR DP 11959.

Campos, N., & Coricelli, F. (2015). *Some unpleasant Brexit econometrics*. VoxEU. org (http://www.voxeu.org/article/some-unpleasant-brexit-econometrics).

Christodoulakis, N., & Sarantides, V. (2016). External asymmetries in the euro area and the role of foreign direct investment. *The World Economy*, 1–31.

Conconi, P., Sapir, A., & Zanardi, M. (2015). The internationalization process of firms: From exports to FDI. *Journal of International Economics, 99*, 16–30.

De Sousa, J., & Lochard, J. (2011). Does the single currency affect foreign direct investment? *Scandinavian Journal of Economics, 113*(3), 553–578.

Dhingra, S., Ottaviano, G., Sampson, T., & Van Reenen, J. (2016). *The consequences of Brexit for UK trade and living standards*. CEP Brexit Analysis No. 2 (http://cep.lse.ac.uk/pubs/download/brexit02.pdf).

Driffield, N., Love, J., Lancheros, S., & Temouri, Y. (2013). *How attractive is the UK for future manufacturing foreign direct investment?* London: HM Government Office for Science.

Egger, P., & Pfaffermayr, M. (2004). Foreign Direct Investment and European Integration in the 1990s. *The World Economy*, 99–110.

Fally, T. (2015). Structural gravity and fixed effects. *Journal of International Economics, 97*, 76–85.

Faeth, I. (2009). Determinants of foreign direct investment–a tale of nine theoretical models. *Journal of Economic Surveys, 23*(1), 165–196.

Glick, R., & Rose, A. K. (2002). Does a currency union affect trade? The time-series evidence. *European Economic Review, 46*(6), 1125–1151.

Glick, R. & Rose, A. K. (2016). *Currency unions and trade: A post-EMU mea culpa*. Mimeo (previous version NBER working paper no. 21535, 2015).

Harrison, A., & Rodríguez-Clare, A. (2010). Trade, foreign investment, and industrial policy. In D. Rodrik & M. Rosenzweig (Eds.), *Handbook of Development Economics* (Vol. 5).

Haskel, J., Pereira, S., & Slaughter, M. (2007). Does inward foreign direct investment boost the productivity of domestic firms? *Review of Economics and Statistics, 89*(3), 482–496.

Havránek, T., & Iršová, Z., (2011). Estimating vertical spillovers from FDI: Why results vary and what the true effect is. *Journal of International Economics, 85*(2), 234–244.

Head, K., & Mayer, T. (2014). Gravity equations: Workhorse, toolkit, and cookbook. In G. Gopinath, E. Helpman & K. Rogoff (Eds.), *Handbook of International Economics* (Vol. 4, pp. 131–195). Elsevier.

Helpman, E., Melitz, M., & Yeaple, S. (2004). Exports versus FDI with heterogeneous firms. *American Economic Review, 94*(1), 300–316.

Imbens, G. W., & Wooldridge, J. M. (2009). Recent development in the econometrics of programme evaluation. *Journal of Economic Literature, 4*(1), 5–86.

Iršová, Z., & Havránek, T. (2013). Determinants of horizontal spillovers from FDI: Evidence from a large meta-analysis. *World Development, 42*, 1–15.

Javorcic, B. S. (2004). Does foreign direct investment increase the productivity of domestic firms? In search of spillovers through backward linkages. *American Economic Review, 94*(3), 605–627.

Mastromarco, C., & Léopold Simar, L. (2015). Effect of FDI and time on catching up: New insights from a conditional nonparametric frontier analysis. *Journal of Applied Econometrics, 30*(5), 826–847.

Motta, M. (1992). Multinational firms and the tariff-jumping argument: A game theoretic analysis with some unconventional conclusions. *European Economic Review, 36*(8), 1557–1571.

OECD. (2016a). *FDI flows (indicator)*. doi:10.1787/99f6e393-en.

OECD. (2016b). *International direct investment statistics Yearbook 2015*. Paris: OECD Publishing.

PWC. (2016). Leaving the EU: Implications for the UK economy. http://www.pwc.co.uk/economic-services/assets/leaving-the-eu-implications-for-the-uk-economy.pdf.

Saggi, K. (2002). Trade, foreign direct investment, and international technology transfer: A survey. *World Bank Research Observer, 17*(2), 191–235.

Sanso-Navarro, M. (2011). The effects on American foreign direct investment in the United Kingdom from not adopting the euro. *Journal of Common Market Studies, 49*(2), 463–483.

Santos Silva, J. M. C., & Tenreyro, S. (2006). The log of gravity. *Review of Economics and Statistics, 88*(4), 641–658.

Straathof, S., Linders, G. J., Lejour, A., and Mohlmann, J. (2008). *The internal market and the Dutch economy: Implications for trade and economic growth*. (CPG Netherlands Document No. 168).

UNCTAD. (2016). *World Investment Report 2016*. Geneva: UNCTAD.

Yeaple, S. (2013). The multinational firm. *Annual Review of Economics, 5*(1), 193–217.

Immigration and the UK–EU Relationship

Professor Jonathan Portes

Abstract This chapter examines the history of free movement within the EU, and in particular the origins and impact of the decision to allow immediate access to the labour market for workers from the new Member States in 2004. It discusses the economic and labour market impacts of migration from elsewhere in the EU to the UK. It then considers the impact of the referendum, and possible options for changes to UK immigration policy after Brexit.

1 Introduction

The question of "what Brexit means" and in particular what those who voted to leave in the June 2016 referendum thought they were voting for remains highly contentious. However, free movement—and the resulting

Professor J. Portes (✉)
Department of Political Economy, King's College London,
London, UK
e-mail: jonathan.portes@kcl.ac.uk

© The Author(s) 2017
N.F. Campos and F. Coricelli (eds.), *The Economics of UK–EU Relations*,
DOI 10.1007/978-3-319-55495-2_7

substantial flows of EU nationals to the UK—was undoubtedly a central theme. The slogan "Vote Leave, Take Control" summed up the entire Leave campaign, whether referring to the fictional £350 million per week that the UK "sends to Brussels", or to our supposed ability to speedily conclude advantageous free trade deals with third countries once freed from the dead hand of EU control of UK trade policy.

However, it was particularly effective and resonant with respect to immigration policy and border control, because, of course, it contained a very large element of truth; free movement of workers is one of the foundational "four freedoms" of the EU, and as long as it remains a member, the UK is obliged to respect this central obligation. So the Remain campaign found it extremely difficult to counter the simple argument that the only way for the UK to control immigration was to leave.

In the run-up to the referendum, negative attitudes to immigration, and in particular free movement within the EU, were by far the strongest predictor of opposition to UK membership. Ashcroft (2016) found that approximately 80% of those who thought that immigration as mostly a force for good voted to Remain, while a similar proportion of those who thought of it as a force for ill voted to Leave. This strong correlation remains when controlling for socio-demographic factors (Vasilopoulou 2016).

Was immigration, either from within the EU or more generally, the key driving factor in the vote to leave? There is already a significant literature on this topic. A number of analyses (e.g. Resolution Foundation 2016; Goodwin and Heath 2016; Carozzi 2016) find that areas with higher levels of immigration were, if anything, somewhat more likely to vote to Remain, but areas which had experienced large recent migrant flows were more likely to vote Leave.

However, alternative explanations also exist—for example, Conlantone and Stanig (2016) show that the Leave vote was correlated with exposure to competition to trade with China, while at an individual level (Kaufmann 2016) shows that social attitudes were more important than economic self-interest (as measured by socioeconomic status).

Clearly monocausal explanations are insufficient, and simple univariate or multivariate regression analysis is insufficient to establish causality (Goodwin and Heath 2016)—but to both any casual observer of the national-level campaign, and to anyone looking at the local level and micro-level data, it is clear that—outside London at least—perceptions of the impact of migration were indeed a key factor in driving the Leave vote.

Immigration has long been a salient and disputed issue in British politics. This was the case 40 years ago; the government's decision to admit a substantial number of refugees of Indian ethnicity from former British colonies in East Africa was hotly disputed, and then as now a large majority favoured much tighter restrictions on immigration to the UK. But it scarcely figured as an issue in the 1975 referendum on whether the United Kingdom should remain a member of the European Union (then the European Economic Community).[1] Indeed, if anything, there was actually a small negative correlation between attitudes to immigration and to the EU (that is, those who thought immigration was too high were slightly more likely to vote to stay in (Evans and Mellon 2015).

So, what changed, and how did the UK get to this position? This chapter looks both forward and backward. It examines the history of free movement within the EU, and in particular the origins and impact of the decision to allow immediate access to the UK labour market for workers from the new Member States in 2004. It discusses the economic and labour market impacts of migration from elsewhere in the EU to the UK. It then considers the impact of the referendum, and possible options for changes to UK immigration policy after Brexit.

2   Free Movement of Workers

Long before the UK joined, the EU was founded on four basic principles: free movement of labour, capital, goods and services. These "four freedoms" were set out in the original Treaty of Rome, which spoke of the "abolition, as between Member States, of obstacles to the free movement of persons" (European Commission 1957). While the primary driver, as with other aspects of the original Treaty, may have been a desire to promote European integration for its own sake, the founders of the EU also believed that there were large economic benefits. In fact, economic theory is ambiguous on whether factor mobility (in this context, the free movement of labour and capital) is a complement or a substitute to free trade (the free movement of goods and services). In a standard

Heckscher–Ohlin model, they are pure substitutes. Either free trade or factor mobility will increase the efficiency of resource allocation and will maximise overall welfare; it is not necessary to have both.

Similarly, capital mobility may in some circumstances be a substitute for labour mobility. But in more recent, and arguably more realistic, trade models the picture is much less clear (see Venables 1999, for a review). The general consensus among economists is that labour mobility, like trade, is welfare-enhancing, and that the benefits are additional to any that result from trade or from capital mobility, although there may be significant distributional effects. Ozden (2015), provides a useful summary of the consensus view.

However, while the economic case may be strong in principle, other free trade areas (for example, the North American Free Trade Area) or even customs unions like Mercosur do not typically involve free movement of people.[2] So, from a purely economic perspective, free movement was not a necessary part of the European project; it would have been possible to have a customs union, and an integrated economic space, without it; the decision to make it one of the founding principles was a political as well as an economic choice. Labour mobility was complementary not just to the economic aspects of European integration but to its wider political objectives. The commitment to free movement of workers set out in the Treaty was bolstered by a further Directive in 1968.

The period from the late 1950s to the early 1970s saw strong economic growth in most of the EU. Demand for labour was strong and unemployment low. However, intra-EU labour mobility remained quite low, compared to, for example, the US, although there were significant flows from Italy to other EU countries, especially France. Labour demand was therefore largely met by immigration from outside the EU, especially Turkish "guest workers" in Germany, North African migrants to France and—although the UK was not yet an EU Member State—Commonwealth migrants to Britain (Kokkailainen 2011).

So when the UK joined the EU in 1973, and subsequently voted to remain a member in 1975, free movement was very much part of the existing EU acquis—subsequent complaints that the British people thought that they were joining a "Common Market" rather than an area of which people could circulate freely missed the point was that the latter was precisely what a "Common (labour) Market" meant. However, at the time, the potential impact on either UK immigration policy, or the level and nature of immigration to the UK, appeared to be relatively small. The UK did not necessarily appear particularly attractive to migrants from existing EU member states, while non-EU migration, as noted above, was an extremely contentious issue. For both politicians and voters, the two were separate.

The economic crisis of the 1970s led to a sharp reduction in labour demand, and most EU countries, including the UK, attempted to reduce labour migration from outside the EU. Intra-EU mobility remained quite low throughout the 1980s and 1990s, despite some concerns in the UK. Indeed, one of my first assignments, as a junior Treasury official working on social security issues in the late 1980s, was to help devise legislative ways to preclude "benefit tourism" from the new Member States (Spain and Portugal). The concerns were misplaced: the 1986 accession did not lead to any significant increase in flows from Spain and Portugal. Although they had traditionally been countries of emigration, EU accession (and large inflows of EU funding) led swiftly to rapid economic growth and ample domestic demand for labour.

The 1980s and early 1990s did see a renewed push for greater market integration, launched, with the strong support of the UK, under the umbrella of the "Single Market". However, the Commission's 1985 White Paper, which identified obstacles to the Single Market and set out proposals to address them, devoted only one relatively anodyne page to free movement: the focus was very much on product markets (European Commission 1985). As far as the UK was concerned, intra-EU labour mobility and the Single Market remained separate issues, economically and politically

So by 2000, although increasingly economically integrated in terms of trade, and despite the political commitment to free movement, only slightly over 1% of EU citizens lived in a country other than their country of birth, and the previous decade had seen only a very modest upward trend (European Commission 2014). Approximately 2% of the UK population was born elsewhere in the EU (a large proportion from the Republic of Ireland), a proportion which had remained relatively stable.

The potential downsides of this lack of mobility, despite the formal right to free movement, became more salient as the EU moved towards monetary union. The standard theory of optimal currency areas suggested that the costs of giving up the exchange rate as an adjustment mechanism (as a consequence of entering into an economic union) would be reduced if other adjustment mechanisms, in particular labour mobility, were able to operate (Mundell 1961). There was therefore considerable concern that the lack of labour mobility posed a threat to the efficient operation of the incipient monetary union; this debate is summarised in European Commission, 2014.

Partly in response to these concerns, the EU undertook a number of initiatives designed to turn "free movement of workers" from a formal right to one that appeared a realistic prospect to EU citizens. In particular, the Free Movement of Citizens Directive (European Commission 2004) simplified, consolidated and considerably extended the right to free movement for EU citizens, not just to take a job but to look for one, and to be accompanied by family members (including non-EU citizens) as long as those exercising free movement were not an "undue burden". This also extended to non-discrimination against EU citizens, except in limited and temporary circumstances, in the operation of the benefit system.

If these extensions to the free movement of workers—effectively turning it, for most practical purposes, into free movement of citizens—was not needed for a *customs* union, but was in large part a response to the need to enhance labour mobility as an adjustment mechanism within a *monetary* union, why did they not only apply to euro Member States, that is excluding the UK? Commission papers of the time are silent on this point. However— ironically in retrospect—it was consistently UK policy throughout this period to insist that the Single Market, including measures related to labour markets and labour mobility, were EU rather than eurozone issues, and to resist any suggestion that the UK was, because of its opt-out from the euro, in any sense a second-tier or outer circle member of the EU.

3   The 2004 and 2007 Accessions

The accession, in May 2004, of 10 new Member States, including a number of members of the former Soviet bloc (often referred to as the "Accession 8", or A8 or EU-8", states—Poland, Hungary, the Czech

Republic, Slovakia, Slovenia, Estonia, Latvia and Lithuania), radically changed the dynamic of intra-EU labour mobility. As set out above, free movement had (from an economic perspective) originally been motivated by, first, theoretical arguments about optimal resource allocation; and, second, by its potential to serve as an adjustment mechanism in the face of asymmetric macroeconomic shocks, particularly in a monetary union. It had not been seen as operating in an area where there were very large, persistent, structural differences in wage levels, as was now the case.

Given these disparities, there was clearly a possibility of much larger intra-EU flows than had previously been the case. A number of Member States therefore took the opportunity permitted by the accession treaties to impose "transitional" restrictions on free movement of workers. The UK (together with Ireland and Sweden), however, did not.

A myth has since emerged that the main reason the UK government granted immediate access was because of a supposed "Home Office forecast" that only 13,000 migrants would arrive. In fact, the forecast in question (Dustmann 2003) was independent external research, commissioned but not produced by government, and was to a certain extent already irrelevant by the time the decision was taken (since the forecast was conditional on all EU countries granting immediate labour market access, which was not the case). Within government, there were three far more important arguments for the decision.

First, the broader geopolitical one. The UK—and Prime Minister Blair in particular—had long been the most vigorous proponent of membership for the countries of the former Eastern bloc; they were seen (correctly) as likely allies for the UK's generally liberal positions in EU debates. So the decision was seen as a way of cementing our relationship with them, and in particular the Polish government. By contrast, the imposition of transitional controls would have been perceived as something of a slap in the face: "we welcome your politicians in the Council of Ministers, but we do not actually want your people to come to our country".

Second, economic and labour market impacts. The UK labour market was buoyant, with unemployment at its lowest level in three decades; and all the analysis suggested that immigrant workers—particularly the reasonably well educated and motivated ones likely to arrive from the new Member States—were likely to boost the UK's economy without doing much if any damage to the prospects of native workers. In the then prevailing macroeconomic framework, the Bank of England regarded (nominal) wage growth as a key indicator in determining the course of monetary policy; to the extent that increased labour supply restrained nominal wage growth, this would allow the Bank to refrain from increasing interest rates (note that in this framework, migration reduces nominal wage growth in the short term, but does not impact real wages; the perception, encouraged by some politicians, that the Bank and Treasury saw migration as a way of reducing *real* wages is simply false; it is based on a confusion between nominal and real).

And third, the practicalities, given the UK's relatively light touch approach to labour market regulation. There was no legal provision which would have allowed the UK to deny the right of visa-free entry to the citizens of the new EU member states: the only available option was to prevent them from working legally as employees. However, unlike many other EU countries, the UK has very limited capacity indeed to enforce employment regulations in general, and restrictions on illegal working in particular. As with the National Minimum Wage, the government largely relies on employers to self-enforce. The assumption within government was therefore that the impact of imposing transitional restrictions would be a very large increase in illegal working. This hardly seemed like an attractive alternative.

In 2007, Bulgaria and Romania joined the EU; this too led to a significant increase in flows, although this time Spain and Italy were major destination countries. The UK and most other countries imposed transitional restrictions, which were finally lifted in all EU countries by 2014, so there is now complete free movement for the EU27 (some Member States still impose restrictions on Croatian nationals).

4   Impacts

The impact of accession on intra-EU migration flows was large and sustained, with substantial increases in migration to all the major economies of the existing EU, even the ones that did impose restrictions, like Germany, but in particular the UK and Ireland. Goodhart (2013) described the influx of A8 nationals to the UK as the "biggest peacetime movement [of people] in European history". Relative to expectations, flows to the UK were particularly large. New estimates from Forte and Portes (2017, forthcoming) find that free movement leads over-time to an increase of nearly 500%—a factor of six—in migration flows to the UK.

The main drivers were economic: Kahanec (2013) found that migration responded both to structural economic differences between Member States, and to short-term economic shocks; and that accession had led to significant increases in mobility, albeit hampered in part by the imposition of transitional restrictions. At an individual level, the vast majority of migrants moved to work, attracted by either higher wages or greater job opportunities. Location decisions were also influenced by cultural factors and network effects (Galogski et al. 2009).

The financial crisis and ensuing recession did temporarily reduce flows to the UK in the 2008–2012 period. However, since 2013, recovery in the UK labour market, continuing economic difficulties in some euro-zone countries, and (in 2014) the ending of transitional restrictions on Bulgarian and Romanian nationals resulted in a further sharp rise in the migration of EU citizens to the UK (Charts 1, 2).

Over the last decade, then, the UK resident population originally from other EU member states has more than doubled, to more than 3 million, and continues to rise rapidly.

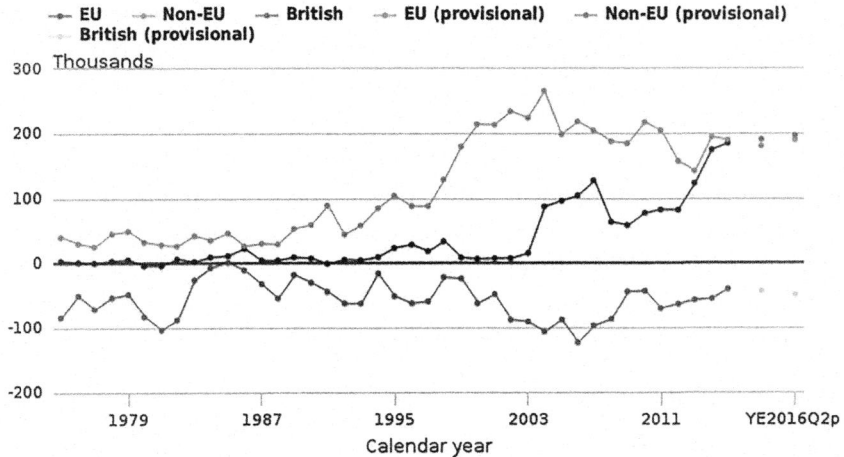

Chart 1 Net migration to the UK by citizenship. *Source* UK Office of National Statistics

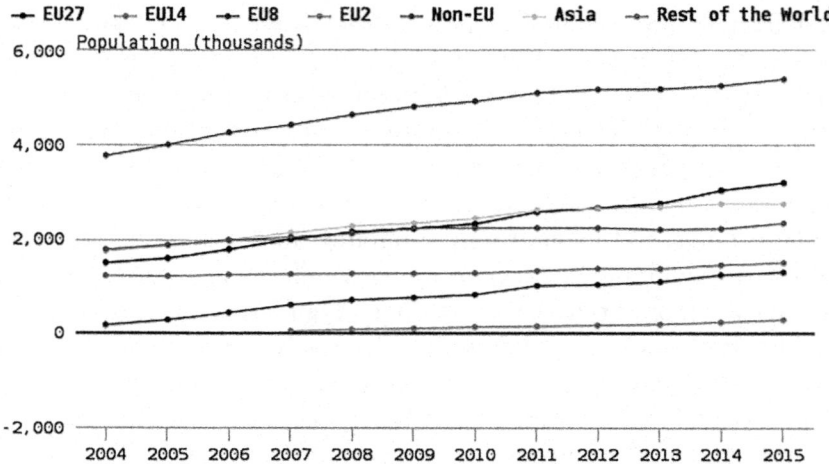

Chart 2   Resident UK population by country of birth. *Source* UK Office of National Statistics

EU nationals currently make up 6–7% of the UK labour force. Even this may understate the possible impacts on the UK labour market: over the last 4 years, more than 2 million EU nationals have registered for UK National Insurance numbers, required for (legal) access to employment. Much of the disparity between this and the official immigration statistics reflects very short-term and seasonal migration, which is not recorded in either the immigration statistics or the Labour Force Survey, which provides almost all the official data on aggregate labour market developments. There is also likely to be some actual under-recording.

As noted above, the primary motivation for migration was work, and most new migrants are in employment, with employment rates for intra-EU migrants well above rates for natives. One notable feature of migrants from the new Member States was that, although they were not necessarily low skilled, they primarily moved into low-skilled employment in destination countries, and were concentrated in certain sectors (for example, construction, retail, hospitality, domestic work, food processing and agriculture) (MAC 2014).

Standard theory predicts that a substantial movement of "low-skilled" workers from relatively low-wage/low-productivity economies to higher wage/productivity economies will (assuming that the workers are employed in relatively low-skilled jobs) result in:

- increased output, although impacts on per capita output will be considerably smaller, and possibly ambiguous
- an increase, possibly temporary, in the skill premium (the wage of a skilled worker relative to an unskilled one) and hence in wage inequality
- depending on labour market institutions, a possible impact on unemployment

Public and policy concern has focused on the distributional impacts—in particular, potential negative impacts on employment and wages for low-skilled workers. Although the broad consensus in the economic literature is that negative impacts of migration for native workers are, if they exist at all, relatively small and short-lived (see, for example, Constant 2014) much of this literature is US based; there was almost no empirical literature on the economic impact of immigration to the UK before 2004. Unsurprisingly, given the size of the migratory flows, this deficiency has now been remedied. There is a now a considerable literature on the impact on the UK economy and labour market.

To the considerable surprise of many economists, including this author, there is now a clear consensus that even in the short-term EU migration does not appear to have had a negative impact on the employment outcomes of UK natives. A comprehensive literature review by the UK government (BIS 2014) found that "To date there has been little evidence in the literature of a statistically significant impact from EU migration on native employment outcomes". Since 2014, the continued buoyant performance of the UK labour market has further reinforced this consensus. Rapid falls in unemployment, now down to about 5%, have been combined with sustained high levels of immigration.

While the evidence on wage impacts is less conclusive, the emerging consensus is that recent migration has had little or no impact overall, but possibly some, small, negative impact on low-skilled workers. Nickell and Salaheen (2015) find that a 10 percentage point rise in the immigrant share leads to approximately a 1.5% reduction in wages for native workers in the semi/unskilled service sector; this would mean that immigration since 2004 would have reduced wages for native workers in that sector by about 1%, or put another way would have depressed annual pay increases by about a penny an hour. Impacts in other sectors are even smaller.

Beyond the aggregate impacts on employment and wages, there may also be other impacts on labour market institutions and structures, positive and negative, particularly if migration results in labour market segmentation (MAC 2014). There is indeed some evidence of dual or segmented labour markets in some low-paid sectors, for example, food and drink manufacturing, where migrants are disproportionately represented in the seasonal, temporary or flexible workforce. Of course, the existence of dual or segmented labour markets in low-paid sectors pre-dates the arrival of EU migrants: the food and drink sector, for example, relied historically on women and itinerant workers in peak periods before it had access to migrants (Rolfe and Hudson-Sharp 2016). However, the prevalence and persistence of these models of employment does appear to have increased, facilitated by access to migrant workers.

Employers argue that the availability of migrants has allowed their businesses to be competitive and to expand in a way which would not have been possible given relatively low levels of unemployment in the last decade (Rolfe and Hudson-Sharp 2016). The needs of employers in low-skilled sectors and of new migrants from the EU have been well-matched: migrants take low-skilled jobs in these sectors because they offer an easy entry to the UK labour market, allowing them to work long hours through over-time without long-term commitment (Anderson et al. 2006; Green et al. 2013; Pauritus 2014). The offer of temporary work with flexible or "zero hours" contracts is, in contrast, unattractive to many UK workers and problematic for those coming off unemployment benefits. An additional feature of Eastern European migration in particular has been a willingness to live and work throughout the UK, while previous migrants have been drawn largely to the South East and to urban conurbations (Rolfe and Hudson-Sharp 2016).

While EU migrants, particularly from the newer Member States, are concentrated in some low-skilled sectors and low-paid occupations, this is of course by no means true of all EU migrants. Particularly in London, EU migrants make up a large proportion of employees in finance and business services, occupations which are generally highly skilled and highly paid. Moreover, in some medium-skilled occupations where, until

2010, non-EU migrants made up a substantial share of employment—for example, nursing—tighter restrictions on non-EU migration have led to a significant shift by employers towards EU migrants for new recruits (Spanish and Romanian nurses rather than Filipino ones). The importance of EU migration to the functioning of the UK labour market therefore goes well beyond certain low-skilled sectors.

The impact on productivity and hence (per capita) growth is methodologically much harder to estimate. It has been argued that EU migration is likely to have depressed productivity growth, either through a simple "batting average" effect (since new EU migrants are on average paid less than the average of the current workforce) or, more tenuously, because the availability of relatively low-paid but flexible workers reduces the incentive to invest in labour-saving and/or productivity-enhancing equipment. It is, however, difficult to see this in the data—the UK's abysmal productivity performance coincides with the financial crisis and its aftermath (which of course in turn led to a fall in migration) rather than the earlier sharp rise in migration.

A recent literature uses cross-country evidence to estimate the impact of migration on growth and productivity in advanced economies. This includes Boubtane et al. (2015) and Jaumotte et al. (2016). Boubtane et al. find that migration in general boosts productivity in advanced economies, but by varying amounts; for the UK, the estimated impact is that a 1 percentage point in the migrant share of the working age population leads to a 0.4–0.5% increase in productivity. This is higher than in most other advanced economies and reflects the relatively high skill levels of migrants to the UK. Their data set, however, only runs up to 2006.

Jaumotte et al. find that a 1% increase in the migrant share of the adult population results in an increase in GDP per capita and productivity of approximately 2%. This result is consistent across a variety of empirical specifications. Perhaps surprisingly, the estimated aggregate impacts of high and low skilled migration are not significantly different (although the distributional implications are). One possible, partial explanation is that low skilled migration appears to increase labour force participation among native women (a result also found in individual country studies, cf. Barone and Mocetti 2011). This is one example of the type of complementarity or spillover effect by which migrants working in low-skilled occupations might indirectly increase productivity and output and is likely to be relevant to the UK.

The implication is therefore that migration to the UK is likely to have boosted productivity (see Forte and Portes for a more detailed discussion).

The overall consensus, then, is that the impact on the UK economy and labour market has been relatively benign. As one recent evidence review (Wadsworth 2015) summarised:

> On balance, the evidence for the UK labour market suggests that fears about adverse consequences of rising immigration in general and EU immigration in particular have still not, on average, materialised. It is hard to find evidence of much displacement of UK workers or lower wages, on average. Immigrants, especially in recent years, tend to be younger and better educated than the UK-born and less likely to be unemployed. But there have been some effects. The less skilled may have experienced greater downward pressure on wages and greater competition for jobs than others, but these effects still appear to have been small.

Given the labour market impacts, fiscal impacts too might be expected to be positive. Dustmann and Frattini (2014) found that migrants from the EU to the UK made a significant positive contribution to the public finances, even during periods when the UK as a whole was running a fiscal deficit. Of course, it is hardly surprising that young migrants in employment make an initial positive fiscal contribution; proper assessment of fiscal impacts requires a life cyle perspective (Preston 2014). In this context, there are various reasons to expect the impact to still be positive (in particular, migrants tend to arrive after they have left compulsory, publicly financed education). This issue is discussed below in the section on the future impacts of immigration policy changes.

However, positive net impact on public finances at the national level does not preclude significant impact on demand (and hence cost) at the local level, particularly if funding allocations do not adjust quickly (or at all) to reflect pressures resulting from migration (George et al. 2011). A notable recent example is the shortage of primary school places in some parts of the UK (especially London); this appears to be largely the result of poor planning on the part of central government, given the rise in the number of young children resulting from recent increases in migration (from both the EU and elsewhere).

But broader concerns about the potential negative impacts on public services appear to be largely unsubstantiated: higher immigration are not associated, at a local level, with longer NHS waiting times (Giuntella et al. 2015), and in schools, increased numbers of pupils with English as a second language does not have any negative impact on levels of achievement for native English speaking students (Geay et al. 2013). If anything, pupils in schools with lots of non-native speakers do slightly better. This does not mean, of course, that citizens do not associate their experience of deterioration in public service quality and availability resulting from other factors (in particular, cuts in funding during the UK's ongoing fiscal consolidation) with the increased demand resulting from higher levels of immigration. The fact that migrants' fiscal contribution could, in principle, at least provide enough funding to cover their marginal impact on demand is not much comfort in practice if those revenues are in fact being allocated elsewhere, for tax cuts or deficit reduction, as in fact has been the case.

5 Benefit Tourism and the UK's Renegotiation

As far back as 1993, Conservative opponents of the European Union focused on the issue of "benefit tourism". In his speech to the Conservative Party Conference, the then Secretary of State for Social Security, Peter Lilley, claimed (referring, apparently, to Italian, French and German nationals):

> Community rules have opened up a new abuse: 'Benefit Tourism'. People travelling around pretending to look for work, but really looking for the best benefits. Not so much a Cook's tour as a Crooks tour. Gordon Brown claims our system is less generous than elsewhere in Europe. Then why do they come and scrounge off us? They certainly don't come here for the climate.

"Benefit tourism" resurfaced as a major political issue in the UK under the Cameron government. However, this was driven by political necessity rather than economic reality. The then Prime Minister, recognising that EU migration was generally unpopular, came to the conclusion that his "renegotiation" would not be credible with the public unless it addressed the issue. However, his original proposal—an "emergency brake" on the number of EU nationals allowed to migrate to the UK—commanded little support in other EU countries, and when Chancellor Merkel informed him it was unacceptable he withdrew it. Restrictions on the access of EU nationals to UK benefits was a—hopefully achievable—fallback position.

Given this background, it was hardly surprising that the UK government was unable to substantiate its position that "benefit tourism" is a significant policy concern. There is no evidence that access to the UK benefit system is a major driver of migration flows. Overall, migrants are underrepresented among benefit claimants, and especially claimants of unemployment and other out-of-work benefits. And while it is EU migrants do claim significant amounts of "in-work" benefits, which are available to low-paid workers, especially those with children, most do so only after they have already been resident for several years, suggesting it has little to do with their original migration decision (Portes 2015). Recent analysis of administrative data by the UK government (HMRC 2016) showed that approximately 750,000 EU migrants who arrived in the four years prior to 2014 paid National Insurance contributions during 2013–2014, suggesting they were in work during this year, while only about 150,000 claimed in-work benefits. This implies that even for low-skilled or low-paid migrants, in-work benefits are not a major factor driving flows to the attraction of the UK. The wider economic literature also supports the view that differences in benefit entitlements are not a significant driver of migration (Giuletti 2014).

Nevertheless, migrant access to benefit entitlements was a key issue in the UK's renegotiation. This would have allowed the UK to phase in entitlements to in-work benefits for new arrivals from the EU over a period of four years, and reduce, but not eliminate, child benefit payments paid to those with children living abroad. It is generally accepted (even within the UK government) that the impact of these provisions on benefit payments will be small, and on migration flows negligible.

This was probably the maximum degree of change to the existing rules that the Prime Minister could have hoped to secure, given the need for the approval of all 27 other Member States—including, of course, the countries whose citizens resident in the UK will be directly affected. However, the renegotiation backfired badly during the campaign. Its real significance proved to be not the details of the changes, but that it clarified that, as set out above, that free movement remains a fundamental principle within the EU; and the UK was forced to accept that remaining within the EU mean broadly accepting the status quo. The UK did not secure any treaty change, now or promised, and the main measures the UK would have been entitled to impose would have been temporary and/or time-limited.

That meant that the dividing lines for the referendum were more clearly drawn, and in a way that very much favoured the Lave campaign. If the UK had voted to stay in, it would have accepted—however reluctantly—that staying entails a commitment to free movement of workers in the EU, both in principle and practice, and the resulting migration flows, with the impacts described above. In the event, forced to confront this logic, the British public voted to leave. In retrospect, the Prime Minister's decision to focus his renegotiation on the largely illusory problem of benefit tourism was a catastrophic political error, which ended not only his own political career but very probably the UK's membership of the EU.

6   Where Next for UK Migration Policy?

So what does the Brexit vote mean for UK immigration policy? The first point to make is that it seems highly probable that EU nationals currently resident will be granted permanent residence rights. There is clearly majority support for this; it is very difficult to see in practice that depriving significant numbers of people who have lived here for any period of time of the right to remain would be politically or administratively sustainable, regardless of the legal position. Another important point is that it does not seem likely or feasible that we would restrict EEA nationals' right to enter the UK without a visa.

Nevertheless, this does not mean that it is infeasible to restrict future EU migration for work purposes. And in the short term, even before any policy change, we might see a significant fall in net migration from the EU, for several reasons.

- Even before the referendum, employment growth in the UK had slowed (whether as a result of Brexit-related uncertainty, or, perhaps more likely, of other factors). Meanwhile, unemployment is falling both in the EU as a whole, and in the Eurozone. Moreover, for some countries at least (in particular Romania and Bulgaria), the very high levels of recent inflows is likely to reflect the impact of the lifting of transitional controls in 2014; this seems likely to run its course. So even if there had been no referendum, immigration might have peaked.
- The referendum could make this fall much sharper. This is not just because of the overall economic impact of Brexit on growth, output and employment, about which we still have little hard data, although there is a strong consensus that the economy is already slowing significantly. A Brexit-related slowdown is likely to impact some sectors/regions—such as the finance sector in London—that employ large numbers of EU migrants. Moreover, migration from some EU countries—e.g. Poland—appears to respond quite quickly and substantially to exchange rate changes, presumably because migrants compare the salaries that they could earn at home to what they can earn here (and, in part, remit back to family). The value of the UK minimum wage, expressed in zlotys, has fallen by almost 15% already.
- To these economic reasons must be added legal and psychological ones. EU citizens already resident here may have a legitimate expectation, supported by most if not all politicians, that they will be allowed to remain legally indefinitely. But there will inevitably be a prolonged period of uncertainty before we know exactly what that means. If people cannot plan with any confidence, not just about themselves but their families, they are less likely to come and less likely to stay. Moreover, not only have we seen isolated but very unpleasant outbreaks of racism, with calls for EU citizens resident here to leave, but there is a much more widespread and more general sense that they are no longer welcome. There is already some anecdotal evidence that

this is leading to some to contemplate returning to their countries of origin.

What will this mean in terms of numbers? Forte and Portes estimate the determinants of migration from other EU countries, including both macroeconomic variables and the impact of free movement, and use the results to construct illustrative scenarios for future migration flows. Their central scenario implies a decline in net migration from the EU of more than 100,000, to less than half its current level. Of course, any such forecast is subject to huge uncertainty and the actual outcome will depend crucially on when and how policy changes as a result of Brexit. It would, of course, be hugely ironic if it was the referendum result—rather than any change in policy—that led to the government hitting its "tens of thousands" target.

So what are the potential outcomes for future UK immigration policy after Brexit? Before the referendum, it appeared that a Brexit vote would mean that the UK faced a clear choice on immigration policy (Portes 2016). If we wanted as far as possible to retain access to the Single Market—either by maintaining membership of the European Economic Area (like Norway) or via a series of bilateral agreements (like Switzerland)—then we would need to accept that freedom of movement would continue much as now. At the same time, as noted above, it is difficult to view the referendum result as anything other than a rejection of free movement in its current form. Some degree of control of EU migration for work purposes would appear to be a political necessity. However, this still leaves a considerable degree of flexibility. In particular, it is helpful to look at the design of a possible new system along two separate (although not unrelated) dimensions: the degree of "European preference", and the restrictiveness of the system.

6.1 European Preference

The first choice then is whether any new system should give preferential treatment to EU (and presumably EEA) citizens, compared to those coming from outside the EU:

- A "non-discriminatory" system, as promised by Vote Leave during the referendum campaign, would simply apply the same system to EU citizens and non-EU ones. At present, this would mean a relatively restrictive regime for skilled workers, with some quotas (but see below); no migration for low and medium-skilled work; and specific restrictions on students and spouses (but no quotas)
- By contrast, a "modified free movement" regime (although it would almost certainly not be called that!) would preserve much of the current degree of labour mobility between the UK and EU, with perhaps some overall annual or monthly limit, requirements for workers to have a job offer before moving, and restrictions on entitlements to benefits and access to public services;
- In between, there are variety of options, but in particular it is possible that the government might seek to create some sector-specific schemes which would be wholly or largely restricted to EU nationals; these might cover some sectors that have been particularly dependent on EU workers who would not qualify under the current rules applying to non-EU nationals (for example, agriculture and social work)

At present some version of the intermediate option appears to be the government's preference—but there is almost no detail as yet as to how such as system might work.

6.2 Liberal or Restrictive Policy

The second choice the government faces is whether the policy should be relatively liberal or restrictive. Note that it is perfectly possible, in theory, to completely abolish free movement—that is to move to a system that treats EU and non-EU citizens the same—while making the system overall as or more liberal than the current one. Equally, applying the current system for non-EU nationals to EU ones would result in a far more restrictive system than at present.

A more liberal alternative would be "downward harmonisation"; that is, the new system for work-related migration would be less restrictive than that currently applying to non-EU nationals (although, obviously, more restrictive for EU nationals to whom free movement currently applies). This would mean that immigration continued to run at historically fairly high levels; it could, however, support a rebalancing from unskilled jobs to skilled migration, as well as from EU to non-EU migration.

A restrictive policy would aim to reduce migration to the government's target of "tens of thousands". At the moment, this appears to be the government's preferred option: Prime Minister May has ruled out any liberalisation of the rules applying to non-EU citizens and has even suggested further restrictions on, for example, international students.

The economic consequences of ending or very significantly restricting free movement, while at the same time maintaining or tightening other rules, would be significant. The Office of Budget Responsibility, in its November 2016 forecast, projected a significant worsening of the government's fiscal position as a result of Brexit. Of this, about £15 billion (over the forecast period to 2020) was the result of assumed reductions in migration flows. Looking at the broader macroeconomic impacts, Forte and Portes estimate that Brexit-induced reductions in migration would (under a central scenario) reduce GDP by 0.6% to 1.2% over the same period.

At a sectoral level, the consequences of restrictions for some industries that rely on migration from within the EU to fill low-skilled jobs would be very large. At least in theory, it is possible to construct a plausible economic rationale; while restrictions would cut growth in the short term, it might over-time incentivise firms into productivity-enhancing investment or training. However, there is little or no evidence that occupational or sectoral usage of migrant labour is associated with lower levels of training (MAC 2010). Other research has focused on migration from outside the EU and in relation to higher-level skills, but has similar findings (George et al. 2012; CIPD 2014). In low-paid sectors the difficulty of attracting and retaining young people appears to act as a disincentive to training, rather than the availability of migrants (Rolfe and Hudson-Sharp 2016).

The evidence on the impact on wages suggests that there a restrictive policy might have some (relatively small) positive direct impact on wages for low-skilled workers, although little or none for medium and highly skilled workers. However, the impact on incomes would be more than offset by the wider negative economic and fiscal impacts. Wadsworth et al. (2016) summarised:

> We cannot be precise about the size of the losses from restricting immigration following a Brexit ... At the national level, falls in EU immigration are likely to lead to lower living standards for the UK-born. This is partly because immigrants help to reduce the deficit: they are more likely to work and pay tax and less likely to use public services as they are younger and better educated than the UK-born. It is also partly due to the positive effects of EU immigrants on productivity.

Analysis of both the impact of the UK's membership of the EU, and the economic consequences of Brexit has to date mostly focused on the UK's trading relationship with the rest of the European Union. However, free movement is perhaps equally if not more important: the movement of people has had, and will continue to have a profound influence on the UK's economy and society, and its ongoing relationship with other European countries, for the foreseeable future.

Notes

1. For simplicity I will refer to the "EU" throughout.
2. The Trans-Tasman Agreement between Australia and New Zealand is an exception.

References

Anderson, B., Ruhs, M., Rogaly, B., & Spencer, S. (2006). Fair enough? Central and Eastern European migrants in low-wage employment in the UK. COMPAS. Retrieved July 31, 2015, from http://www.irr.org.uk/pdf/Fair_Enough.pdf.

Ashcroft. (2016). How the UK voted on Thursday, and why. Retrieved from http://lordashcroftpolls.com/2016/06/how-the-united-kingdom-voted-and-why/.

Barone, G., & Mocetti, S. (2011). With a little help from abroad: The effect of low-skilled immigration on the female labour supply. *Labour Economics, 18*(5), 664–675.

Carozzi, F. (2016, July). Brexit and the location of migrants. Spatial Economics Research Centre, LSE. Retrieved from http://spatial-economics.blogspot.de/2016/07/brexit-and-location-of-migrants.html.

Chance, M., Pytliková, M., Zimmermann, K. F. (2014). The free movement of workers in an enlarged European Union: institutional underpinnings of economic adjustment, IZA discussion paper 8456. Available at http://ftp.iza.org/dp8456.pdf.

CIPD. (2014). The growth of EU labour: Assessing the impact on the UK labour market. CIPD. Retrieved from http://www.cipd.co.uk/binaries/the-growth-of-eu-labour-assessing-impact-uk-labour-market_2014.pdf.

Colantone, I., & Stanig, P. (2016). The real reason the U.K. voted for Brexit? Jobs lost to Chinese competition. *Washington Post.* https://www.washingtonpost.com/news/monkey-cage/wp/2016/07/07/the-real-reason-the-u-k-voted-for-brexit-economics-not-identity/.

Constant, A. F. (2014). Do migrants take the jobs of native workers? IZA World of Labor. Available at https://www.gov.uk/government/publications/impacts-of-migration-on-uk-native-employment-an-analytical-review-of-the-evidence.

Dustmann, C., & Frattini, T. (2014). The fiscal effects of immigration to the UK. *Economic Journal, 124*(580).

Dustmann, C., Casanova, M., Fertig, M., Preston, I., & Schmidt, C. M. (2003). *The impact of EU enlargement on migration flows.* Home Office Online Report 25/03.

European Commission. (1957). Retrieved from http://europa.eu/eu-law/decision-making/treaties/index_en.htm.

European Commission. (1985). Completing the internal market: White paper from the Commission to the European Council. Available at http://europa.eu/documents/comm/white_papers/pdf/com1985_0310_f_en.pdf.

European Commission. (2004). *Free movement of citizens directive.* Available at http://eur-lex.europa.eu/legal-content/EN/TXT/PDF/?uri=CELEX:32004L0038&from=EN.

Evans, G., & Mellon, J. (2015). *Immigration and the EU: Attitudes and perceptions, myths and realities.* Paper presented to NIESR conference on Immigration and the EU–UK relationship. Available at http://www.niesr.ac.uk/sites/default/files/civicrm/persist/contribute/files/Presentation%208th%20december%20NIESR.pptxview.

Forte, G., & Portes, J. (2017, March 1). The economic impact of Brexit-induced reductions in migration. *Oxford Review of Economic Policy, 33*(1), S31–S44.

Galogski, B., Leschke, J., & Watt, A. (2009). *EU labour migration since enlargement: Trends, impacts and policies.* Farnham: Ashgate Publishing. Available at http://books.google.co.uk/books/about/EU_Labour_Migration_since_Enlargement.html.

Geay, C., McNally, S., & Telhaj, S. (2013). Non-native speakers of English in the classroom: What are the effects on pupil performance? *The Economic Journal, 123*(570): F281–F307. ISSN 0013-0133.

George, A., Meadows, P., Metcalf, H., & Rolfe, H. (2011). *Impact of migration on the consumption of education and children's services and the consumption of health services, social care and social services.* Report to the Migration Advisory Committee. London: MAC. Available at http://www.ukba.homeoffice.gov.uk/sitecontent/documents/aboutus/workingwithus/mac/27-analysis-migration/02-research-projects/impact-of-migration?view=Binary.

George, A., Lalani, M., Mason, G., Rolfe, H., & Rosazza, C. (2012). *Skilled immigration and strategically important skills in the UK economy.* London: Migration Advisory Committee.

Giuletti, C. (2014). The welfare magnet hypothesis and the welfare take-up of migrants. IZA World of Labour. Available at http://newsroom.iza.org/de/wp-content/uploads/2014/06/welfare-magnet-hypothesis-and-welfare-take-up.pdf.

Giuntella, O., Nicodemo, C., & Vargas Silva, C. (2015). *The effects of immigration on NHS waiting times* (Working Paper 5). Oxford: Blavatnik School of Government.

Goodhart, D. (2013, July). National citizen preference in an era of EU free movement, submission to the government's review of the balance of competencies (updated December). Available at www.demos.co.uk/files/DavidGoodhartSubmissionJuly2013.pdf.

Goodwin, M., & Heath, O. (2016, August). Brexit vote explained: Poverty, low skills and lack of opportunities. Joseph Rowntree Foundation. Retrieved from https://www.jrf.org.uk/report/brexit-vote-explained-poverty-low-skills-and-lack-opportunities.

Green, A., Atfield, G., Adam, D., & Staniewicz, T. (2013). Determinants of the composition of the workforce in low skilled sectors of the economy. Warwick Institute for Employment Research report to MAC. Retrieved from https://www.gov.uk/govemment/uploads/system/uploads/attachment_data/file/257272/warwick-insti.pdf.

Her Majesty's Revenue and Customs. (2016). Further statistics on the tax contributions of EEA nationals in 2013–14. Retrieved from https://www.gov.uk/government/statistics/further-statistics-on-tax-contribution-of-eea-nationals-for-2013-to-2014.

Kahanec, M. (2013). Labor mobility in an enlarged European Union. In A. F. Constant & K. F. Zimmermann (Eds.), *International Handbook on the Economics of Migration* (pp. 137–152). Cheltenham, UK, and Northampton: Edward Elgar.

Kaufman, E. (2016). It's not the economy, stupid, LSE Brexit blog. Retrieved from http://blogs.lse.ac.uk/politicsandpolicy/personal-values-brexit-vote/.

Koikkalainen, S. (2011, April). Free movement in Europe, past and present. Washington, DC: Migration Policy Institute. Retrieved from http://www.migrationpolicy.org/article/free-movement-europe-past-and-present.

Migration Advisory Committee. (2014). *Migrants in low skilled work.* Retrived from https://www.gov.uk/government/publications/migrants-in-low-skilled-work.

Mundell, R. A. (1961). A theory of optimum currency areas. *American Economic Review, 51.*

Nickell, S., & Salaheen, J. (2015). *The impact of immigration on occupational wages: Evidence from Britain* (Staff Working Paper No. 574). Available at http://www.bankofengland.co.uk/research/Pages/workingpapers/2015/swp574.aspx.

Ozden, C. (2015, March). A long commute: IMF, Finance and Development, 52, 1. Available at http://www.imf.org/external/pubs/ft/fandd/2015/03/ozden.htm.Google/Scholar.

Pauritus, V. (2014). "Economic migrants" or "middling transnationals"? East European migrants' experiences of work in the UK. *International Migration, 52*(1), 36–55.

Portes, J. (2015). Labour mobility in the European Union. In S. N. Durlaf & L. E. Blume (Eds.), *The New Palgrave dictionary of economics. Online Edition,* Basingstoke: Palgrave Macmillan. Retrieved from http://www.dictionaryofeconomics.com/article?id=pde2015_L000248. doi:10.1057/9780230226203.3943.

Portes, J. (2016). Immigration, free movement and the UK Referendum, *National Institute Economic Review, 236.*

Preston, I. (2014, November 5). The effect of immigration on public finances. VOX EU: Retrieved from http://www.voxeu.org/article/immigration-and-public-finances.

Resolution Foundation. (2016, July). *Why did we vote to leave*. Retrieved from http://www.resolutionfoundation.org/media/blog/why-did-we-vote-to-leave-what-an-analysis-of-place-can-tell-us-about-brexit/.

Rolfe, H., & Hudson-, Sharp N. (2016). *The impact of free movement on the labour market: Case studies of hospitality, food processing and construction.* London: NIESR.

Vasilopoulou, S. (2016). UK Euroscepticism and the Brexit Referendum. *The Political Quarterly, 87*(2), 219–227. doi:10.1111/1467-923X.12258

Venables, A. J. (1999). Trade liberalization and factor mobility: An overview. In R. C. Faini, J. de Melo, & K. Zimmermann (Eds.), *Migration: The controversies and the evidence* (pp. 23–48). Cambridge: Cambridge University Press.

Wadsworth, J., Dhingra, S., Ottaviano, G., & Van Reenen, J. (2016). Brexit and the impact of immigration on the UK. Brexit Analysis No. 5 London: Centre for Economic Performance.

Wadsworth, J., & Vaitilingam, R. (2015). Immigration, the European Union and the UK Labour Market, LSE, CEP Policy Analysis. Available at http://cep.lse.ac.uk/pubs/download/pa015.pdf.

EU Regional Policy and the UK

Sascha O. Becker, Peter H. Egger
and Maximilian von Ehrlich

1 Introduction

The UK referendum on EU membership on 23 June 2016 re-ignited
debates about the economic costs and benefits of EU membership. In
1973, Britain joined the European Community, the predecessor of the
European Union (EU) principally because participating in the European
project was seen as a way to halt its relative economic decline (Crafts
2012). The economic benefits of the UK's EU membership have been
questioned again and again, but studies generally concluded that the

S.O. Becker (✉)
University of Warwick, Coventry, UK
e-mail: s.o.becker@warwick.ac.uk

P.H. Egger
ETH Zurich, Zurich, Switzerland
e-mail: egger@kof.ethz.ch

M.v. Ehrlich
University of Bern, Bern, Switzerland
e-mail: maximilian.vonehrlich@vwi.unibe.ch

© The Author(s) 2017
N.F. Campos and F. Coricelli (eds.), *The Economics of UK–EU Relations*,
DOI 10.1007/978-3-319-55495-2_8

201

membership in the Community and Union continued to be beneficial (see, e.g. Pain and Young 2004). After David Cameron's announcement that he planned to re-negotiate the terms of Britain's EU membership and hold a referendum on it, new and updated estimates were produced. Campos, Coricelli, and Moretti (2014), using the synthetic control method where the UK is compared to a "synthetic" UK (i.e. a weighted average of comparison countries), estimate the cumulated benefit, in terms of GDP per capita, of EU membership to the UK in the four decades after 1973 at 24%. The UK Treasury (HMRC 2016), in their central estimate (the so-called "Canada" option), predicts a 6.2% fall in GDP, i.e. £4300 per household, in the long run, if Britain were to leave the EU. A variety of other estimates produced by leading research centres and economists are in the same range, if not higher (see Dhingra et al. 2016, for an overview).[1] All estimates of the macroeconomic costs (or benefits) of Brexit clearly depend on which door out of the EU the UK takes or will be permitted to take by the EU member countries, i.e. what the exact option of relationship with the remaining members of the EU and other countries will be (see Dhingra and Sampson 2016, for an overview of the exit options).

Many observers are more directly, and to some extent more narrowly, concerned about the fiscal dimension of EU membership. Even though the EU budget makes up only 1% of the gross national income (GNI) of its 28 member states, the worry that Brussels "wastes our money" resonates with many voters. Notably, the UK pays less into the Brussels pot due to the well-known UK rebate. But the UK is still a net contributor, so it was and is fair to ask whether money from the EU budget was well spent.

Our chapter focuses on EU Regional Policy, which makes up more than one-third of EU spending, being a major budget item. The regional dimension is particularly interesting because of the tremendous inequality in per-capita incomes not only across the EU, but also across the UK. We will ask three related questions. First, since EU Regional Policy is, to some extent, "foreign aid" for the poorer regions of the EU, has it worked at all, and have all recipient regions benefited to the same degree, so have UK contributions to the EU budget been well spent, even when disregarding the fact that some funding came back to the UK anyways? Second, have UK regions benefited from the EU spending at all and in the same way as other EU regions? Third, what would replace EU regional spending in the UK? This last question is related to the political economy of regional policy and we will argue that it is far from clear whether and to which extent UK regions that did in the past and currently do benefit from EU funding will be supported by the British government after Brexit.

This chapter is organized as follows. In Sect. 2, we describe the historical and institutional background of EU Regional Policy. In Sect. 3, we summarize research on the effectiveness of EU Regional Policy for the EU as a whole. In Sect. 4, we look at how UK regions have benefited from EU Regional Policy. In Sect. 5, we consider the potential consequences of Brexit for UK regions, focusing particularly on political-economy aspects. Section 6 concludes.

2 Historical and Institutional Background of EU Regional Policy

EU Regional Policy was introduced during the tenure of the UK's first EU commissioner, Lord George Thomson, Baron Thomson of Monifieth (1921–2008) who said:

> I am on the side of the underprivileged, and it doesn't matter which country they work in.

He campaigned as regional affairs Commissioner for Europe's worst-off areas, and he was as depressed by bad economic conditions in Sicily as in his native Scotland. In order to foster the reduction of poverty and the catching up of the poorest regions in the European Community, the European Regional Development Fund was created in 1975. Initially, operations remained purely national, financing predetermined projects in the Member States with little European or subnational influence. With the enlargement of the EU to Greece in 1981, and Portugal and Spain in 1986, and the adoption of the Single European Act in 1986, discussions about a truly European regional policy started. In 1988, the European

Council decided to double the annual resources to be spent on regional policy: Structural Funds under the umbrella of Cohesion Policy were to be spent focusing on the poorest and most backward regions, via multi-annual programming, strategic orientation of investments, and the involvement of regional and local partners. Interestingly, the implementation of this enhanced Regional Policy was overseen by yet another British Commissioner, Bruce Millan, in the same role of Commissioner for Regional Policy. So, important milestones in EU Regional Policy are closely connected with UK politicians as EU Commissioners.

Starting with the programming or budgetary period 1989–1993, EU Regional Policy followed roughly the same principles: Objective 1 transfers (after 2006 renamed: "Convergence Objective") were reserved for the poorest regions of Europe, defined as being ones with a purchasing-power-adjusted per-capita GDP of below 75% of the European Community (or Union) average. Those Objective 1 transfers have made up about 70% of all regional transfers for the last 25 years, demonstrating that the major aim of EU Regional Policy was and still is to support the poorest regions of Europe. The remaining part of the EU Regional Policy budget is spent on regions with GDP per capita above the 75% threshold. Spending targets various other policy objectives, such as giving support to the economic and social conversion of areas experiencing structural difficulties (so-called Objective 2) and giving support to the adaptation and modernization of education, training and employment policies and systems (so-called Objective 3). After the first programming period 1989–1993, subsequent ones covered the years 1994–1999, 2000–2006 and 2007–2013, and the ongoing programming period which is supposed to run from 2014 to 2020.

To get a sense of magnitudes, in the budget over the 2007–2013 programming period, funding for the Regional and Cohesion Policy amounted to €347 billion (35.7% of the total budget for that period—or just over €49 billion per year). All cohesion policy programmes are co-financed by the member states, bringing total available funding to almost €700 billion.

3   Does EU Regional Policy Give Value for Money?

EU Regional Policy is a kind of "foreign aid". The UK has traditionally put a lot of emphasis on foreign aid. For instance, in 2010, the government ring-fenced the foreign aid budget while the vast majority of UK ministries saw their budgets slashed by 20% or more. Even after Brexit, the UK could still be inclined to support the poorest regions of Europe in the same way as it supports poor countries around the world.

Clearly, as EU Regional Policy entails costs, it is fair to the financing tax payer to ask to which extent it achieves its major goal, namely closing the gap in purchasing-power-adjusted per-capita income between net donor and net recipient countries and regions. Since the policy explicitly is about redistribution, one should expect positive effects at least in the recipient regions but not necessarily everywhere (as it is the case in general with untargeted aid). More than that, one would expect the policy to induce economic effects in excess of the transfers. To the extent that even net donating countries and regions get some funding under various objectives of the policy, some positive effects should even materialize in net donating regions.

With EU Regional Policy, an assessment of its effectiveness is possible based on data for the past 25 years. The primary outcome of interest which permits a more or less straightforward benchmark vis-à-vis the costs is per-capita-income growth. As with foreign aid in general, assessing growth effects of EU Regional Policy is difficult because poor regions are more likely to receive transfers according to the policy but, on average, they tend to grow faster anyway also without those transfers due to convergence. Hence, a positive correlation between receiving EU transfers and economic growth per se is not evidence of a causal effect of the former on the latter.

Early work on the effectiveness of EU Regional Policy came to generally negative conclusions regarding its effects, since linear regressions did not reveal statistically significant positive effects of the policy on per-capita-income growth (see Sala-i-Martin 1996; Boldrin and Canova 2001). However, the studies were criticized along three lines: (i) that they were focused on countries, while transfers were given to smaller, sub-national units (NUTS2 or NUTS3 regions) so that effects might be concealed by regional aggregation; (ii) linear regressions which include a number of control variables (i.e. drivers of economic growth) might not be well suited to identify causal effects of the Policy; and (iii) while a large part of the funding explicitly targets per-capita-income growth, there are also other objectives, and those could induce indirect effects on economic growth by changing some of its fundamental drivers (whereby some of the effects ascribed to fundamental drivers of economic growth should in fact be ascribed to the policy).

Indeed, subsequent research to the aforementioned one revealed some positive effects of the programmme, e.g. on agglomeration and industry location (see Midelfart-Knarvik and Overman 2002), on countries with favourable institutions (see Beugelsdijk and Eijffinger 2005; Ederveen et al. 2006), and on subnational regions (see Ederveen et al. 2002; Cappelen et al. 2003; however, Dall'erba and Gallo (2008), remarked that the evidence on regional economic growth effects was much weaker when taking cross-regional-border spillover effects of the Policy into account). Mohl and Hagen (2010) provide a good overview of the early research on EU Regional Policy.

Fortunately for identification, it turns out that some aspects of EU Regional Policy follow a design which facilitates establishing a causal link between transfer recipience and economic growth that had been overseen by the aforementioned work. In particular, the biggest part of EU Regional Policy is devoted to directly fostering economic catching up of the poorest regions under *Objective 1* or *Convergence*. The associated funds are assigned according to a simple rule: regions with a (purchasing-power-adjusted) per-capita GDP level below 75% of the EU average are eligible for such transfers and others are not. This somewhat arbitrary rule gives rise to a (quasi-)experimental situation and to potential anomalies that can be exploited in order to estimate causal effects of the policy. For example, a NUTS2 region with a GDP per capita of 74.99% of the EU average is eligible for Objective 1 (which we use interchangeably with Convergence) transfers, while one with a GDP per capita of 75.01% of the EU average is not. In absence of transfers and all other things being equal, we would expect two such regions to have nearly identical growth prospects.

However, only one of these regions can benefit from millions of Euros in Objective 1 transfers. Close to the 75% threshold, it is a bit like flipping a coin whether nearly equally rich EU regions receive millions more or less of EU funding, and focusing on such similar regions in the statistical analysis provides for a setting which permits an identification of the policy's causal effects on economic outcomes.

Using this design, Becker et al. (2010) found that Objective 1 transfers induce per-capita-income growth in recipient regions. However, this would not be enough to justify the programme, as transfers might induce a shallow consumption effect and even some crowing out of private investment without positive medium- and long-term consequences for economic growth. However, the analysis in Becker et al. (2010) suggests that Objective 1 transfers trigger changes in recipient-region income beyond a simple consumption effect: one Euro of transfers generated between 1.00 and 1.20 Euros on average during the EU budgetary periods 1989–1993, 1994–1999 and 2000–2006. Hence, on average, Objective 1 transfers have been effective, contrary to popular belief, and the corresponding budget was not generally wasted. Pellegrini et al. (2013) largely confirm these results using the approach of Becker et al. (2010) and data for two programming periods—1994–1999 and 2000–2006—on GDP data from Eurostat (Becker et al. 2010, had used GDP data from Cambridge Econometrics).

Yet, while this evidence is supportive at large, it does not mean that there would not be an even better use for the corresponding money. An interesting related question to the one on the policy general effectiveness is about where it triggered the largest effects and where the smallest in terms of broad categories of regions. For instance, if the poorest regions —i.e. ones in the South and the East of the EU (plus Ireland) responded most sensitively to transfers reallocating some of the budget from somewhat better-off to somewhat worse-off regions could raise the value for money of transfers. Becker et al. (2013) found that Objective 1 transfers affect regional per-capita income growth quite differently, and in a systematic way: Objective 1 recipient regions with a better educated workforce ("technological absorptive capacity") and/or better-run local government with less corruption and better local administration ("institutional absorptive capacity") do better than the average recipient region; conversely, regions with below-average technological and institutional absorptive capacity do not grow faster than regions that receive no transfers at all (these results were found for the same EU budgetary periods 1989–1993, 1994–1999 and 2000–2006 as in Becker et al. 2010). As it happens, the poorest regions of the Union on average are also the ones with the lowest levels of technological and institutional absorptive capacity. Hence, the positive average per-capita-income growth effects of Objective 1 transfers are mainly generated by strong growth effects of regions in the vicinity of the transfer threshold of a purchasing-power-adjusted per-capita income of 75% the EU average in western European countries.

One might comment in this regard that treating Objective 1 recipient and non-recipient regions as to represent two classes of regions with similar within-class transfer levels is not quite adequate. Indeed, the level of transfers varies starkly among NUTS2 and NUTS3 regions both absolutely as well as in percent of recipient-region GDP. It could be that some regions perform poorly since they do not receive enough funds to finance investments to cause larger medium—and long-term effects on economic growth. Hence, an interesting question with regard to all EU Regional Policy transfers (not just Objective 1 or Convergence) is whether higher transfers lead to bigger economic benefits. Becker et al. (2012) assessed this question at the level of NUTS3 regions for the budgetary periods 1994–1999 and 2000–2006 and concluded that providing bigger transfers is not necessarily better in terms of the generated per-capita-income-growth effects: some regions seem to struggle with the amount of transfers received and above a certain transfers-to-GDP ratio further additional growth is by no means ensured; also, some regions did not get enough funding for high-enough growth effects to materialize. Overall, there appears to be a concave relationship between transfers-to-GDP ratios and the average effects on per-capita-income growth which suggests an optimal transfers-to-GDP ratio on average: below this ratio an additional Euro of transfers generates more than a Euro of GDP, whereas above this ratio an additional Euro of transfers generates less than a Euro of GDP. In an RDD based on the 75% rule with continuous measures of transfer intensity (Pellegrini and Cerqua 2015) also find a maximum desirable transfer amount above which additional funds do not generate additional per-capita-income growth.

These results suggest three broad sets of policy conclusions: one for transfer pessimists, one for transfer pragmatists, and one for transfer reformists. The transfer pessimist might say that the European Commission should save money by voiding transfers to recipient regions where, at least statistically, they do not do any good. The transfer pragmatist might say that transfers work well on average and they might work better when reallocating transfers from regions where statistically they do not do any good to those where they do. The transfer reformist might say that the denomination of funds should be changed. Apparently, the technological and institutional absorptive capacity levels are not homogeneous and tend to be worse in poorer than in richer regions. For EU funding to be productive, one would first have to establish sufficiently high levels of absorptive capacity. Hence a reallocation of funds from financing physical capital and infrastructure towards human capital and measures that improve the functioning of the local public sector (through training and monitoring) would increase the effectiveness and efficiency of funding, at least in the medium to the long run.

4   EU Regional Policy in the UK

An assessment of the effectiveness of EU Regional Policy for Objective 1 regions in the UK is harder than an assessment of the effectiveness on average, since the number of treated regions in the UK is small. Figure 1 shows the UK's Objective 1 regions: in 1989–1993: Northern Ireland; in 1994–1999: Northern Ireland, Merseyside, Highlands and Islands; in 2000–2006: Merseyside, South Yorkshire, West Wales and the Valleys, Cornwall and Isles of Scilly; in 2007–2013: West Wales and the Valleys, Cornwall and Isles of Scilly. This means that of all NUTS2 regions in the UK, one received Objective 1 treatment in 1989–1993, three in 1994–1999, four in 2000–2006 and two in 2007–2013. Note that West Wales and the Valleys as well as Cornwall and the Isles of Scilly are still Objective 1 regions in the current programming period 2014–2020. Hence, because of the small number of UK Objective 1 regions, we may not conduct an

UK Objective 1 Regions 1989-1993   UK Objective 1 Regions 1994-1999

UK Objective 1 Regions 2000-2006   UK Objective 1 Regions 2007-2013

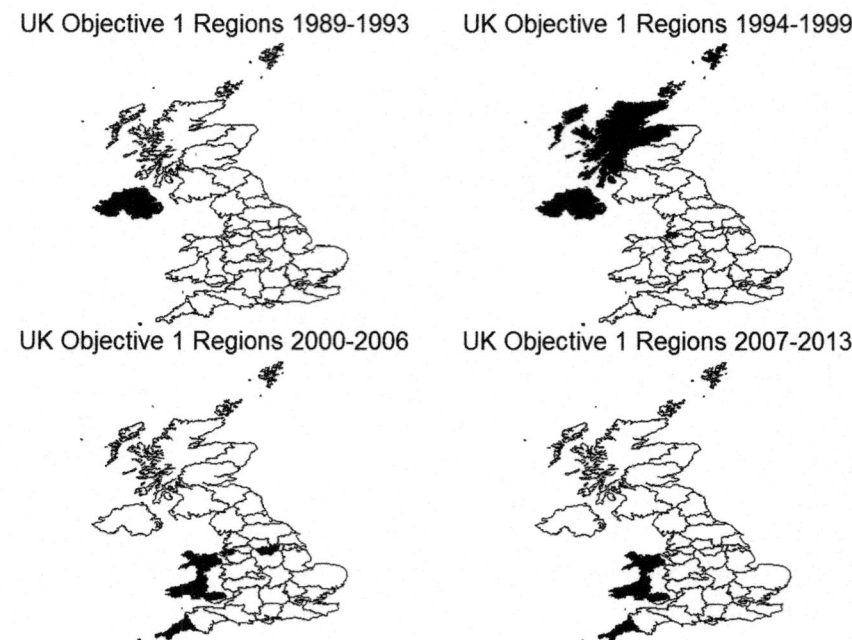

Fig. 1 UK Objective 1 regions. *Notes* Author's own maps. Objective 1 treatment is available directly from the European Commission, from various Council Regulations, in particular the Regulations numbered 2052/88, 2082/93, and 502/1999, and in editions of the Official Journal. Objective 1 regions are marked in *black*

analysis as in Becker et al. (2010, 2013) for UK regions alone. However, we may pool the data for all NUTS2 regions in the EU and the three programming and consider a deviation of the effect on UK regions from the average effect.

Let us briefly sketch the econometric set-up using i and t to refer to a region and budgetary period. Let us denote per-capita income growth by $Growth_{it}$, computed as a log-difference of per-capita income of i at the end of period t versus prior to t. We denote by $\widetilde{GDPPC}_{it}$ the log GDP per capita in relevant years determining treatment eligibility, measured as a deviation from the log GDP per capita corresponding to the 75% threshold. O_{it} denotes Objective 1 treatment status, and $\widetilde{UK}_i$ denotes normalized (as a deviation from the average) UK region status (1 for UK regions and 0 else). Then, what can be estimated is

$$Growth_{it} = \alpha_{(i)} + f_0\left(\widetilde{\text{GDPPC}}_{it}\right) + O_{it}\left[\beta + \gamma \sim \widetilde{\text{UK}}_i + f_1\left(\widetilde{\text{GDPPC}}_{it}\right)\right] + \varepsilon_{it},$$

$$(1)$$

where ε_{it} is a disturbance term, $\alpha_{(i)}$ is either a region fixed effect or a common constant, $f_0(\cdot)$ and $f_1(\cdot)$ are linear or quadratic functions of $\widetilde{\text{GDPPC}}_{it}$ for Objective 1 untreated and treated regions, respectively, β is the local average treatment effect of Objective 1 treatment for average EU regions, and γ measures the deviation from this local average effect for the average treated UK NUTS2 region.

Tables 1 and 2 summarize the local average treatment effect and the deviation from that for UK regions for Objective 1 treatment for the last two completed budgetary periods, 2000–2013. We use the two most recent budgetary periods here, since data on a much broader set of outcomes are available than for earlier budgetary periods which permits a greater scope of the analysis. These outcomes are: GDP per capita growth; Employment growth; Investment per GDP, Public investment per GDP; Growth in total compensation of employees; Growth in total hours worked of employees; Growth in number of patent applications; and Participation rate in education and training.

The numbers in the two tables suggest that there was a statistically significant effect of Objective 1 transfers for the average region, in particular, on GDP per capita growth but also on Employment growth and on Growth in total compensation of employees. The comparable coefficients are smaller than in Becker et al. (2010, 2013)—as an outcome not of the inclusion of the UK effect but due to the different sample period. For instance, (Becker et al. 2016) report results for the same set of budgetary periods as in Tables 1 and 2 but without including $\widetilde{\text{UK}}_i$ (i.e. setting $\gamma = 0$), where the estimates of the local average treatment effect of Objective 1 are very similar to the ones in Tables 1 and 2. Hence, the lower treatment effects in the recent budgetary periods suggest that the Economic and Financial Crisis did not only affect economic growth,

Table 1 Effects of Objective 1 treatment in the UK (I)—(2000–2013)

	Linear		2nd. order polynomial	
	(1)	(2)	(3)	(4)
GDP per capita growth				
Objective 1	0.006***	0.012**	0.006*	0.012**
	(0.002)	(0.006)	(0.003)	(0.006)
UK dev. from EU avg. Obj.	−0.001	−0.006	−0.001	−0.007
1 Effect	(0.005)	(0.015)	(0.005)	(0.014)
Fixed effects	No	Yes	No	Yes
Observations	506	506	506	506
AIC	−3020.067	−3271.576	−3026.953	−3343.203
Employment growth				
Objective 1	0.006**	0.020***	0.003	0.017***
	(0.002)	(0.006)	(0.003)	(0.006)
UK dev. from EU avg. Obj.	0.009**	−0.016	0.010**	−0.016
1 Effect	(0.005)	(0.015)	(0.005)	(0.014)
Fixed effects	No	Yes	No	Yes
Observations	506	506	506	506
AIC	−3049.622	−3329.024	−3055.529	−3355.676
Investment per GDP				
Objective 1	0.007	0.010	0.004	0.008
	(0.008)	(0.009)	(0.010)	(0.009)
UK dev. from EU avg. Obj.	−0.004	−0.013	−0.004	−0.013
1 Effect	(0.017)	(0.024)	(0.017)	(0.023)
Fixed effects	No	Yes	No	Yes
Observations	506	506	506	506
AIC	−1756.271	−2844.728	−1755.830	−2844.650
Public investment per GDP				
Objective 1	0.001	0.004	0.002	0.003
	(0.004)	(0.004)	(0.004)	(0.004)
UK dev. from EU avg. Obj.	0.032***	−0.038***	0.032***	−0.037***
1 Effect	(0.005)	(0.007)	(0.005)	(0.007)
Fixed effects	No	Yes	No	Yes
Observations	274	250	274	250
AIC	−1757.186	−2038.005	−1767.265	−2040.540

Notes ***, **, * denote significance at the 1-, 5- and 10% level, respectively. All estimates are based on a two-stage least squares approach using eligibility as the instrument and controlling for the forcing variable and its interactions. Growth rates refer to log differences divided by the number of years. Investment rates refer to the sum of investments divided by the sum of GDP over the respective programming period. Lower AIC indicates better model-fit
Source Authors' own calculations

Table 2 Effects of Objective 1 treatment in the UK (II)—(2000–2013)

	Linear		2nd. order polynomial	
	(1)	(2)	(3)	(4)
Growth in total compensation of employees				
Objective 1	0.004*	0.018***	0.002	0.016***
	(0.002)	(0.006)	(0.003)	(0.006)
UK dev. from EU avg. Obj.	0.009*	−0.011	0.009*	−0.011
1 Effect	(0.005)	(0.016)	(0.005)	(0.015)
Fixed effects	No	Yes	No	Yes
Observations	506	506	506	506
AIC	−2985.229	−3252.954	−2986.388	−3278.683
Growth in total hours worked of employees				
Objective 1	0.007**	0.001	0.004	0.000
	(0.003)	(0.007)	(0.003)	(0.007)
UK dev. from EU avg. Obj.	0.006	0.011	0.006	0.011
1 Effect	(0.005)	(0.018)	(0.005)	(0.018)
Fixed effects	No	Yes	No	Yes
Observations	506	506	506	506
AIC	−2898.057	−3124.450	−2909.387	−3127.824
Growth in number of patent applications				
Objective 1	0.022	0.112*	0.024	0.105
	(0.023)	(0.064)	(0.028)	(0.065)
UK dev. from EU avg. Obj.	−0.023	−0.012	−0.024	−0.009
1 Effect	(0.042)	(0.140)	(0.042)	(0.140)
Fixed effects	No	Yes	No	Yes
Observations	480	474	480	474
AIC	−780.996	−1006.778	−780.938	−1007.858
Participation rate in education and training				
Objective 1	−0.002	−0.013	−0.005	−0.015
	(0.004)	(0.010)	(0.005)	(0.011)
UK dev. from EU avg. Obj.	0.011	0.074***	0.011	0.075***
1 Effect	(0.008)	(0.026)	(0.008)	(0.026)
Fixed effects	No	Yes	No	Yes
Observations	475	454	475	454
AIC	−2305.982	−2484.357	−2307.705	−2483.871

Notes ***, **, * denote significance at the 1-, 5-, and 10% level, respectively. All estimates are based on a two-stage least squares approach using eligibility as the instrument and controlling for the forcing variable and its interactions. Growth rates refer to log differences divided by the number of years. Lower AIC indicates better model-fit

Source Authors' own calculations

per-capita income, and employment directly, but it also might have had a detrimental effect on the effectiveness of regional transfers within the EU.

What is interesting concerning the results in Tables 1 and 2 relative to the earlier ones in Becker et al. (2010, 2013) is that the per-capita-income-growth effect appears to be fully driven by the employment effect. Hence, to the extent that Objective 1 transfers affected GDP per capita growth, this was mediated by employment growth, which also showed in the growth in total compensation of employees. For these insights, it is of small importance whether NUTS2 region fixed effects are included or not (which points to the validity of the assumptions underlying the identification design) and whether the control functions of prior-to-budgetary-period per-capita-income levels are linear or quadratic. Interestingly, while there is no significant effect of Objective 1 transfers on Public investment per GDP, there is a negative effect on UK regions once conditioning on fixed NUTS2 region effects. This indicates that Objective 1 status in the UK came with significantly lower public investment. This seems to be the only noticeable UK-specific effect in Table 1. But we caution that public investment data are available for only a smaller number of regions than the other outcomes. The only UK-specific finding in Table 2 is the positive effect of Objective 1 status on the participation rate in education and training in the fixed effects specifications.

It is also interesting to look at EU regional transfers more broadly, beyond Objective 1 status. Our data cover regional transfers to all NUTS3 regions, a more disaggregated regional level than NUTS2, and all different objectives of EU regional transfers. Table 3 summarizes the moments of the distribution of transfer intensities across NUTS3 regions for the EU as a whole and for the UK across three programming periods, 1994–1999, 2000–2006 and 2007–2013 for those regions that actually received transfers. Moreover, this table provides information on the share of regions that received any funding out of the EU's Regional Policy budget. It is apparent from this table that the UK is similar to the average EU country in terms of the fraction of funded regions across all programming periods covered. However, the funding intensity is much smaller in the UK than on average. This does not come as a surprise, since the fraction of regions which were eligible for Objective 1 funding—the biggest

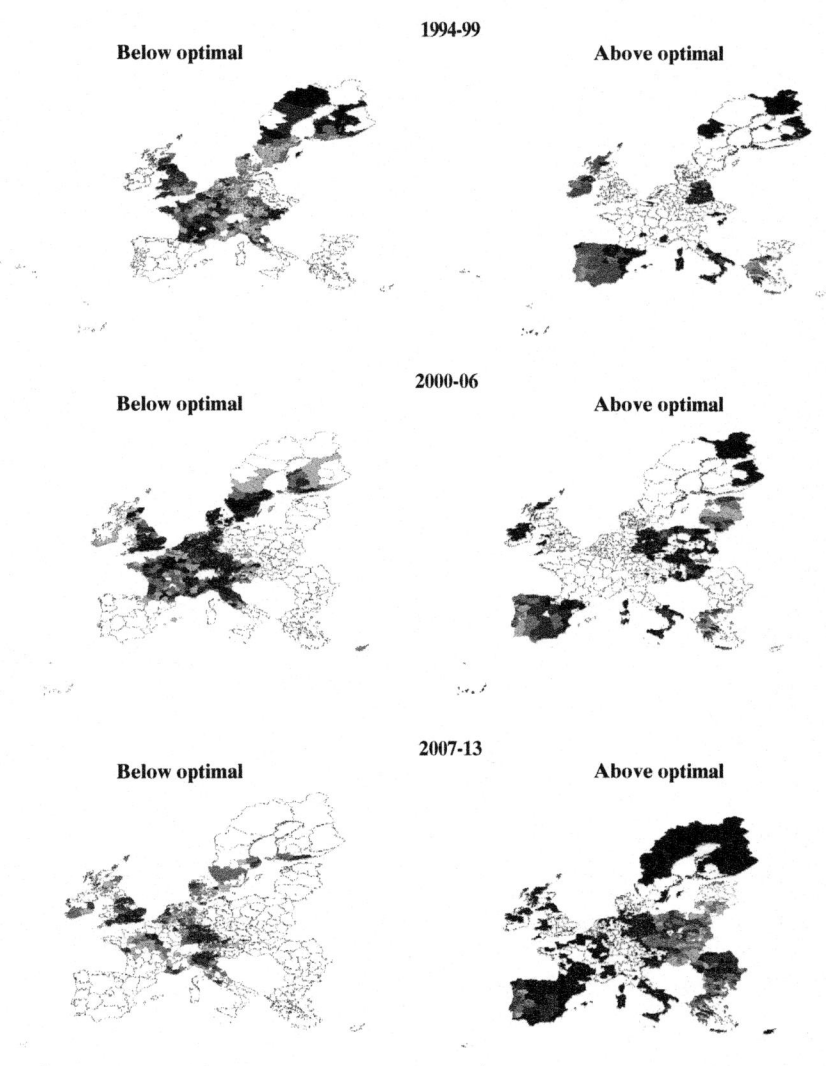

Fig. 2 Optimal transfer intensity. *Notes* Author's own maps. Transfer intensity below the optimal level are on the left, transfer intensities above the optimal level are shown on the right. For both deviations above and below the optimal level, lighter colors depict transfer intensities further from the optimum. For instance, dark on the left means below but close to the optimum transfer intensity. Light on the right mean transfer intensities far above the optimal level. Regions that are white in the left and right panel are those not belonging to the EU during the respective period or regions with missing data

Table 3 Distribution of annual transfers in the EU as a whole and in the UK—(1994–2013)

	Mean	SD	Min	Max
	(1)	(2)	(3)	(4)
European Union (EU)				
Annual expenditure per initial GDP (1994–1999)	0.007	0.017	0.0000171	0.29
Annual expenditure per initial GDP (2000–2006)	0.005	0.008	1.73e–06	0.09
Annual expenditure per initial GDP (2007–2013)	0.005	0.01	5.49e–07	0.07
Share of regions receiving transfers (1994–1999)	0.90			
Share of regions receiving transfers (2000–2006)	0.77			
Share of regions receiving transfers (2007–2013)	0.99			
United Kingdom (UK)				
Annual expenditure per initial GDP (1994–1999)	0.003	0.004	0.000427	0.018
Annual expenditure per initial GDP (2000–2006)	0.002	0.001	0.0000181	0.007
Annual expenditure per initial GDP (2007–2013)	0.0005	0.0009	2.63e–06	0.005
Share of regions receiving transfers (1994–1999)	1			
Share of regions receiving transfers (2000–2006)	0.77			
Share of regions receiving transfers (2007–2013)	1			

Notes Transfer intensity is defined as total annual expenditure over all Structural and Cohesion Fund transfers as a share of GDP in the initial year of the respective programming phase
Source Authors' own calculations

spending category in the EU's Regional Policy budget—is below average in the UK.

Figure 2 provides information on the relative effectiveness of funding across regions. We perform two separate estimations to account for the fact that the last programming period, 2007–2013, was affected by the financial crisis. First, we pool data from 1994–1999 and 2000–2006 as in Becker et al. (2012) to estimate dose-response functions that replicate their results. Second, we pool data from 2000–2006 and 2007–2013 to produce analogous dose-response function estimates. In all cases, dose-response functions try to condition out observable differences between regions other than the ones related to the transfer intensity and thereby to isolate the causal effect of the transfer intensity on economic outcomes. For an interpretation of the figures, the following background information is important. First, since the regional definition of NUTS3 regions changes over time, the regional definitions are made homogeneous for the couples of periods 1994–1999 and 2000–2006 on the one hand and 2000–2006 and 2007–2013 on the other hand. Hence, we need to draw separate maps for 1994–1999, 2000–2006 (both based on Becker et al. 2012) and 2007–2013. Second, we use the same software and routine to estimate the dose-response function as in Becker et al. (2012) for 1994–1999 and 2000–2006 on the one hand and for 2000–2006 and 2007–2013 on the other hand. Third, we determine the level of the *optimal transfer intensity*—i.e. the one where one Euro of funding generates exactly one Euro of GDP. At lower transfer-intensity levels, increasing transfers would have generated more than a one-for-one effect on GDP in 1994–1999 and 2000–2006 according to Becker et al. (2012). At higher transfer-intensity levels than the optimum, increasing transfers would have generated less than a one-for-one effect on GDP in 1994–1999 and 2000–2006 according to Becker et al. (2012). The same is true for the period 2007–2013 as it turns out. However, while the optimum transfer-intensity level was estimated at about 0.4% of NUTS3-recipient-region GDP for 1994–1999 and 2000–2006 in Becker et al. (2012), it is estimated at about 0.25% for the more recent sample period 2000–2006 and 2007–2013 together, here. For practical purposes, we use the optimum level of 0.4% for 1994–1999 and 2000–2006 and 0.25% just for 2007–2013 in the figures. This can be rationalized, as also other results suggest that the response to funding has changed during the years of the Economic and Financial Crisis which affects the period 2007–2013.

The left and right panels of Fig. 2 point to NUTS3 regions with a transfer intensity that is below and above the period-specific optimum level, respectively. Moreover, we generally draw regions darker for transfer intensities which are closer to the period-specific optimum level.

Hence, darker regions are ones with a transfer intensity that is relatively close to 0.4% in 1994–1999 and 2000–2006 and close to 0.25% in 2007–2013, while light colours refer to regions with a transfer intensity that is very distant from the optimum transfer intensity. According to the results, much could be gained in terms of efficiency, if transfers to light regions in the left panel would be expanded at the cost of ones to light regions in the right panel.

5 Selected examples of EU regional transfers in the UK

Some selected examples of projects funded from the EU Regional Policy budget in the UK are Birmingham's International Convention Centre, roads in the Scottish Highlands, and the upgrade of Liverpool's John Lennon airport. Also, many UK firms have benefited from EU transfers over the last decades, as widely documented.

The fact that EU Regional Policy overall has generated positive growth effects, and that the effects on UK Objective 1 regions have largely been in line with those on average EU Objective 1 regions does not mean that all is well and that EU transfers should continue without any changes. In fact, an independent report focusing on the evaluation of the Cornwall and Isles of Scilly 2007–2013 European Regional Development Fund (ERDF) by AMION Consulting (2015) found that 3557 jobs were created in Cornwall, well short of the targeted 10,000 jobs. The report concludes (p. 6) that there is a "significant projected under-performance of the Programme in achieving its target results regarding jobs, Gross Value Added (GVA) and private sector investment". This particular case of under-performance can probably be explained by the Financial Crises which hit the UK just after the ERDF targets for Cornwall were set, but it goes to show that EU Regional Funds were and are, of course, not a magic bullet.

It is also important to note the following: while EU Regional Funds are assigned following rules agreed by EU member states, their spending is nationally administered. So, the potential ineffectiveness of EU funding in UK or EU regions is not to be blamed on "Brussels", except maybe for a potential lack of rigorous evaluation in past decades before the institution of an Evaluation Unit in the European Commission.

For comparison, it is interesting to note the effectiveness of a prominent *domestic* regional policy in the UK as a benchmark. Einiö and Overman (2016) recently evaluated the UK's Local Enterprise Growth Initiative (LEGI), which spent 418 million pounds on 30 deprived areas during the period 2006–2011 (DCLG 2010). This was a major funding programme to support local businesses. Eligibility for the programme was based on a deprivation index rank rule: an eligible area had to rank 50th or below against at least one of a set of predetermined deprivation indices. Einiö and Overman use these features of the programme to identify the causal effects on employment, net business creation and unemployment. While this place-based policy helped businesses in supported regions, the benefit came at the expense of businesses in neighbouring regions. Criticizing the EU is one thing. Doing better is another thing.

In summary, EU Regional Policy transfers to the UK have been substantial, and growth effects similar to those in the rest of EU recipient regions. Still, EU funding sometimes achieved less than targeted, especially during the 2007–2013 programming period when the effectiveness of EU Regional Policy was hampered all over the EU. EU regional policy is not a magic bullet, and neither are domestically designed policies in the UK and elsewhere. Yet, funded regions clearly crave for the regional transfers, as the case of Cornwall shows, where NUTS2 boundaries were changed in order for Cornwall to become eligible for EU funding. Will UK regions currently receiving EU funding lose out after Brexit?

6   UK Regional Policy After Brexit: Speculations Based on Past Evidence

The question of how Brexit will affect regional policy is interesting. Clearly, at this point the answer to this question is even more uncertain than the one to the question of how exactly Brexit will affect the UK macro economy, although most established economists predict that the UK economy as a whole will not gain from Brexit.

The reason is that it is unclear what would replace EU funding. From the viewpoint of a UK region that currently benefits from EU funding, what are its future prospects of being supported? After Brexit, will Cornwall continue to be supported at the same level as before? Or did EU funding serve a purpose because rule-based transfers of EU money in the UK were less controversial than money distributed by Westminster? A similar uncertainty surrounds EU agricultural policy. Channelling transfers via the Brussels budget is an elegant way to "hide" transfers to farmers. Will the UK government continue to support British farmers to the same extent after Brexit as the EU did before Brexit? Noting that both EU regional funding and agricultural funding are highly regionally concentrated, the fiscal consequences of Brexit are concentrated in certain areas. As argued by the Centre for Economic Reform (2014, p. 86), "people in those areas will urge Westminster to replace EU funds with national spending if the UK leaves the Union".

How UK regions that are about to lose EU funding will fare in the absence of this funding is up to their bargaining power and Westminster's goodwill. We can only speculate about the matter based on past experience.

What happened to UK regions that lost access to Objective 1 funding in the past? Did the UK government step up and provide regional support at the same or a lower level? In the case of regions in Scotland, Wales and in Northern Ireland, a comparison of domestic regional transfers with EU regional transfers is difficult if not impossible, due to devolution, which brings in an additional layer of regional redistribution: e.g. from Westminster to Edinburgh and from there within Scotland.

For this reason, let us elaborate on two case studies of English Objective 1 regions: South Yorkshire which had held Objective 1 status only from 2000–2006, but neither before nor after that; and Cornwall and the Isles of Scilly (for short, just "Cornwall") which had gained[2] Objective 1 status in 2000–2006, maintained it in 2007–2013, and continued to hold it in the ongoing programming period 2014–2020. For this analysis, we use data on EU Structural Funds (including commitments) from the ONS Regional Trends Reports (Office for National Statistics 1995–2008).

While we have data on EU funding at the NUTS2 level, data on domestic regional funding for the UK is only available for the more aggregated NUTS1 level for the considered time span. In the case of South Yorkshire, this means that the UK data are measured for the NUTS1 region at the level of UKE ("Yorkshire and the Humber") which comprises East Yorkshire and Northern Lincolnshire (Humberside), North Yorkshire, South Yorkshire and West Yorkshire. In the case of Cornwall, the corresponding (more aggregated) NUTS1 region is UKK ("South West England") which comprises Gloucestershire, Wiltshire, Bristol, Dorset, Somerset, Cornwall and Devon.[3]

The following two graphs, at the NUTS1 level, are thus far from ideal. However, the figures show that EU regional funding gave a transfer boost

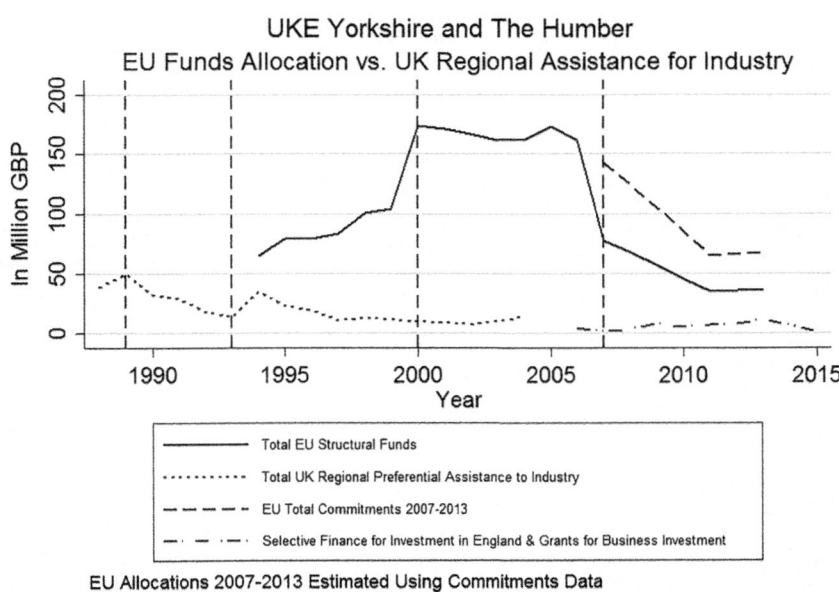

Fig. 3 South Yorkshire EU Objective 1 and Yorkshire and Humber UK domestic funding. *Notes* Author's own chart

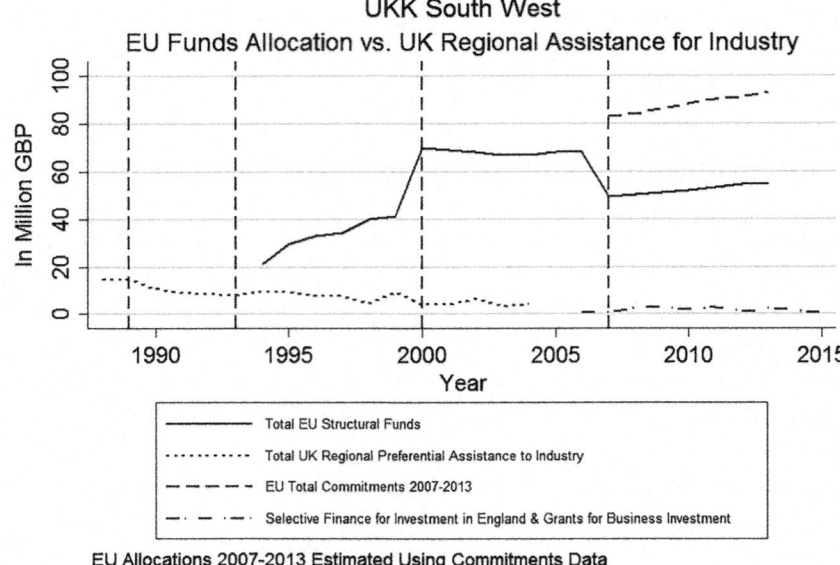

Fig. 4 Cornwall EU Objective 1 and South West UK domestic funding. *Notes* Author's own chart

to the two sample regions that went well beyond the domestic transfers these regions had received before.

South Yorkshire Looking at Fig. 3, when South Yorkshire lost Objective 1 status in 2006, the whole (aggregate) region of "Yorkshire and the Humber" lost a significant amount of EU funding and returned to the domestic funding level it had before the 2000–2006 period. At the time, the local press noted this as a crucial break in regional support for the region: see http://www.sheffieldtelegraph.co.uk/news/business/objective-1-bows-out-after-eight-years-of-investment-1-450485.

Cornwall It is noticeable that Cornwall was likely turned into a separate NUTS2 region not only because of Cornwall's push to be recognized as a cultural entity of its own, but also because Cornwall, being the poorer half of the combined NUTS2 region of Cornwall and Devon could expect to receive Objective 1 status after the split, as argued before. And, in fact, it did. Figure 4 shows how EU funding to the whole

Southwest NUTS1 region shot up after 2000, to a level far higher than domestic transfer schemes.

7 Conclusion

We looked at three important questions relating to EU Regional Policy and the UK. First, is the UK taxpayer money that is spent on EU Regional Policy, especially to the poorest regions of the EU, money well spent? The answer to this questions is multi-faceted:

- Objective 1 transfers to the poorest regions of the EU (i.e. regions with per-capita GDP of <75% the EU average) induce growth and income beyond a simple consumption effect: one Euro of transfers generates between 1.00 and 1.20 Euros on average. So, on average, Objective 1 transfers have been effective. Contrary to popular belief, money paid into the EU regional policy budget was not generally wasted.
- However, this average positive effect is not necessarily uniform across regions. Transfers affect regional per-capita-income growth quite differently, and in a systematic way: those regions receiving Objective 1 transfers that have a better educated workforce ("technological absorptive capacity") and/or better-run local government, i.e. less corruption and better local administration ("institutional absorptive capacity"), do better than the average recipient region, and regions below average in terms of education of the workforce and/or quality of local government, do not grow faster than regions that receive no transfers at all. This points to potential efficiency gains for future EU regional policy if EU regional transfers were targeted at improving absorptive capacity with beneficial long-run effects rather than just catching up in the short run.
- Regarding EU regional transfers as a whole more spending does not generally lead to higher economic benefits: some regions seem to struggle with the amount of transfers received and above a certain transfer intensity further additional growth is by no means ensured.

Again, future EU regional policy might consider capping transfers to avoid inefficiencies.

Second, have the UK's poorest regions, those receiving Objective 1 transfers, benefited from those transfers? We find that the generated effects in terms of growth and investment are similar to those of other EU recipient regions, so there is no UK specialism.

Third, what would replace EU Regional Policy if the UK left the EU? The answer to this question has to be speculative because there is no automatic domestic rule that kicks in for regions that no longer receive EU funding. We looked at case studies of UK regions that lost their Objective 1 status in the past, after they crossed the 75% threshold. In those historic cases, the UK national funding that replaced EU funding was substantially lower than what those regions had before. UK regions currently in receipt of substantial amounts of EU funding might also lose substantially after Brexit, unless they negotiate a Growth Deal with Westminster. Any such negotiation will likely be subject to political bargaining because other interest groups will also battle to get a share of Britain's contribution to the EU budget.

Notes

1. The only estimates coming up with overall economic *gains* from Brexit is from a group appropriately called *Economists for Brexit*.
2. Interestingly, this was the result of the split of the former combined NUTS2 region of Cornwall and Devon, which was above 75% of the EU average in terms of per-capita income, into Cornwall and Devon as two regions, with the poorer Cornwall falling below the 75% threshold.
3. We would have clearly preferred to single out UK domestic funding at exactly the same NUTS2 level, i.e., only for South Yorkshire and for Cornwall. The use of the more aggregate NUTS1 level constitutes a necessary compromise to depict EU funding in comparison to UK domestic transfer schemes. In the period 1988–2004, this is captured by the Government Regional Preferential Assistance to Industry measure, as reported in the ONS Regional Trends Reports. This is a composite measure, including assistance from (i) Regional Development Grants,

(ii) Regional Selective Assistance and (iii) Regional Enterprise Grants (and several other transfer schemes in the case of Wales and Scotland). After 2004, this aggregated data was no longer available, leading us to look at the main funding programmes instead. First, the Selective Finance for Investment in England (SFIE) scheme was active after 2006, providing financial assistance to industries in Great Britain. It was replaced by the Grants for Business Investment scheme in 2008, which was thereafter in effect until 2011. Data for both is taken from the "Industrial Development Act of 1982" Annual Reports (Department for Business Innovation and Skills 1982–2015).

Acknowledgements We thank the ESRC "UK in a Changing Europe" initiative for financial support.

References

AMION Consulting. (2015). *Cornwall and isles of scilly 2007–2013 ERDF convergence programme: Thematic evaluation.* http://erdfconvergence.org.uk/_userfiles/files/C&IoSERDF2000-2013EvaluationOverviewReport.pdf.

Becker, S. O., Egger, P. H., & von Ehrlich, M. (2010). Going NUTS: The effect of EU structural funds on regional performance. *Journal of Public Economics, 96*(9–10), 578–590.

Becker, S. O., Egger, P. H., & von Ehrlich, M. (2012). Too much of a good thing? On the growth effects of the EU's regional policy. *European Economic Review, 56*(4), 648–668.

Becker, S. O., Egger, P. H., & von Ehrlich, M. (2013). Going NUTS: The effect of EU structural funds on regional performance. *American Economic Journal: Economic Policy, 5*(4), 29–77.

Becker, S. O., Egger, P. H., & von Ehrlich, M. (2016). *Effects of EU regional policy: 1989–2013* (CAGE Online Working Paper Series No. 271).

Beugelsdijk, M., & Eijffinger, S. C. (2005). The effectiveness of structural policy in the European Union: An empirical analysis for the EU–15 in 1995–2001. *Journal of Common Market Studies, 43,* 37–51.

Boldrin, M., & Canova, F. (2001). Europe's regions—Income disparities and regional policies. *Economic Policy, 16*(32), 207–253.

Campos, N. F., Coricelli, F., & Moretti, L. (2014). *Economic growth and political integration: Estimating the benefits from membership in the European Union using the synthetic counterfactuals method* (CEPR Discussion Paper No. 9968).

Cappelen, A., Castellacci, F., Fagerberg, J., & Verspagen, B. (2003). The impact of EU regional support on growth and convergence in the European Union. *Journal of Common Market Studies, 41,* 621–644.

Centre for European Reform. (2014). *The economic consequences of leaving the EU: The final report of the CER commission on the UK and the EU single market.* http://www.cer.org.uk/sites/default/files/smc_final_report_june2014.pdf.

Crafts, N. (2012). British relative economic decline revisited: The role of competition. *Explorations in Economic History, 49*(1), 17–29.

Dall'erba, S., & Le Gallo, J. (2008). Regional convergence and the impact of structural funds over 1989–1999: A spatial econometric analysis. *Papers in Regional Science, 87,* 219–244.

DCLG. (2010). *National evaluation of the local enterprise growth initiative programme—appendices.* London: Department for Communities and Local Government.

Department for Business Innovation and Skills. (1982–2015). *Industrial development act of 1982 Annual Report.* London: The Stationery Office Limited.

Dhingra, S., & Sampson, T. (2016). *Life after BREXIT: What are the UK's options outside the European Union?* CEP Brexit Analysis No. 1. http://cep.lse.ac.uk/pubs/download/brexit01.pdf.

Dhingra, S., Ottaviano, G., Sampson, T., & Van Reenen, J. (2016). The UK Treasury analysis of 'The long-term economic impact of EU membership and the alternatives': CEP Commentary, CEP Brexit Analysis No. 4. http://cep.lse.ac.uk/pubs/download/brexit04.pdf.

Ederveen, S., Gorter, J., deMooij, R., & Nahuis, R. (2002). *Funds and games: The economics of European cohesion Policy.* Amsterdam: CPB & Koninklijke De Swart.

Ederveen, S., de Groot, H. L., & Nahuis, R. (2006). Fertile soil for structural funds? A panel data analysis of the conditional effectiveness of European cohesion policy. *Kyklos, 59,* 17–42.

Einiö, E., & Overman, H., G. (2016, February). *The (displacement) effects of spatially targeted enterprise initiatives: Evidence from UK LEGI* (SERC Discussion Paper No. 0191).

Midelfart-Knarvik, K. H., & Overman, H. G. (2002). Delocation and European integration—is structural spending justified? *Economic Policy, 17* (35), 323–359.

Mohl, P., & Hagen, T. (2010). Do EU structural funds promote regional growth? New evidence from various panel data approaches. *Regional Science and Urban Economics, 40*(5), 353–365.

Pain, N., & Young, G. (2004). The macroeconomic impact of UK withdrawal from the EU. *Economic Modelling, 21*(3), 387–408.

Pellegrini, G., & Cerqua, A. (2015, November 27). *Measuring the impact of intensity of treatment using RDD and covariates: The case of structural funds.* Paper presented at Rome workshop.

Pellegrini, G., Terribile, F., Tarola, O., Muccigrosso, T., & Busillo, F. (2013). Measuring the effects of European regional policy on economic growth: A regression discontinuity approach. *Papers in Regional Science, 92*(1), 217–233.

Sala-i-Martin, X. (1996). Regional cohesion: Evidence and theories of regional growth and convergence. *European Economic Review, 40,* 1325–1352.

The Office for National Statistics. (1995–2008). Regional trends. Basingstoke: Palgrave Macmillan.

UK Treasury. (2016). HM Treasury analysis: The long-term economic impact of EU membership and the alternatives.

Brexit and EU Regulation

John Springford

1 Introduction

Britain has been a comparatively economically liberal and sceptical participant in the EU's regulatory process, and many EU member-states have a greater appetite for regulating markets than the UK, which means that the British government must sometimes implement EU rules that are more restrictive than those it would have chosen itself. But the claim that leaving the EU's single market will liberate the supply-side of the British economy is wishful thinking. The truth is that the factors that weaken Britain's long-term economic growth are overwhelmingly domestic, not European; the impact on output from repealing European legislation would be minimal; and the economy's supply capacity would be impaired if divergent regulations between the EU and the UK curbed trade and investment.

The EU is to a large extent in the business of regulation, and some rules emanating from Brussels do indeed impose more costs than they confer benefits. For example, the cost of recycling waste electrical equipment, mandated by a 2012 directive, outweighs the savings from

J. Springford (✉)
Director of Research, Centre for European Reform, London, UK
e-mail: John@cer.org.uk

© The Author(s) 2017   **229**
N.F. Campos and F. Coricelli (eds.), *The Economics of UK–EU Relations*,
DOI 10.1007/978-3-319-55495-2_9

reduced landfill and recycled materials, according to an impact assessment by the British government.[1] And the Bank of England has found that capping bankers' bonuses at 100% of their annual salary has increased risk in the financial system: banks find it more difficult to slash salaries than bonuses in a downturn, which makes them more fragile.[2]

However, it is an extremely difficult task to calculate the economic effects of all EU rules to arrive at a 'net cost (or benefit) of Europe'. Some analysts have added up the costs and benefits of major EU regulations that can be found in UK impact assessments, in which civil servants attempt to quantify the economic impact of individual regulations. The think-tank Open Europe, for example, found that EU rules lead to marginally more benefits for the British economy than costs.[3] However, all impact assessments are uncertain estimations, and many do not calculate benefits, as these can be difficult to quantify.

Meanwhile, the method favoured by the EU's most trenchant critics can be crude: assign largely arbitrary, but invariably inflated costs to regulations; then imply that the UK would face none of these costs if it quit the EU.[4] It is a method designed to produce conclusions that have been determined before the exercise has been carried out.

The British debate about EU regulation accords with Dani Rodrik's globalisation 'trilemma'. Countries cannot pursue democracy, national self-determination and globalisation at the same time; one has to give.[5] The reason for this trilemma is that globalisation—that is, rapid growth in trade, as well as in capital and labour flows across national borders—requires countries to adopt common policies such as financial rules to govern capital flows across borders. Therefore, the democratic nation-state cannot simply tailor policies to domestic needs and preferences—a process which threatens democracy at the national level. To tackle this trilemma, governments have three choices. First, policy-making could move one level up, to a supranational democracy, with countries ceding national self-determination but preserving democracy and globalisation. Second, nation-states can act in ways that violate electorates' preferences in order to make their policies compatible with a globalised world. Or third, governments can limit the flow of goods, capital and people across their borders, and so preserve democracy at the level of the nation-state.

The EU is a regional form of high-intensity globalisation: a single market, common regulation, combined with, for some, a common currency. As a result, some policies—external trade agreements and some regulations—are entirely decided at the EU level. And, in terms of the single market at least, the EU and its member-states have ended up somewhere between Rodrik's first and second choice. The European Parliament is a supranational democratic institution in which MEPs, representing their constituents, amend and ratify the European Commission's proposed regulations and directives. The Council of Ministers and the European Council do the same, since ministers and heads of state of national governments vote on EU legislation or agree it by consensus. But, since 28 countries with varying political cultures are involved in the process, EU regulation is inevitably a compromise—and so the EU's member-states sometimes violate their electorates' preferences in pursuit of common rules, intended to reduce barriers to trade, investment and the movement of workers across national borders.

The 2016 referendum result showed that, alongside disatissfaction at high rates of immigration from newer EU member-states, the UK public were persuaded by the Leave camp's appeals to democracy and national self-determination. What is less clear, however, is whether the public understood—or if they did understand, agreed with—the economic rationale behind the EU's attempt to create common regulation. This chapter discusses whether the EU's single market process, launched in 1992, has done much to reduce the cost of trade in goods and services across the EU, and whether it has done much to boost trade flows. It also considers whether, if the UK decides to leave the single market as well as the EU, it would be something of a liberation to the supply-side of the British economy—a key argument of the Leave campaign. To understand whether an exit from the single market might reduce the cost of regulation, one must establish why regulations exist in the first place; appraise the extent to which the EU has a legitimate interest in regulation; honestly assess the effects of EU regulation on British economic performance; and consider whether the UK would escape the regulatory costs attributed to membership if the country chose to leave the EU.

1.1 Why the EU Regulates

Regulations can and do impose costs on companies, and ultimately on consumers (because companies often pass on these costs). When they are badly designed, the costs of such regulations can be unnecessary and damaging. But there are legitimate reasons why governments regulate markets. Markets are not perfect: they sometimes fail, producing sub-optimal outcomes. An unregulated market may, for example, generate negative externalities (such as pollution or congestion) because the social costs of activities are not borne fully by those who engage in them. In such cases, governments have a responsibility to intervene to correct the failure. If the end result is that a firm is made to internalise social costs which it had previously managed to externalise, the fact that its costs have risen is no bad thing.

The EU has employed three tools to boost trade. First, it eliminated tariffs on goods. Second, it established the right of companies and people to sell their goods, services or labour, or to invest, in other member-states —the so-called 'four freedoms'. This right is enforced by the European Commission and European Court of Justice, institutions tasked with preventing national governments from passing laws—or providing subsidies or tax relief—that give domestic companies or workers a competitive advantage against companies or workers from other countries. Third, it has sought to reduce the cost of potential exporters having to comply with 28 national sets of regulations. The EU creates minimum regulatory standards, and then requires all member-states to allow goods that comply with those standards to be sold unhindered across the single market. It also harmonises product regulations.

Thus the EU largely sets the common minimum standards that are necessary for mutual recognition—the animating principle of the single market—to work. This basic premise is widely misunderstood in the British debate. For example, one recommendation of the British government's 'Business taskforce on EU red tape', which was asked to find regulations to scrap, was to push for the full implementation of the EU's services directive.[6] But deepening the EU market for services would be impossible without more EU regulation. Services markets tend to be more highly regulated than markets in goods. Consumers find it more difficult to assess the quality of a lawyer than an apple before they make a purchase, so the state intervenes to ensure legal standards are high. Member-states would not allow foreign companies, operating under foreign rules, to provide services to their citizens without common standards at the EU level.

Confusion also reigns over the reach of EU regulation. Before the referendum, Business for Britain, a cross-party business campaign for a renegotiation of Britain's EU membership, suggested that UK companies that do not export to the rest of the EU should be exempted from EU regulation.[7] That would be unworkable: many UK firms who opt against exporting are still part of the single market: they compete for British customers with firms from elsewhere in the EU. Meanwhile, some companies do not export directly, but supply parts, components and services to firms that do. By exempting non-exporters from EU rules, the UK would effectively be withdrawing from the single market.

Another reason why the EU has a legitimate interest in regulation is that there are times when collective action at a European level may produce better outcomes than countries acting independently at a national level. In policy areas like climate change, for example, collective action at an EU level should, in principle at least, produce superior outcomes by reducing the opportunity for individual member-states to 'free ride'.

Nonetheless, the EU's member-states retain broad powers to regulate their economies. Some of the costs that firms complain about arise when national legislatures impose regulatory burdens over and above those required by EU legislation (a practice known as 'gold-plating'). And if the EU did not exist, member-states would have to make their own rules: it is misleading to imply that all the regulatory costs associated with EU legislation would simply disappear if the UK left the EU. British banks, for example, would not cease to be regulated. The regulatory burden on them might not even fall, because the era of 'light touch' financial regulation is over: UK standards are now often stricter than those required by the EU.[8]

In short, if a regulatory requirement in force in Britain is to count as a cost of EU membership, at least two conditions must be satisfied. First, it must be shown that its costs outweigh its benefits. And second, it must be proved that the UK would have no such requirements outside the EU.

1.2   Has the Single Market Programme Achieved Its Objectives?

How much of the economic integration between the UK and the EU is down to shared regulation, as opposed to the absence of tariffs—or geographic proximity? The Bertelsmann Foundation in Germany has found that the UK's GDP was 1% larger thanks to the EU's single market programme, which started in 1992.[9] For its part, the Centre for Economic Policy Research concluded that the EU's single market programme boosted EU GDP by 2.2%.[10] The European Commission estimates that the single market programme produced around 2% growth in EU output. Facing greater competition, companies cut margins by around 1%. Productivity in labour, capital and land use increased by half a percentage point.[11]

The single market programme, then, is likely to have modestly raised national incomes of the participating member-states a little. And it is possible to directly observe changes in trade costs over time, which offers some evidence of the single market programme's effectiveness. Economists at the World Bank have put together a database that measures how costly trade in goods is between countries.[12] Trade costs can come in various forms. One cost is taxes on imports: tariffs. Another arises from non-tariff barriers, like quotas restricting imports or national regulations that prevent imported goods, made to different standards, from being sold. Still another is distance. It costs money to transport goods from one country to another, so distant countries will tend to trade less than neighbouring ones.

Chart 1 shows the World Bank's estimates of trade costs between Britain, the EU, the rest of the OECD and the eight emerging economies with which Britain conducts most trade: China, India, South Africa, Russia, Nigeria, Brazil, Malaysia and Indonesia (listed in order of how much they trade with Britain). Britain's trade with non-European members of the OECD is more costly than it is with the EU: barriers to trade with these countries are equivalent to 98% of the value of the goods traded, compared to the EU's 85%. In other words, these trade costs would add 98 pence to the price of a good produced in Britain for £1. The cost of trade with emerging economies is higher still. And costs have fallen less with Britain's most important trade partners outside Europe—both developed and emerging—than with the EU since 1995, the first year for which there is data.

The cost of Britain's trade with the EU, on the other hand, dropped by 15 percentage points between 1995 and 2010—although the decline stopped after 2006. And since the EU is Britain's largest trading partner, this fall is more valuable than the smaller reduction in the cost of trade with the non-EU members of the OECD (trade costs with emerging economies have been static). Chart 2 shows by exactly how much. It weights trade costs between Britain and other countries by the amount of

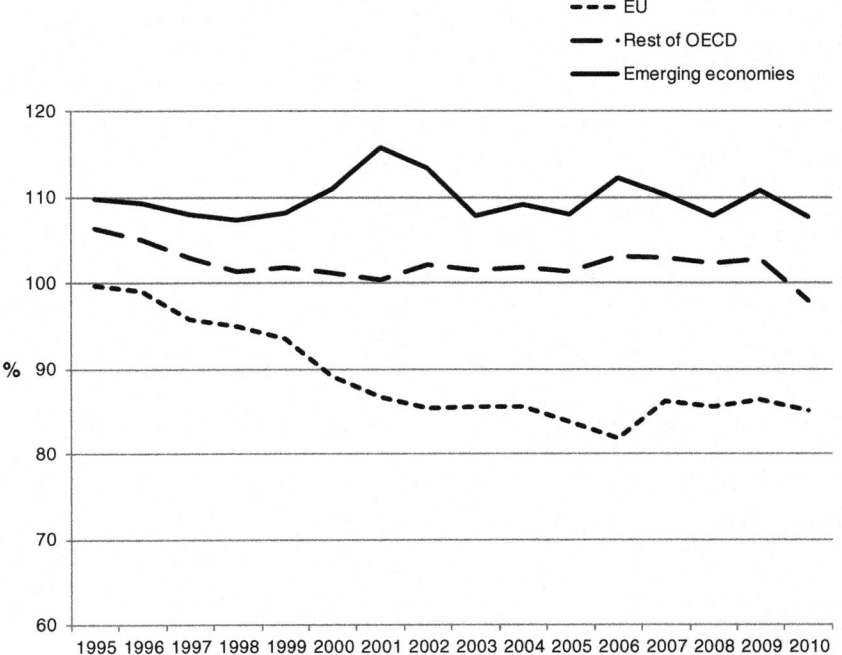

Chart 1 Trade costs between Britain and the EU, the rest of the OECD, and emerging economies. *Source* World Bank ESCAP dataset

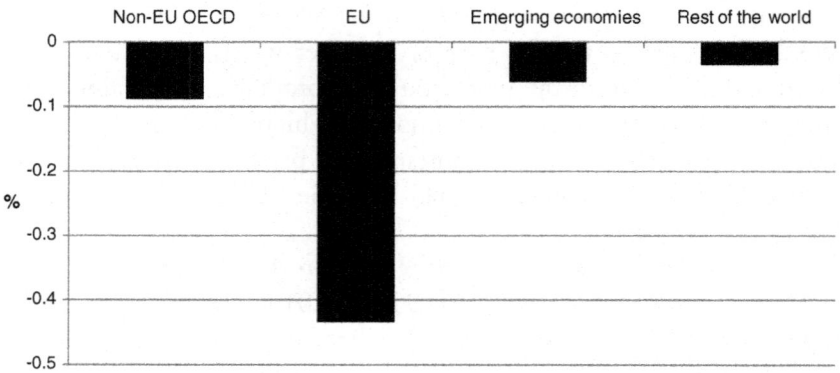

Chart 2 Annual average change in trade costs between Britain and the EU, the rest of the OECD, emerging economies and the rest of the world. *Source* World Bank ESCAP dataset

trade conducted with them. Since around a half of all Britain's trade is with the EU, that fall has cut the total cost of Britain's trade by 0.4 percentage points a year. The small declines in the cost of trade with the rest of the OECD, emerging economies and the rest of the world are less valuable, not only because they have been smaller, but also because Britain conducts less trade with those economies.

However, this is all about the past: one might argue that, after it left the EU, the UK could simply sign an FTA with the Union to secure the existing economic benefits of European integration. Although a Britain outside the EU might be able to negotiate such an agreement, British goods and services could only be sold in EU markets if they met European rules. If Britain's antipathy to EU rules led over time to its adopting different rules for products sold on the domestic market, trade costs with the EU would increase.

Consider an optimistic scenario after a British exit. The EU does not impose the common external tariff on Britain's goods, but trade costs do not fall as quickly with the EU as they had before, because Britain refuses to sign up to all future rules of the single market in order to secure access. And let us assume that the fall in trade costs forgone would only be worth 0.2 percentage points a year, since initiatives to deepen the single market have stalled since 2007. In 10 years, this would amount to a missed opportunity in the form of a 2 percentage point reduction in the total cost of Britain's trade.

Furthermore, it is unlikely that the UK can easily sign FTAs with the rest of the world to make up for any forgone reduction in the cost of trade with the EU. While Britain's trade with the rest of the world is growing faster than with the EU, Europe will continue to be its largest trade partner for decades to come. The rest of the world's contribution to the total reduction of Britain's trade costs was less than one-third that of the EU, between 1996 and 2010 (Chart 3). This means that any attempts to reduce the cost of trade through FTAs with non-EU countries would have to be very comprehensive to make up for forgone trade with Europe.

The preceding analysis has focussed on goods. But is there any evidence that the EU has boosted Britain's services exports? The UK has a strong comparative advantage in the trade of services, with its leading exports being financial and related business services, such as accountancy, law and consulting. In 2015, services exports made up 44% of Britain's total exports.[13] Free movement of capital and unrestricted trade in services constitute two of the four freedoms of the EU's single market, and the EU has made successive attempts to reduce barriers to trade in these areas. Have these attempts worked?

Britain's services trade with the EU has grown at 1.4 times the rate of EU economic growth since 1998 (see Chart 4)—a faster rate than with most other countries and regions. (Since fast-growing economies trade

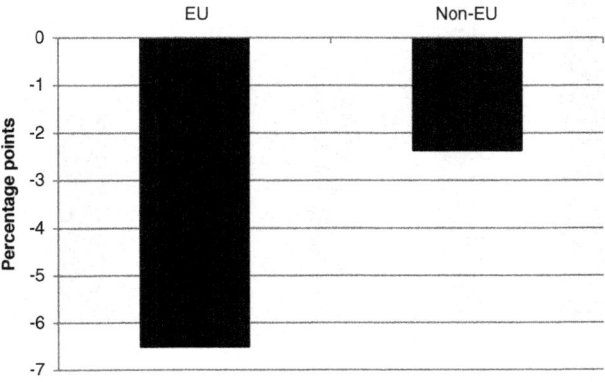

Chart 3 Countries' total contribution to falling UK trade costs, 1996–2010. *Sources* World Bank ESCAP database and ONS UK trade data

more with each other, the only way to tell whether efforts to free up trade are working is to compare the rates of growth in services trade and GDP.) Services trade with the US grew at a similar rate. Britain's services trade with emerging economies rose rapidly between 1998 and 2015, but trade with these countries did not grow at a faster rate than GDP.

However, while Britain's services trade has grown faster with the EU than with any other region, it is not especially impressive. Given the EU's attempts to liberalise services, trade might be expected to be growing at a faster pace. While the EU has made some progress in lowering barriers to trade—the 2004 services directive reduced them by about one-third—there is more that could be done.[14]

The rationale for the fourth freedom of the single market—the free movement of capital—is twofold. First, by allowing financial institutions to move into new markets, it is intended to raise the level of competition, and so drive down prices for consumers. Second, international capital flows allow savings to flow to where they may be most profitably invested, giving savings-constrained but potentially fast-growing countries more capital to invest.[15] How much integration has occurred in retail and inter-bank markets, and with what economic consequences?

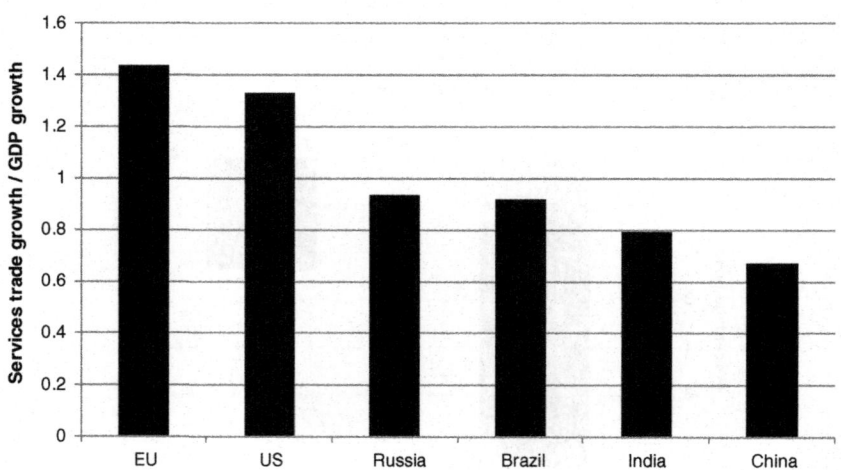

Chart 4 UK services trade growth with major partners, 1998 to 2015. *Source* ONS Pink Book and IMF World Economic Output database

Declining transport and communication costs have driven globalisation. But their impact across economic sectors has not been uniform. In the manufacturing sector, for example, supply chains have displayed a tendency towards increased geographical dispersal across the globe. In the financial sector, by contrast, the reverse has often been the case: lower communications costs have coincided with financial services—and wholesale financial services in particular—becoming increasingly concentrated in a small number of 'global cities'.[16] The City of London has been one of the principal beneficiaries of this trend.

For Britain, the biggest impact of the single market in services and capital has been on the City of London as an international financial centre. The development of the single market, as well as the reduction in barriers to capital flows across the developed world, led to larger cross-border flows of savings looking for investments, and the growth of European bond and equity markets. (The British government and its officials were leading advocates for the single market programme, and its architects: the advantages of a liberalised European financial system for the City of London were obvious.) UK-based banks now preside over a quarter of all EU banking assets.[17]

As well as being the largest global financial centre in the EU, the City of London is also at the centre of the eurozone's financial system. Over the last economic cycle, the City integrated faster with the EU than with markets elsewhere. Chart 5 shows British banks' lending to the EU, the US, Japan and emerging and developing economies.[18] UK-based banks built up heavy exposures to both the eurozone and other EU member-states, with the scale of flows growing much faster than eurozone or EU GDP between 1999 and 2008. The financial integration between the UK and the eurozone was five times greater than with the US, adjusted for economic size, in the depths of the euro crisis in 2012.

In sum, the evidence suggests that the single market programme has achieved some of its aims—although the degree of integration in goods markets has been markedly higher than that achieved in services sectors. The result has been a modest boost to UK national income, and to that of the EU as a whole.

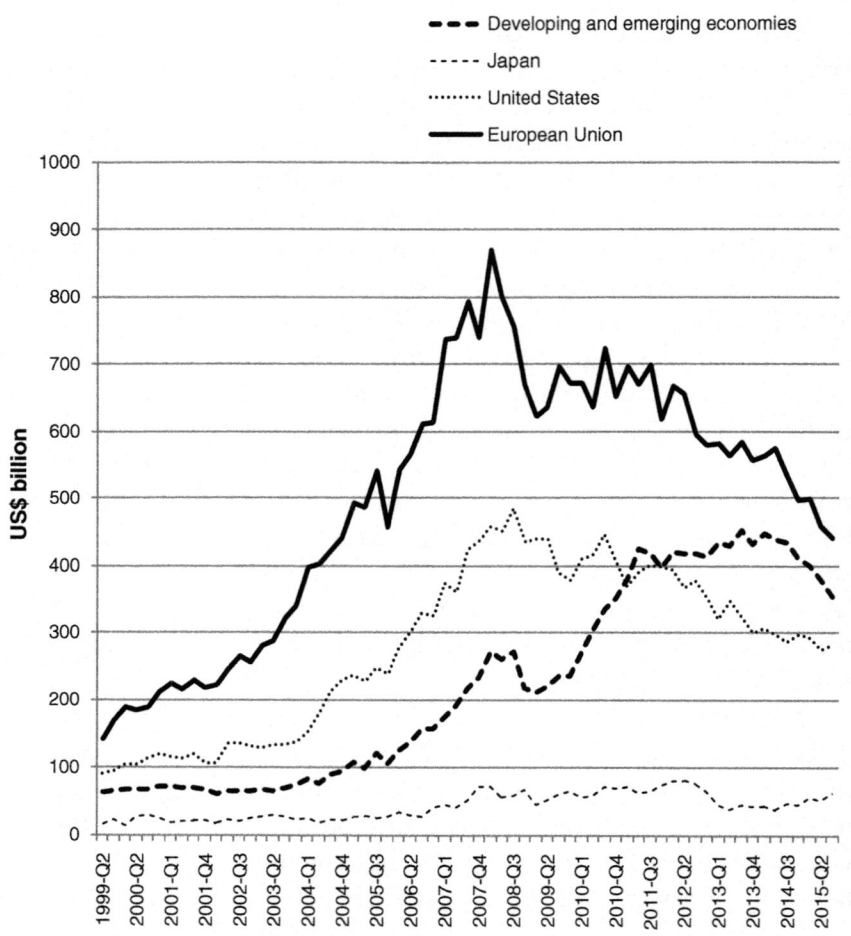

Chart 5 UK banks' international assets. *Source* Bank of International Settlements

1.3 The Gains from 'de-Europeanising Britain'

It follows, then that the gains from 'de-Europeanising Britain' are unlikely to be as large as British critics of EU regulation imply—and, if British and EU regulation after Brexit diverges in a manner that raises trade costs, national income is likely to be lower than would otherwise be the case, not higher. The evidence that follows suggests that the EU does not impose rigid harmonisation upon its member-states economies; some of its most iconic directives, such as the 'working time directive', are not as costly as its opponents argue; the largest supply-side constraints on the British economy are the result of domestic policy; and Britain, out of necessity, is likely to retain many EU rules even after it leaves the Union.

After Brexit, the UK could in theory be freed to regulate its own product and labour markets as it sees fit (although if it wanted to continue to export to the continent, its firms would have to match many European standards). There may be some benefits from less costly rules in some sectors. But the comparative indices of the OECD for product and labour market regulation show that British markets are already among the least regulated in the developed world.

Chart 6 shows the overall level of product market regulation for the UK, the EU and the OECD. British markets for goods and services are the second least regulated in the OECD, behind the Netherlands, another EU member-state. Rules at the EU level are designed to create common standards in order to make products more tradable: a lawn-mower made in the UK can be sold in Germany without having to be manufactured according to German specifications, for example. But the chart shows that EU rules do not appear to impose rigid harmonisation upon the union as a whole: under EU directives, member-states are able to impose higher standards on their own firms if they wish, and over time, other member-states have moved towards Britain's liberal approach, rather than the other way round. It is hard to argue that Britain's product and services markets are highly regulated as a result of EU membership.

The same story broadly holds true for the labour market (see Chart 7). The OECD's indices of employment protection legislation show a greater level of diversity among the countries surveyed, with continental European countries embracing markedly higher levels of employment protection than the English-speaking countries outside Europe. So where does this leave the UK? The answer is that membership of the EU does not prevent the UK from belonging firmly to the Anglophone camp. According to the OECD's indices, employment protection legislation is only slightly more restrictive in the UK than it is in the US or

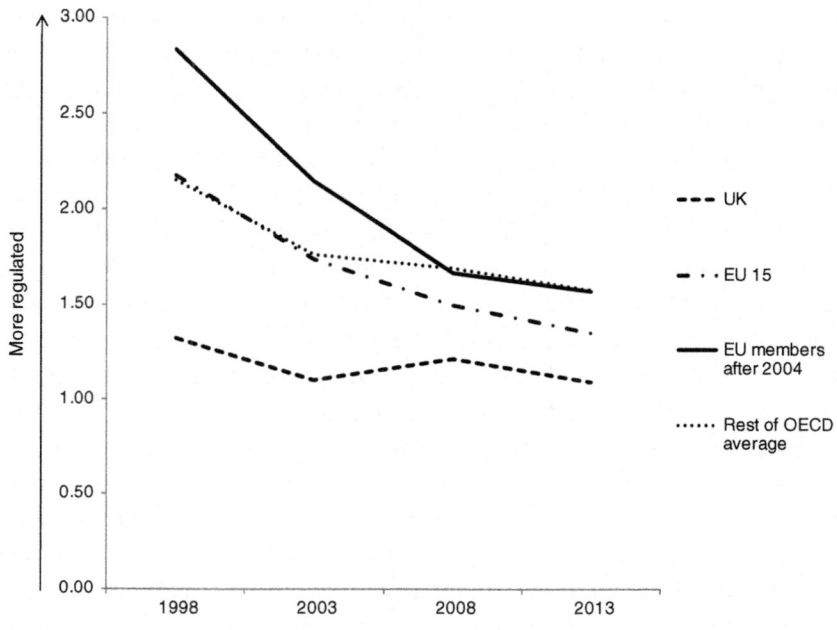

Chart 6 Levels of product market regulation. *Source* OECD

Canada, and less so than in Australia. It is, of course, much less restrictive than in continental European countries like France or Spain.

Some totemic EU rules, such as the 'working time directive', have a surprisingly limited impact. This directive violates the principle of subsidiarity: there was no need to regulate working hours or conditions at EU rather than national level, because there was little evidence that EU member-states were trying to improve economic competitiveness by driving down labour standards. Working hours across the EU were in decline even before the introduction of the directive.[19] Nonetheless, the working time directive's negative effects are marginal at best, not least because of the opt outs the UK has negotiated.[20] Chart 8 shows how many British people work more than 40 h per week. There is a spike at 40 h: 14% of British workers work 8 h a day. There are further spikes at 45, 50, 55 h and so on (because people tend to work 9, 10 or 11 h days, 5 days a week). But there is also a spike at 48 h—the working time limit under the directive. This is evidence that it has an impact on the labour

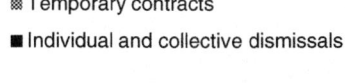

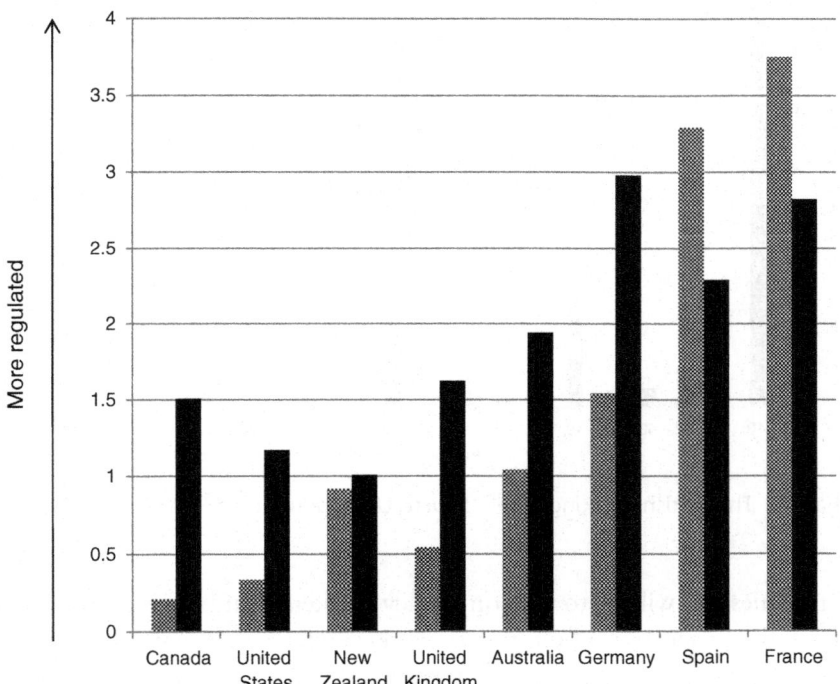

Chart 7 Levels of employment protection. *Source* OECD

market: there is no other reason why a larger proportion of people work 48 h rather than 46. But the spike is small, making up only 1.5% of workers. It follows that the gains in economic output that would flow from the abolition of the working time directive would be small: at best, 1.5% of British workers may work a few more hours a week.

The other bugbear, the Agency Workers Directive, has also had a surprisingly modest impact. The rules, which came into force in 2011, give employment agency workers the right to the same pay, holidays and working conditions as equivalent permanent workers once they have worked for the same company for 12 weeks. Before it came into force, businesses and the Conservative leadership warned that it would make

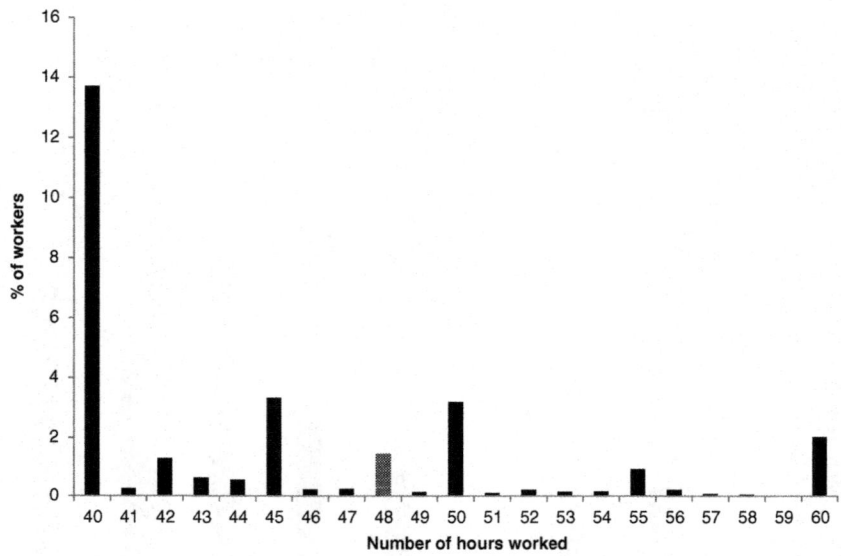

Chart 8 The British working week. *Source* UK Labour Force Survey, Q1-Q4 2013

companies less willing to take on agency workers. But between 2011 and 2015, the proportion of temporary workers who found work through an agency grew from 19 to 20%: the regulations did not lead employers to switch from agency temps to other temporary workers.[21] Chart 9 shows that agency employment continued to climb after the rules came into force. The chart also shows that businesses continued to make use of a loophole that allows an exemption from the right to equal pay if workers are formally employed by the agency, not the company they are working for. Two-thirds of agency workers were employed by agencies, not employers. The largest potential cost of the regulations—equal pay— therefore only applies to a minority of agency temps.

All this suggests that the most valid criticism one can make of the Working Time and Agency Workers directives is that, thanks to opt outs and loopholes, they fail to meet their stated objectives.

Alongside its labour and product market indices, the OECD has compiled an index of the quality of countries' regulatory regimes

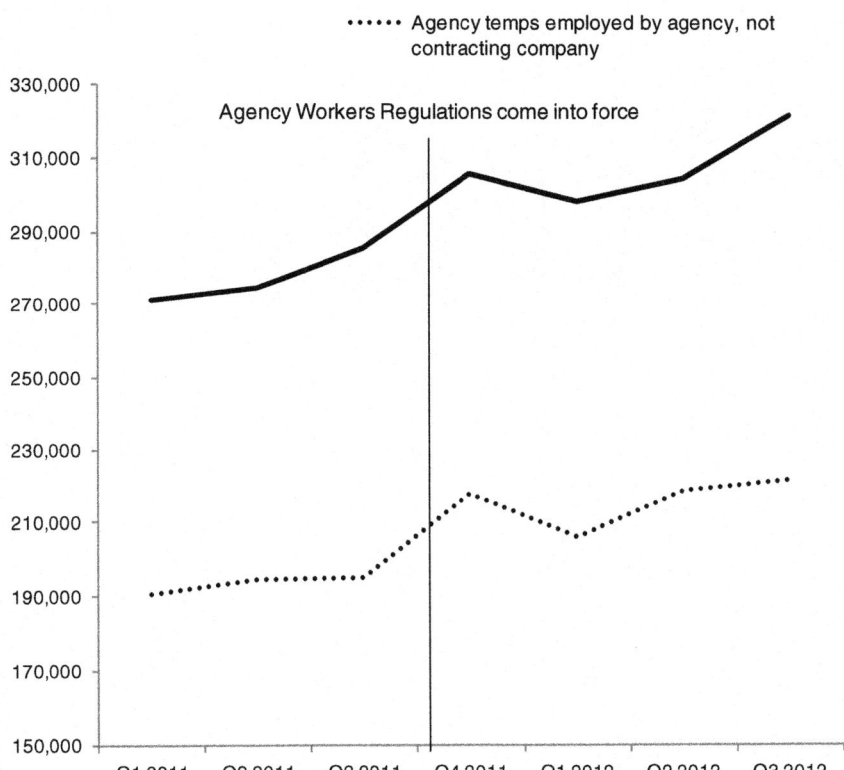

Chart 9 The impact of the agency workers directive. *Source* Chris Forde, 'The effects of Agency Workers Regulations on agency and employer practice', ACAS, 2014

(Chart 10). The OECD tested the European Commission's rule-making process alongside those of other countries, and found that it is of better quality than the OECD average—and similar to that of UK and Australia, which the OECD ranks highest. There can be little doubt that some proposals are forced through the EU's legislative machinery without proper assessment of the potential costs, but it is far from clear, on the basis of the OECD's index at least, that the EU does this more than the UK itself.

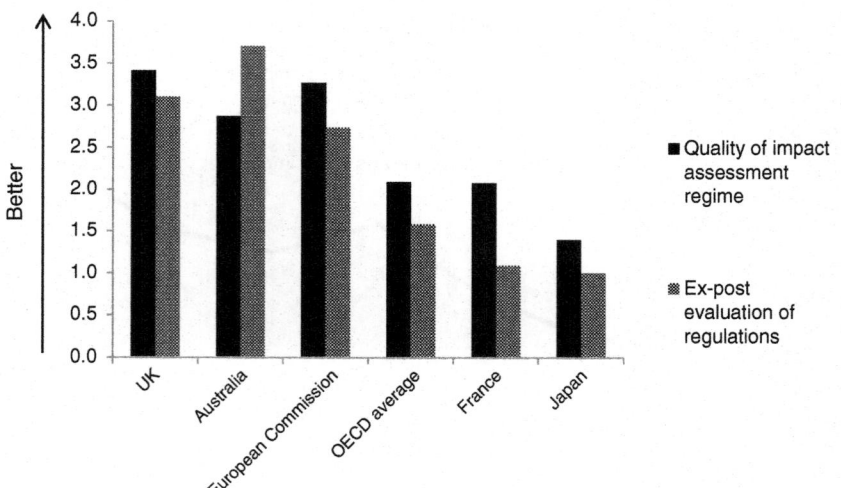

Chart 10 The quality of regulatory regimes. *Source* OECD

At a macroeconomic level, then, any gains from leaving the EU are likely to be limited: a bonfire of European rules would not transform Britain's economic prospects. European rules are not major supply-side constraints upon the British economy: according to the OECD, the largest of these constraints are the result of poor domestic policy.[22] The OECD is especially critical of Britain's rigid planning rules and its restrictions on making land available for development. These rules help to explain why, despite rapid growth in the population, housing construction is running at half the level of the 1960s; why the average size of new homes built is smaller than anywhere else in the EU; why office rents are the highest in the EU; and why Britain's transport infrastructure is so congested and expensive to build.[23]

The OECD also criticises Britain's education system, which is a vital public good, given the importance of human capital to economic prosperity. The UK's record in this area is patchy. It has assets, such as the best of its universities, which are world class. But its rates of literacy and numeracy at age 15 are only around the EU average, as are its rates of graduation from secondary education. Add to this the longstanding weaknesses in vocational training, and the result is that Britain has a comparatively large number of people with low skills—a failing that constrains Britain's labour supply to a far greater degree than EU employment rules.

Is it not possible that the UK could become more attractive as an investment location after Brexit? Outside the Union, would the British authorities not be free to reduce the cost of doing business in the UK, by lowering social and environmental standards, for example? Britain would certainly be freer to introduce less onerous regulatory requirements for new technologies, such as nano-technologies, the life sciences, genetically modified agriculture, space vehicles and interactive robots. This could increase the attractiveness of the UK as an investment location for these sorts of activities.[24]

There may, therefore, be some gains from more relaxed standards in particular sectors, especially in technologies that may drive up productivity. But any small benefits that arose from better regulation must be set against the costs incurred by British exporters and the loss of foreign investment.

Besides, it is far from certain that Britain will reduce most environmental and social standards after withdrawal. After all, some environmental standards in the UK are more stringent than those required by the EU. Britain has, for example, introduced a far more ambitious system of carbon pricing than that countenanced by the EU as a whole. And any UK government would face fierce domestic opposition to further erosion of labour and social standards. It could, of course, choose to live without any equivalent to the EU's working time directive, but it would be a brave government that explained to Britons why they should lose their statutory right to 4 weeks' paid holiday a year.

Brexit will force the British government to choose either lose further sovereignty in order to maintain single market access—or gain power over regulation and lose that access. If it seeks a close economic relationship with the EU, Britain will have to sign up to many of the EU's rules. As a non-participant in the EU's institutions, it will have little say over the rules' drafting—and without the UK's liberal principles informing the regulation-setting process, EU rules may be more restrictive than they are now. If it leaves the single market entirely, the British government will be unconstrained by EU regulations and directives, but will face higher barriers to trade with the EU. The politics points in one direction and the economics in another: the British government faces a Herculean labour to satisfy both.

Notes

1. Department of Business, Innovation and Skills, 'Waste electrical and electronic equipment system impact assessment', October 2013.
2. Marilena Angeli and Shahzad Gitay, 'Bonus regulation: Aligning reward with risk in the banking sector', Bank of England Quarterly Bulletin, Q4 2015.
3. Stephen Booth and others, 'Still out of control? Measuring eleven years of EU regulation', Open Europe, June 2010.
4. Tim Congdon, 'How much does the EU cost Britain?', UK Independence Party, 2012 and Taxpayers' Alliance, 'The great European rip-off: a background note explaining the new estimated total cost of the EU', March 2009.
5. Dani Rodrik, 'The future of European democracy', Institute of Advanced Studies, December 2014. The argument is presented in depth in Dani Rodrik,' The globalization paradox: democracy and the future of the world economy', W.W. Norton, February 2011.
6. UK Department of Business, Innovation and Skills, 'Cut EU red tape: Report from the Business Taskforce', February 2014.
7. Business for Britain, 'Setting out the British option: Liberating 95 per cent of UK businesses from EU red tape', January 2014.
8. Philip Whyte, 'Britain, Europe, the City of London: Can the triangle be managed?', Centre for European Reform, July 2012.
9. Bertelsmann Stiftung, '20 Jahre Binnenmarkt: Wachstumseffekte der zunehmenden europäischen Integration', 2014.
10. Centre for Economic Policy Research, 'Twenty years on: The UK and the future of the single market', 2012.
11. Fabienne Ilzkovitz and others, 'Steps towards a deeper economic integration: The internal market in the 21st century—A contribution to the Single Market Review', European Commission, European Economy Economic Papers, January 2007.
12. World Bank, ESCAP International Trade Costs dataset. http://databank.worldbank.org/data/reports.aspx?source=escap-world-bank-international-trade-costs

13. Office of National Statistics, 'UK trade: June 2016', Statistical bulletin, August 9, 2016.
14. John Springford, 'How to build EU services markets', Centre for European Reform, October 2012.
15. See, for example, Dirk Schoenmaker and Wolf Wagner, 'The impact of cross-border banking on financial stability', Tinbergen Institute Discussion Paper, 2011; Claudia Buch and others, 'Cross-border diversification in bank asset portfolios', International Finance, 2009; and Barba Navaretti and others,' Multinational banking in Europe: Financial stability and regulatory implications', Economic Policy, 2010.
16. Saskia Sassen, 'The global city: New York, London, Tokyo', Princeton University Press, 1991.
17. International Monetary Fund, 'Technical note on financial integration and fragmentation in the European Union', March 2013.
18. By controlling for GDP growth, this provides a more accurate assessment of financial integration than gross figures.
19. European Trade Union Confederation, 'Trends in working time', 2010 (European Trade Union Confederation 2010).
20. Katinka Barysch, 'The working time directive: What's all the fuss about?', Centre for European Reform, April 2013.
21. Office of National Statistics, 'Temporary employees' data, November 2015.
22. OECD, 'Going for growth country notes: United Kingdom', 2013 (Organisation of Economic Co-operation and Development 2013).
23. Simon Tilford, 'Why British prosperity is hobbled by a rigged land market', Centre for European Reform, 2013.
24. David Willetts, 'Eight great technologies', Policy Exchange 2013.

Bibliography

Marilena Angeli and Shahzad Gitay, 'Bonus regulation: Aligning reward with risk in the banking sector', Bank of England Quarterly Bulletin, Q4 2015.
Katinka Barysch, 'The working time directive: What's all the fuss about?', Centre for European Reform, April 2013.
Stephen Booth and others, 'Still out of control? Measuring eleven years of EU regulation', Open Europe, June 2010.

Claudia Buch and others, 'Cross-border diversification in bank asset portfolios', International Finance, 2009.

Business for Britain, 'Setting out the British option: Liberating 95 per cent of UK businesses from EU red tape', January 2014.

Centre for Economic Policy Research, 'Twenty years on: The UK and the future of the single market', 2012.

Tim Congdon, 'How much does the EU cost Britain?', UK Independence Party, 2012.

European Trade Union Confederation, 'Trends in working time', 2010.

Fabienne Ilzkovitz and others, 'Steps towards a deeper economic integration: The internal market in the 21st century - A contribution to the Single Market Review', European Commission, European Economy Economic Papers, January 2007.

International Monetary Fund, 'Technical note on financial integration and fragmentation in the European Union', March 2013.

Barba Navaretti and others, 'Multinational banking in Europe: Financial stability and regulatory implications', Economic Policy, 2010.

Office of National Statistics, 'UK trade: June 2016', Statistical bulletin, August 9, 2016.

Organisation of Economic Co-operation and Development, 'Going for growth country notes: United Kingdom', 2013.

Dani Rodrik, 'The globalization paradox: democracy and the future of the world economy', W.W. Norton, February 2011.

Dani Rodrik, 'The future of European democracy', Institute of Advanced Studies, December 2014.

Saskia Sassen, 'The global city: New York, London, Tokyo', Princeton University Press, 1991.

Dirk Schoenmaker and Wolf Wagner, 'The impact of cross-border banking on financial stability', Tinbergen Institute Discussion Paper, 2011.

John Springford, 'How to build EU services markets', Centre for European Reform, October 2012.

Bertelsmann Stiftung, '20 Jahre Binnenmarkt: Wachstumseffekte der zunehmenden europäischen Integration', 2014.

Taxpayers' Alliance, 'The great European rip-off: a background note explaining the new estimated total cost of the EU', March 2009.

Simon Tilford, 'Why British prosperity is hobbled by a rigged land market', Centre for European Reform, 2013.

UK Department of Business, Innovation and Skills, 'Cut EU red tape: Report from the Business Taskforce', February 2014.

UK Department of Business, Innovation and Skills. (2013, October). Waste electrical and electronic equipment system impact assessment.

Philip Whyte, 'Britain, Europe, the City of London: Can the triangle be managed?', Centre for European Reform, July 2012.

David Willetts, 'Eight great technologies', Policy Exchange, 2013.

Deep Integration and UK–EU Trade Relations

Alen Mulabdic, Alberto Osnago and Michele Ruta

1 Introduction

What is the impact of undoing trade agreements on trade? In this article, we try to address this question by focusing on the effect that EU membership had on trade of the UK, most notably with its European partners, and then use this information to assess the future of UK–EU

The findings interpretations and conclusions expressed in this paper are entirely those of the authors. They do not necessarily represent the views of the International Bank for Reconstruction and Development/World Bank and its affiliated organizationsor those of the Executive Directors of the World Bank or the governments they represent.

A. Mulabdic (✉)
Economist, Trade and Competitiveness Global Practice,
World Bank Group, Washington, D.C., USA
e-mail: amulabdic@worldbank.org

A. Osnago
Policy Analyst, Trade and Competitiveness Global Practice,
World Bank Group, Washington, D.C., USA
e-mail: aosnago@worldbank.org

M. Ruta
Lead Economist, Trade and Competitiveness Global Practice,
World Bank Group, Washington, D.C., USA
e-mail: mruta@worldbank.org

© The Author(s) 2017
N.F. Campos and F. Coricelli (eds.), *The Economics of UK–EU Relations*,
DOI 10.1007/978-3-319-55495-2_10

trade under different scenarios. While the EU is a complex institution, the outcome of a (still ongoing) project of economic and political integration which had its founding moment with the Schumann Declaration in the aftermath of World War II, in this article we see it through the lenses of trade agreements. This allows to anchor the analysis of Brexit, the exit of the United Kingdom (UK) from the European Union (EU), to a well-established economic literature that studies the trade impact of Preferential Trade Agreements (PTAs).

The landscape of trade and trade agreements has radically changed in the last 25 years. First, we have seen a surge in the number of preferential arrangements: in 1990, only 51 PTAs were in force, while there were 279 agreements in force and notified to the WTO in 2015. In addition, modern PTAs are increasingly "deeper" in the sense that they cover many regulatory issues and policy areas that go beyond tariff reduction such as services, investment, competition, and intellectual property rights protection.[1] The nature of trade has also dramatically changed since the early 1990s, particularly as a result of the growing internationalization of production and the rise of Global Value Chains (GVCs). Deep provisions in PTAs may potentially influence trade relations among members either directly, as services commitments, or indirectly as investment and competition provisions may make it easier to operate production activities that span multiple borders. The letter sent by the Japanese government to the UK and the EU in the aftermath of Brexit outlining a number of requests by Japanese businesses operating in the UK on the content of a future UK–EU PTA illustrates the importance of a finer understanding of what Brexit entails, beyond a focus on changes in tariffs and gross goods trade flows.[2]

The EU has been a precursor of deep integration. We use new information on the content of trade agreements from the World Bank (Hofmann et al. 2016) to build a measure of "depth" based on the number of provisions covered by the agreement.[3] The data indicate that the EU is the deepest PTA among the 279 currently in force. The relationship between the UK and the rest of the EU members before Brexit will actually happen is regulated by the European Community (EC)

Treaty and the following enlargement agreements which cover 44 policy areas ranging from standards to movements of capital, to labor mobility. Europe is also the region that has the largest share of intra-regional trade. The UK economy is part of this intense network of trade relations. First, the EU is the most important trade partner of the UK accounting for 52% of UK's exports of goods and services. Second, the UK is closely integrated in regional value chains. For instance, the share of intermediates value added on total domestic value added in UK exports (the majority of which goes to the EU) is close to 70%.

We first investigate the extent to which the depth of the EU contributed to boost trade between the UK and other EU members. We use data from the World Input Output Database (WIOD) on goods, services and value-added trade and the World Bank data on the content of deep agreements to estimate a gravity equation augmented with a measure of depth for the period 1995–2011. By interacting the depth of PTAs with dummies identifying the UK, we can quantify the effect of the depth of trade agreements on UK imports and exports of goods, services and value added. Deep trade agreements are found to increase goods and services trade by 42% on average. The depth of UK's trade agreements strongly increased trade in services: as a result of its EU membership and its participation in deep PTAs signed by the EU with third countries, UK services trade more than doubled. Deep PTAs also increased domestic value added in gross exports of the UK. This effect is mainly driven by stronger GVC relationship of the UK with its EU partners: UK's intermediates value added in gross exports (forward linkages) increased by 31% thanks to deep PTAs. In addition, foreign value added in UK exports (backward linkages) was boosted by EU membership by 37%. Finally, breaking down the EU into "new" and "founding" members reveals that EU membership has been particularly important to increase UK exports of services directed to the latter.

We then analyze the impact that changes in the UK–EU trade agreement can have on UK–EU trade relations going forward. This is a difficult task, as the only certainty on the future institutional setting is its uncertainty. We address this problem by considering three distinct scenarios, with decreasing depth of the future agreement between the UK and the rest of the EU. The first scenario assumes that the PTA between the UK and the EU will be as deep as the agreement the EU has with Norway. In the second scenario, the UK and the EU will sign a PTA as deep as the average PTA the EU currently has with third countries. Finally, the third scenario has no agreement. We find that bilateral UK–EU trade declines under all scenarios and that this drop is sharper the lower the depth of the future arrangement relative to the depth of the EU agreement. In terms of value-added trade, the decline ranges from 6% of the "Norway" scenario to 28% of no agreement. In all scenarios, the largest declines are for UK services and GVC trade with the rest of the EU. These predictions should be seen as average effects. As it takes time for trade flows to respond to changes in trade costs, we expect the impact in the short-run to be smaller than in the longer term.

Our work is closely related to two strands of economic literature. The first is the large body of literature that investigates the impact of trade agreements on members' trade relations which has recently been summarized in Limão (2016). As many of these studies, we use a gravity framework to guide our analysis of the trade effects of PTAs. Second, our work also relates to the small and recent literature that focuses on the economic and trade effects of Brexit (e.g., Dinghra et al. 2016; Kee and Nicita 2016). Our paper differs from others in two main respects. First, we employ an explicit new measure of depth based on the content of PTAs. Second, we do not just focus on goods (or total) trade, but assess the impact of UK membership of the EU and its exit on goods, services and value-added trade. Our study also relates to the economic literature that aims at assessing the economic effects of European economic and political integration (e.g., Brou and Ruta 2011; Campos et al. 2014). Differently from this literature, we focus on EU trade-related institutions and trade effects.

The rest of the paper is organized as follows. Section 2 presents a number of stylized facts on UK–EU trade agreements and trade relations. The empirical analysis of the impact of trade agreements on UK trade with the EU and other partners is in Sect. 3. The future scenario analysis is presented in Sect. 4. Concluding remarks follow.

2   Trade Agreements and UK–EU Trade

This section presents some key stylized facts on UK–EU trade relations. The first subsection looks at the trade policy regime, while the second one focuses on trade flows.

2.1   Trade Agreements

Part of the current public debate on trade policy presents trade agreements merely as institutions aimed at lowering tariffs among member countries and thus sees the trade effects of undoing trade agreements as the result of changes in preferential market access in goods. Modern trade policy institutions are, however, more complex than this. How have trade agreements evolved? How does the EU compare to other agreements?

A new database by the World Bank (Hofmann et al. 2016) reviews 279 PTAs offering new insights on the changing nature of trade agreements. The approach followed by Hofmann et al. (2016) for the identification of provisions and their legal enforceability follows closely the seminal paper by Horn et al. (2010) and the World Trade Report (2011) (WTO 2011). Horn et al. (2010) identify 52 policy areas included in PTAs signed by the EU and US. They consider a policy area to be legally enforceable if the language is sufficiently precise, implying clear legal obligations, and if the area is not excluded from dispute settlement procedures under the PTA. Using this approach, WTO (2011) constructed a dataset mapping the same set of provisions for 100 PTAs in force in 2011 signed by mostly developed countries that contribute to more than 90% of world trade. In an effort to include a larger number of developing countries, Hofmann et al. (2016) updated the WTO dataset and coded all the remaining agreements notified to the WTO and in force until 2015.

The number of trade agreements and their content changed dramatically since the early 1990s (Fig. 1). The number of PTAs in force increased slowly in the 1960s and 1970s and then remained constant until the beginning of the 1990s when a large number of agreements entered into force. The number of PTAs has increased more than fivefold

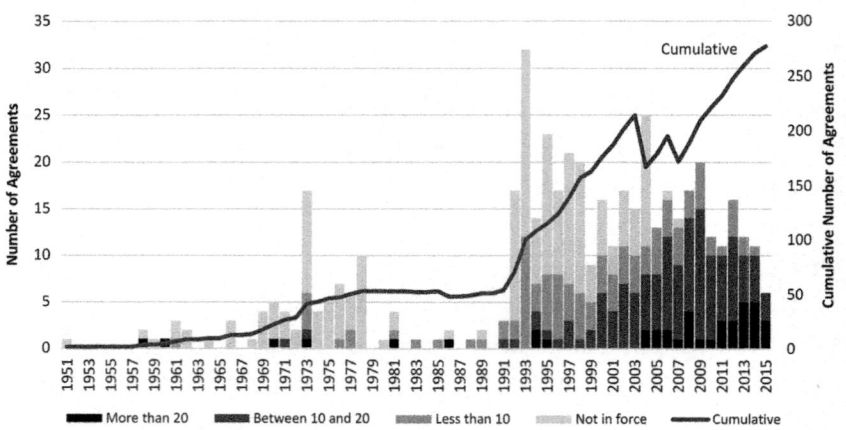

Fig. 1 Number of trade agreements over time and depth

from 51 agreements in 1990 to 279 in 2015. Along with the number, the content of trade agreements has changed. The number of provisions included in PTAs raised over time suggesting an increase in the "depth" of agreements. The majority of PTAs signed after 2003 include at least 10 legally enforceable provisions. That is, modern PTAs are "deep" in the sense that they cover substantially more policy areas than traditional (or "shallow") PTA that focused mostly on tariff liberalization.

Europe has been a precursor of this process. The EC Treaty signed in 1958 and successive enlargement of the European Union already included more than 20 legally enforceable provisions. Thanks to the EU, European countries are among the most integrated countries in terms of number and depth of PTAs. At the end of 2015, EU members were involved in 36 trade agreements. Each EU member has on average more than 25 enforceable provisions with its PTA partners (see Fig. 2). As discussed below, the high average number of provisions in force for EU countries is mainly due to the strong integration inside the EU. As a comparison, each European Free Trade Area (EFTA) country (Iceland, Liechtenstein, Norway and Switzerland) has around 30 agreements in force in 2015 with an average depth of 23. Also, PTAs signed by Japan and Korea are quite deep and include on average 21 and 20 provisions, respectively. Other non-European countries such as the United States

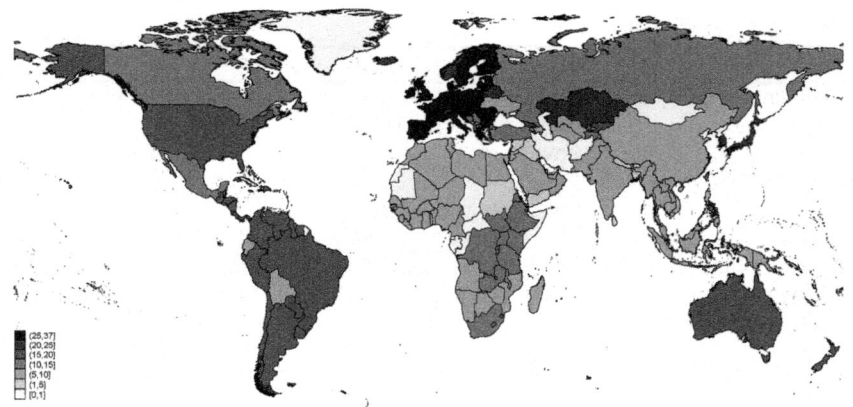

(25,37]
(20,25]
(15,20]
(10,15]
(5,10]
(1,5]
[0,1]

Fig. 2 Average depth across countries (2015)

and Australia, Taiwan and most Latin American countries established relatively deep relationships with their partners, although shallower compared to European countries. On the other hand, South East Asian countries do not seem to be involved in very deep agreements.

The provisions identified by Horn et al. (2010) can be divided into two categories: "WTO plus" or WTO+ and "WTO extra" or WTO-X. WTO+ covers policy areas that fall under the current mandate of the WTO, while WTO-X refers to obligations outside the WTO's mandate. A complete list of provision can be found in Table 1. Not surprisingly, the two most frequent provisions included in PTAs are tariffs on manufacturing and agricultural goods. Other important WTO+ policy areas are customs procedures, export taxes, anti-dumping, countervailing measures, Technical Barriers to Trade (TBT), and Sanitary and Phytosanitary Standards (SPS). WTO-X policy areas most frequently included in PTAs encompass investment, competition policy, movement of capital and Intellectual Property Rights (IPR) protection.

The relationship among EU members is the deepest when we use as a measure of depth the number of legally enforceable provisions. The EC Treaty and the EU enlargements encompass 44 legally enforceable provisions. They include all WTO+ provisions and a large number of WTO-X areas. In addition, the EU is a member of 36 trade agreements

Table 1 List of provisions

WTO+	WTO-X	
Tariffs Industrial goods	Anti-corruption	Financial assistance
Tariffs agricultural	Competition policy	Health
goods	Environmental laws	Human Rights
Customs administration	IPR	Illegal immigration
Export taxes	Investment measures	Illicit drugs
SPS measures	Labor market regulation	Industrial cooperation
State trading enterprises	Movement of capital	Information society
TBT measures	Consumer protection	Mining
Countervailing measures	Data protection	Money laundering
Anti-dumping	Agriculture	Nuclear safety
State aid	Approximation of	Political dialogue
Public procurement	legislation	Public administration
TRIMS measures	Audiovisual	Regional cooperation
GATS	Civil protection	Research and
TRIPS	Innovation policies	technology
	Cultural cooperation	SMEs
	Economic policy dialogue	Social Matters
	Education and training	Statistics
	Energy	Taxation
		Terrorism
		Visa and asylum

with third countries. Some of these PTAs are also very deep. This is the case for the agreements with Moldova, Ukraine and the European Economic Area (EEA), an agreement that includes the EU and all EFTA members except Switzerland. These PTAs, respectively, include 44, 43, and 36 legally enforceable provisions. All the other PTAs signed by the EU are shallower. Table 2 lists all the provisions in the dataset and identifies those included in the EU and the number/share of EU agreements with third countries that include these provisions.

2.2   Trade Relations

To illustrate the UK–EU trade relations we use the information available in the World Input–Output Database (WIOD). There are two important advantages in using this dataset: (i) it covers trade in services at the bilateral level, and (ii) it allows the decomposition of gross exports in

Table 2 Provisions in the EU agreement and number and share of EU's PTAs with third countries including each provision

Provision	EU28	EU-3rd Countries PTAs	
	Legally enforceable	Number	Share (%)
Tariffs on manufacturing goods	Yes	35	100
Tariffs on agricultural goods	Yes	35	100
Anti-dumping	Yes	34	97
Customs	Yes	33	94
Export taxes	Yes	32	91
Countervailing measures	Yes	29	83
Competition policy	Yes	28	80
State aid	Yes	26	74
TRIPS	Yes	23	66
IPR	Yes	22	63
STE	Yes	21	60
Movement of capital	Yes	19	54
Public procurement	Yes	14	40
TBT	Yes	10	29
GATS	Yes	10	29
Investment	Yes	10	29
SPS	Yes	9	26
Social matters	Yes	9	26
Data protection	Yes	8	23
Environmental laws	Yes	5	14
Labor market regulations	Yes	5	14
Approximation of legislation	Yes	5	14
Financial assistance	Yes	5	14
Cultural cooperation	Yes	4	11
Illegal immigration	Yes	4	11
Audiovisual	Yes	3	9
Energy	Yes	3	9
Health	Yes	3	9
Visa and asylum	Yes	3	9
Consumer protection	Yes	2	6
Economic policy dialogue	Yes	2	6
Education and training	Yes	2	6
Industrial cooperation	Yes	2	6
Research and technology	Yes	2	6
Statistics	Yes	2	6
Terrorism	Yes	2	6
Anticorruption	Yes	1	3
Agriculture	Yes	1	3

(continued)

Table 2 (continued)

Provision	EU28	EU-3rd Countries PTAs	
	Legally enforceable	Number	Share (%)
Mining	Yes	1	3
Regional cooperation	Yes	1	3
SME	Yes	1	3
Taxation	Yes	1	3
TRIMS	Yes	0	0
Nuclear safety	Yes	0	0
Civil protection	No	2	6
Public administration	No	2	6
Illicit drugs	No	1	3
Information society	No	1	3
Money laundering	No	1	3
Political dialogue	No	1	3
Innovation policies	No	0	0
Human rights	No	0	0

value-added terms. The main limitation of the dataset is that it provides data for a restricted number of countries, 40 plus an aggregate for the rest of the world, limited to the 1995–2011 period.

The UK accounts for 3.8% of world exports and 3.9% of world imports. In 2011, the UK exported $440 billion of goods and it imported $550 billion.[4] In terms of services, the UK exported $260 billion and it imported $163 billion. Table 3 highlights the importance of the EU as UK's trading partner. Trade in goods with the EU accounts for more than half of the UK's exports and imports. The EU is also an important market destination for UK services absorbing almost half of UK exports. The importance of the EU as a source of services for the UK is instead much smaller: only one-third of imports of services come from the EU.

While the share of UK exports to the EU remained constant in the period under consideration, the composition of trade changed substantially. In 1995, more than 80% of UK exports were goods. This share declined to around 63% in 2011. The reshaping of UK exports toward services is even clearer when looking at trade with the EU. The share of exports of services to the EU more than doubled in 16 years, going from

Table 3 UK trade in goods and services

		UK Exports			UK Imports		
		Services	Goods	Total	Services	Goods	Total
2011	Extra-EU	$135,599 M 19%	$212,739 M 30%	$348,338 M 49%	$108,268 M 15%	$243,531 M 34%	$351,799 M 49%
	EU28	$124,412 M 18%	$228,725 M 33%	$353,137 M 51%	$55,527 M 8%	$308,208 M 43%	$363,735 M 51%
	Total	$260,012 M 37%	$441,464 M 63%	$701,476 M 100%	$163,795 M 23%	$551,739 M 77%	$715,534 M 100%
1995	Extra-EU	$33,866 M 11%	$121,579 M 40%	$155,445 M 51%	$21,048 M 7%	$95,116 M 33%	$116,164 M 40%
	EU28	$24,437 M 8%	$123,086 M 41%	$147,524 M 49%	$23,275 M 8%	$146,607 M 51%	$169,882 M 59%
	Total	$58,304 M 19%	$244,665 M 81%	$302,969 M 100%	$44,323 M 15%	$241,723 M 85%	$286,045 M 100%

8 to 18% of total exports. The pattern for exports outside the EU is similar but the increase is more moderate. This evidence suggests a "servicification" of UK exports.

Germany is both the main destination and source country of goods, accounting for 13% of UK's exports and 15% of UK's imports (see Fig. 3). The other top 4 destination countries in the EU are France, the Netherlands, Ireland and Spain. As to the source of UK imports, the Netherlands, France, Belgium and Italy are in the top 5. Outside the EU, the US is the main destination country absorbing 12% of UK exports, followed by China, Canada, Russia and Australia. UK imports from outside the EU come mainly from China (8%), US, Japan, India, and Canada. The main markets for UK services are US, Ireland, Germany, Luxemburg, and the Netherlands, all importing more than 5% of UK

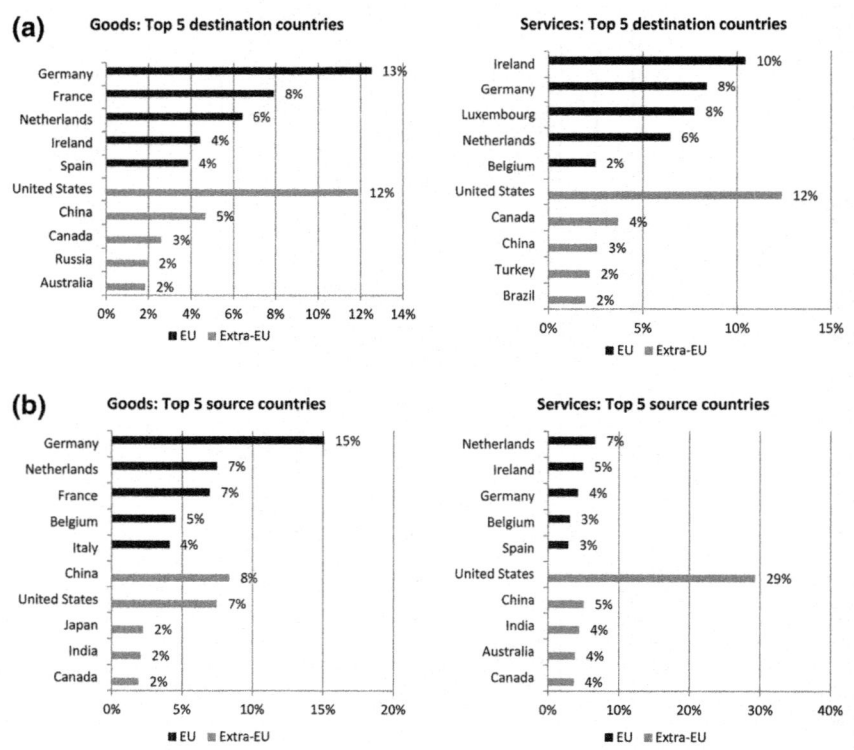

Fig. 3   Top trading partners

services. Other top destination markets are Canada, China, Belgium, Turkey,s and Brazil. The most relevant source of services for the UK is the US representing 29% of UK imports. All other sources are much less relevant being lower than 7%.

The most important exporting sector for the UK is transport equipment followed by chemicals and electrical equipment (see Fig. 4). More than half of transport equipment exports go outside the EU while chemicals are exported mainly to other EU countries. Fuels and machinery complete the list of the top 5 exported goods. Transport and electrical equipment are also the largest imported goods in the UK and

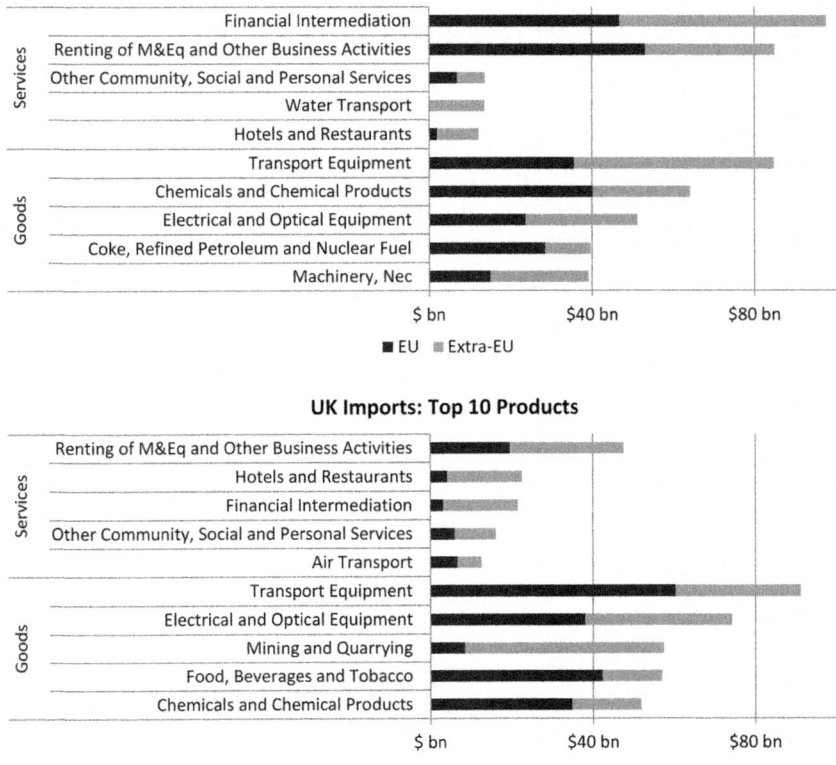

Fig. 4 Top traded sectors

more than half of the value comes from other EU countries. Imports of mining, food, and chemicals are also relatively important for the UK. In terms of services, two sectors stand out as the most important exports: financial intermediation and business services. While roughly half of the value of financial intermediation is provided to the EU, almost two-thirds of the value of business activities is consumed by other EU countries. Renting of machinery and equipment and other business services are the most imported services and more than half of the value comes from non-EU countries. Tourism-related and financial services are among the top imported sectors, mainly from outside the EU, but in terms of value they account for only about half of the business services sector.

We next look at the extent to which the UK economy is integrated in global value chains with the EU and other non-EU partners. In a world of international production networks, gross trade statistics are inflated by the double counting of goods and services that cross borders multiple times. Wang et al. (2016) offer a decomposition of gross exports based on the work by Koopman et al. (2014). This decomposition allows to analyze the extent of GVC integration of an economy. Specifically, gross exports are decomposed into different value-added components that distinguish whether the value has been created domestically, abroad or it has been double counted. Figure 5 gives a graphical representation. The components from 1 to 4 represent the domestic value-added content of gross exports. The sum of the components 2, 3 and 4 is the value added of intermediate goods in exports (i.e., forward linkages). Foreign value added (component 5) is the foreign content of exports and it represents

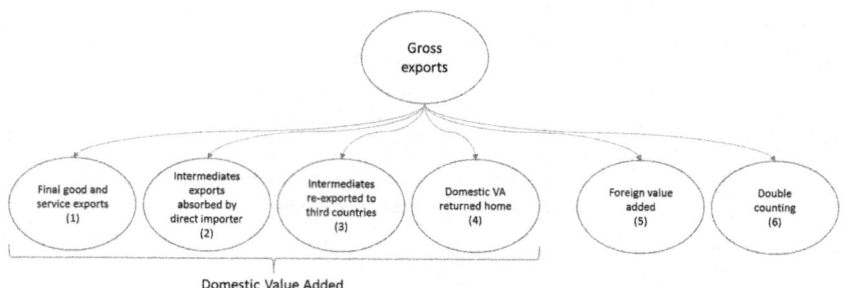

Fig. 5 Decomposition of gross exports (Wang et al. 2016)

backward linkages. The last component is pure double counting due to goods crossing border multiple times.

We use this decomposition of WIOD data to explore where the value of UK exports has been created and how UK is integrated in GVCs. The data suggest that the UK is highly integrated in global value chains. Backward linkages account for 16% of gross exports. Forward linkages are even more important for the UK. The share of intermediates value added in total domestic value added of UK exports is almost 70% in 2011 (Fig. 6).[5] This share increased by 7 percentage points since 1995. The increase is mainly due to an expansion of the integration of the UK in European GVCs after 2004 as suggested by the increase of the value of intermediates value-added exported to other EU members. UK's integration in GVCs with other countries also slightly increased over time.

A deeper look at the decomposition of value-added sheds more light on the structure of GVCs in which the UK is involved. While intermediate value added of UK exports to the EU is similar to that of exports to non-EU countries, the re-exported value-added content of exports, a measure of how much intermediates value added are used as inputs to produce exports in other countries, is much higher. This suggests that UK exports to the EU are an important element of EU exports, whereas they are important for domestic consumption in non-EU countries.

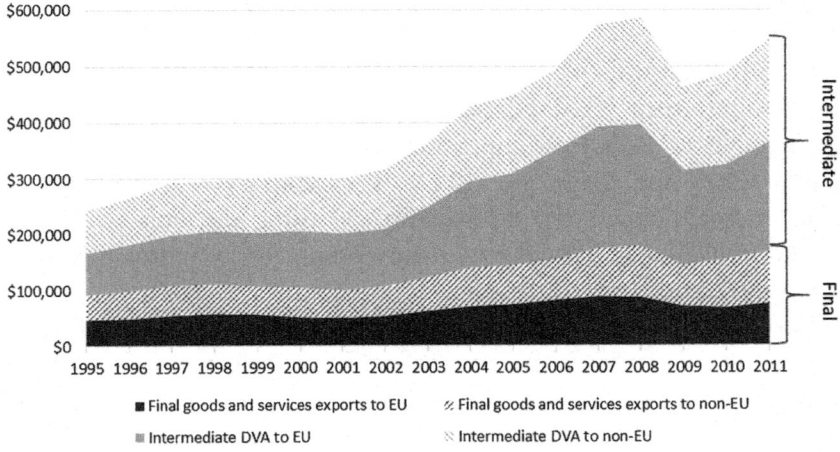

Fig. 6 UK value added of final and intermediate goods and services

3 Depth of Trade Agreements and UK–EU Trade

This section empirically investigates the extent to which the depth of the EU and of the PTAs the EU has with other countries had an impact on UK trade. The empirical estimation of the trade effect of PTAs is based on a gravity model similar to Mattoo et al. (2016); Osnago et al. (2016). Differently from the large body of literature on trade agreements (see Head and Mayer 2014; Limão 2016), we explicitly account for the depth of PTAs exploiting the novel information on the content of trade agreements presented in Sect. 2. Moreover, we include an interaction term to accommodate heterogeneous effects of deep PTAs for the UK. Specifically, we estimate the following gravity equation:

$$\text{Trade}_{ijt} = \exp\left\{\beta_1 \text{Depth}_{ijt} + \beta_2 \text{Depth}_{ijt} * \text{UK}_{ij} + \mu_{ij} + \delta_{it} + \rho_{jt}\right\} + \varepsilon_{ijt} \tag{1}$$

where Trade_{ijt} is bilateral exports from country i to country j in year t, Depth_{ijt} is the number of legally enforceable provisions in the PTA between i and j (normalized between 0 and 1), UK_{ij} is a dummy variable equal to 1 if the exporting or importing country is the UK, ρ_{jt} and δ_{it} are importer-time and exporter-time fixed effects that account for country-time-specific shocks and the multilateral resistance terms (Anderson and van Wincoop 2003, 2004). Finally, μ_{ij} is a set of *undirected* country-pair fixed effects that captures all the time-invariant determinants of trade costs and addresses the endogeneity in PTAs formation (Baier and Bergstrand 2007). To account for the presence of zeroes in trade flows, we estimate Eq. (1) using the Poisson pseudo maximum-likelihood (PPML) estimator proposed by Santos Silva and Tenreyro (2006).

We analyze the effect of deep agreements on different types of trade. First, using data from WIOD, we define Trade_{ijt} as the total exports of goods and services from i to j. Second, we estimate Eq. (1) for export of goods and services separately to allow for heterogeneous effects of depth. Finally, we use the decomposition of gross trade into value-added components proposed by Wang et al. (2016) to measure the effect of deep PTAs on GVC-related trade.

The Depth$_{ijt}$ variable comes from the content of PTAs dataset constructed by Hofmann et al. (2016) and is defined as the count of legally enforceable provisions included in each agreement. To identify the effect of depth on exports, we include country-pair fixed effects and exploit the within county-pair variation, while controlling for any country-year shocks. The coefficient β_1 in Eq. (1) captures the effect of signing the deepest agreement in the sample.[6] While the coefficient of the interaction term β_2 tests if UK's exports or imports are more or less sensitive to deep agreements than other countries. A positive (negative) and significant coefficient implies that for the same level of depth the UK exported or imported relatively more (less) than the average country in the sample. Both coefficients capture the average effect of depth after the agreements enter into force and assume linear effects on trade, with a percentage point increase in depth having similar effects for deep and shallow agreements.

Two caveats need to be kept in mind. First, the model assumes that the marginal effect of an additional provision is the same regardless of what type of provision is included. It is well possible that provisions in deep trade agreements have a different impact depending on how relevant they are for trade. Provisions on standards, investment or competition are likely to have a larger impact on trade than provisions that do not pertain to trade or economic cooperation (e.g., statistics, cultural cooperation). In addition, we expect the short-run impact to be smaller than in the longer term because it takes time for trade flows to respond to changes in trade costs (Johnson and Noguera 2014; Baier and Bergstrand 2007).

3.1 Goods and Services Trade

We begin our investigation from a more conventional analysis of gross trade flows. The first 3 columns of Table 4 report the PPML estimates of our baseline regressions of depth on gross trade. The gravity equation is augmented with the interaction of depth with a dummy that identifies observations for the UK as importer or exporter. The results in column 1

Table 4 Trade and depth

	(1)	(2)	(3)	(4)	(5)	(6)	(7)	(8)	(9)
	Total	Goods	Services	Total	Goods	Services	Total	Goods	Services
Depth	0.353***	0.522***	0.182***	0.353***	0.522***	0.182***	0.326***	0.483***	0.184***
	(0.022)	(0.036)	(0.037)	(0.022)	(0.036)	(0.037)	(0.039)	(0.05)	(0.056)
Depth* UK exp/imp	0.017	0.128	0.693***						
	(0.098)	(0.106)	(0.145)						
Depth* UK exp				−0.002	0.129	0.712***	0.062	0.211	0.530***
				(0.102)	(0.111)	(0.16)	(0.118)	(0.144)	(0.161)
Depth* UK imp				0.037	0.126	0.670***	0.09	0.051	0.665***
				(0.102)	(0.118)	(0.149)	(0.124)	(0.161)	(0.134)
Depth* founding EU imp							0.073	0.062	−0.021
							(0.056)	(0.074)	(0.084)
Depth* founding EU exp							0.011	0.058	0.02
							(0.056)	(0.073)	(0.089)
Depth* UK exp* founding EU imp							−1.286	1.544	3.529***
							(1.04)	(0.994)	(1.299)
Depth* UK imp* founding EU exp							−1.206	1.767*	3.208**
							(1.013)	(0.988)	(1.261)
Observations	27,200	27,200	27,200	27,200	27,200	27,200	27,200	27,200	27,200

The estimator is PPML. All specifications include bilateral fixed effects and country-time fixed effects. Robust standard errors, clustered by country-pair, are in parentheses

*** $p < 0.01$, ** $p < 0.05$, * $p < 0.1$

suggest that country-pairs that signed the deepest PTA increased their total bilateral trade by 42%. The UK was not affected more than the average since the coefficient of the interaction is not significantly different from zero. In other words, the depth of UK trade agreements with the other EU members and with other partners with which the EU had signed PTAs increased UK trade by 42%—not differently from other countries.

The data in WIOD allow to split total trade into trade in goods and trade in services. Columns 2 and 3 report the coefficients of depth and the interaction with the UK dummy for goods and services, respectively. Depth seems to have a much stronger average effect on trade in goods than trade in services. Signing the deepest PTA increases members' trade in goods by 69% and trade in services by 20%. The larger effect for trade in goods could be explained by GVC trade, in which intermediate goods cross the borders many times before they are assembled into final products. We come back to the link between deep PTAs and GVCs in the next subsection. The interaction with the dummy UK reveals an interesting result. While the depth of UK's trade agreements did not increase trade in goods more than the average country, it strongly increased trade in services. The UK more than doubled its trade in services as a result of its EU membership and its participation in deep PTAs signed by the EU with third countries.

So far the analysis did not distinguish the gains for the UK as an importer or an exporter. The second three columns of Table 4 explore if the UK was affected by deep PTAs depending on being an importer or an exporter. We split the dummy UK into two variables that identify if the UK is an importer or an exporter and we include in the regression the interactions of these dummies with depth. Columns 4 and 5 show that the depth did not increase UK imports and exports of goods more than the average country. Column 6 instead, shows that the UK both imported and exported more services than the average after signing deep agreements. The comparison of the coefficients of the two interaction terms suggests that the UK's services exports increased more than its imports.

Where did the gains from deep PTAs for the UK come from? Did deep PTAs increase trade with the original members of the EU or the new members? In order to address these questions, we add additional interaction terms to Eq. 1. The interaction of depth with UK exporter dummy is further interacted with a dummy equal to one if the partner is one of the founding EU members (Belgium, France, Germany, Italy, Luxemburg and the Netherlands). The coefficient of the triple interaction tests for differences between UK's exports to the original and newer EU members as depth increases. A positive coefficient would suggest that the UK exported disproportionally more to the founding EU members as the EU agreement deepened. Similarly, we also add the triple interaction of depth with the UK importer and the original EU importer dummies. The results in column 8 and 9 suggest that the deepening of the EU was particularly important for exports of services directed to the original members that in turn exported relatively more goods to the UK.

3.2 GVC Trade

A body of economic literature suggests that the rise of deep agreements and the increasing importance of GVCs are tightly related. Intuitively, the unbundling of stages of production across borders creates new forms of cross-border policy spillovers and time-consistency problems. This, in turn, generates a demand for deeper forms of integration as certain national policies need to be disciplined in PTAs for GVCs to operate smoothly. Lawrence (1996), Baldwin (2010), WTO (2011) are some of the first studies that look at how deep PTAs are related to GVCs from an informal theoretical perspective. A first formal model of how GVCs affect the design of trade agreements is presented in Antras and Staiger (2012). More recently, a number of studies have also provided empirical evidence of such relationship (Orefice and Rocha 2014; Johnson and Noguera 2014; Osnago et al. 2015).

Here we build on Osnago et al. (2016) and estimate the specific effect of deep PTAs on different measures of trade in value added for the UK. We estimate the gravity Eq. (1) for four left hand side variables of trade in value added with country-pair, importer-year and exporter-year fixed effects. From WIOD, we use the decomposition of gross exports in value-added components by Wang et al. (2016) to measure the domestic value added of exports (i.e., the total value produced in the exporting country), intermediates value added (i.e., the value of all intermediate goods created in the exporting country), re-exported value added (i.e., the value produced in the exporting country that is processed by the importing country and re-exported to third countries or to the source country) and foreign value added (i.e., the total value produced by foreign countries included in exports).

As before, the coefficients of depth is the average effect of signing the deepest PTA in our sample. The interaction of depth with dummies identifying the UK tells whether the UK increased GVC trade more or less than the average country by signing deep PTAs. The PPML estimates of the gravity equation are reported in Table 5. Odd columns are results for the UK independently of it being an importer or an exporter; even columns instead distinguish the additional effect of deep PTAs for the UK as exporter and importer. The comparison of the effects of depth on domestic value added with the effects of depth on intermediates value added sheds light on the importance of forward linkages in GVCs for the UK. The interaction term of depth with UK for foreign value added exports identifies the impact of EU membership on UK's backward linkages in GVCs.

The domestic value added in gross exports increased on average by 14% for the country-pairs that signed the deepest PTA. The effect for the UK is larger by an additional 21%. Splitting the UK dummy into importer and exporter suggests that the effect of deep PTA increased both UK's value-added imports and exports. Deep PTAs are also found to have a positive effect on intermediates value added. Signing the deepest PTA increased domestic intermediates value added by 14% on average and by an additional 17% for the UK. The close similarity of these coefficients with those for domestic value added and the fact that intermediates represent around two-thirds of UK's value added in exports (Fig. 6) suggest that deep agreements increased the relative importance of value added of intermediate goods with PTA members. In other words, the depth of UK's trade agreements with the EU and with the third countries the EU had signed PTAs largely contributed UK's forward integration into GVCs.

Table 5 Value-added trade and depth

Variables	(1)	(2)	(3)	(4)	(5)	(6)	(7)	(8)
	DVA		Intermediates VA		Re-exported VA		FVA	
Depth	0.130**	0.131**	0.127**	0.127**	0.176***	0.177***	0.0786	0.0786
	(0.0548)	(0.0548)	(0.0626)	(0.0626)	(0.0672)	(0.0672)	(0.0545)	(0.0545)
Depth* UK	0.189***		0.160***		0.0436		0.315***	
	(0.0582)		(0.0594)		(0.06)		(0.0814)	
Depth* UK exporter		0.169**		0.152**		0.0337		0.309***
		(0.0749)		(0.0762)		(0.0821)		(0.109)
Depth* UK importer		0.213***		0.172**		0.0599		0.318***
		(0.0745)		(0.0849)		(0.104)		(0.0913)
Observations	26,520	26,520	26,520	26,520	26,520	26,520	26,520	26,520

The estimator is PPML. All specifications include bilateral fixed effects and country-time fixed effects. Robust standard errors, clustered by country-pair, are in parentheses
*** $p < 0.01$, ** $p < 0.05$, * $p < 0.1$

The estimates for re-exported value added and foreign value added shed more light on the structure of UK GVCs. Comparing the coefficient of the interaction term in column 3 with that in column 5 indicates that the additional increase in domestic intermediate value added for the UK is driven by the value of intermediates that are directly absorbed by the importer. In fact, the left-hand side variable of columns 5 and 6 is a subset of on the variable in columns 3 and 4 since it includes only the value of intermediates that are re-exported by the importer to third countries or returns home. Deep PTAs increased the foreign value-added content of UK exports by 37%.[7] Column 8 shows that depth had an additional effect on both the foreign content of UK exports and imports. This result suggests that the UK used more foreign inputs to produce its exports after signing deeper PTAs and, at the same time, also countries that export to the UK increased foreign value added in their exports to the UK.

4 Possible Future Scenarios

In this section, we use the estimates of our econometric analysis to investigate the future of UK–EU trade relations after Brexit. Once Britain invokes Article 50 it has 2 years to negotiate a withdrawal agreement from the EU (unless a unanimous decision of all remaining members is reached to extend the period). Given the high uncertainty about the future of the UK–EU trade relationship we evaluate the results of the empirical analysis assuming several post-Brexit scenarios, characterized by different degrees of depth. In the first case, we assume that the negotiations lead to the UK signing an agreement similar to the one in force between the EU and Norway, while the least optimistic scenario evaluates the trade impact of the outcome being no agreement between the UK and EU.

In the "Norway" scenario, we assume that the UK bargains an agreement with the EU as deep as the EEA, which covers 36 policy areas. This agreement would allow the UK to be part of the European Single Market and to retain the "four freedoms:" free movement of goods, capital, services, and people. In addition, the UK would have to comply

Table 6 Changes in UK's trade with the EU under different scenarios

	"Norway" scenario	"Average PTA" scenario	"No-agreement" scenario
	(36)	(14)	(0)
Goods	−12%	−38%	−50%
Services	−16%	−48%	−62%
Domestic value added	−6%	−20%	−28%
Intermediates value added	−5%	−18%	−26%
Foreign value added	−7%	−25%	−34%

Notes Depth decreases from 44 to 36 in the "Norway" scenario, to 14 in the "average PTA", and to 0 in the "no-agreement" scenario. Calculations are based on estimates in Table 3, column 5 for goods and column 6 for services trade, while results for value added trade use estimates from column 2 in Table 5

with competition and state-aid rules and horizontal areas related to the four freedoms without being able to influence them. Based on estimates from the empirical analysis, this scenario would lead to a 12% decrease in gross exports of goods from the UK to the EU (see Table 6).[8] While the estimates for services and domestic value added suggest decreases of 16% and 6% in exports, respectively. Forward and backward GVC participation would decline by 5% and 7%, respectively. These results need to be interpreted with caution. Since, as discussed in Sect. 3, we do not identify the impact of the inclusion of specific provisions and assume the marginal effect on trade to be log-linear, the model may be over-estimating the trade effect of the "Norway" scenario.

The "average PTA" scenario assumes an agreement between the UK and the EU with a depth equal to the average depth of EU's agreements with non-member countries. By looking at the agreements that the EU signed in the past, we would expect the new agreement to include around 14 provisions. Agreements with this depth guarantee market access for goods and, to some extent, services but do not usually go beyond areas that are not covered by the WTO (i.e., WTO-X areas) other than competition policy and investment. Estimates suggest that the sharp drop in the agreement's depth between the UK and the rest of the EU would lead to a 38% drop in gross exports of goods, 26 percentage points more than in the "Norway" scenario. The largest decrease would be for exports of services that are estimated to fall by 48%. Intermediates value-added exports are predicted to drop by 18%, almost four times the drop of the "Norway" scenario. The sharp reduction in intermediates and foreign value-added trade (25%) implies that the UK would participate substantially less in international production networks.

In the "no-agreement" scenario, the UK and the EU do not sign any preferential agreement. In this case, the variable depth would drop to zero, meaning that areas such as investment, competition policy and movements of capital (just to name key ones) would no longer be regulated by the agreement and the UK would have to pay Most Favored Nation (MFN) tariffs to access the EU market. In this scenario, gross trade in goods from the UK to EU countries would be halved, while export of value added would be reduced by 28%. According to the estimates services exports would fall by 62%, which implies a 14 and 46 percentage points drop with respect to the intermediate and "Norway" scenarios. Intermediates value-added exports would decrease by about a quarter and foreign value added in UK's exports would by one third.

To better understand these magnitudes, we use the 2011 data from WIOD to obtain the dollar equivalent of the losses for the three different scenarios. It should be noted that these back-of-the-envelope calculations account for the partial effects and do not have general equilibrium or welfare implications since they do not account for possible re-direction of exports to non-EU countries (i.e., trade diversion and deflection), price adjustments or changes in wages. Although the largest percentage changes are for service exports, in terms of dollar equivalents we find that export of goods would decrease the most in all the three scenarios. The "Norway" case, in which the UK signs an agreement similar to the EEA, suggests that export of goods would decrease by $27.447 billion, while services and value-added exports would drop by $19.906 billion and $16.445 billion, respectively. To put this numbers in perspective, the impact on total (goods and services) trade is equal to 1.83% of UK's GDP and 0.63% for value-added exports. In the worst case scenario, we find that goods exports would decrease by $114.363 billion, which is equivalent to 4.41% of UK's GDP.[9] For services and value-added exports the values are lower, around $78 billion each, which accounts for 3% of GDP.

We compare our results with estimates from earlier studies that either use a different approach or use different data. Baier et al. (2008) adopt a methodology similar to ours based on a gravity model to identify the effect of various agreements, among which are the EU and the EEA, using PTA specific dummy variables. Their estimates suggest that if the UK were to exit the EU and sign the EEA, its gross exports of goods would fall by 25%.[10] One possible explanation for the difference in effects is that in our database the EEA is one of the deepest agreements, as it covers 36 policy areas. Instead, Baier et al. (2008) capture the trade impact of the EEA as the average effect of the trade agreement between the European Economic Community and the EFTA countries, signed in 1973, and the EEA of 1994.[11]

A more recent study by Dhingra et al. (2016), based on a general equilibrium trade model à la Costinot and Rodriguez-Clare (2013), finds that the losses associated with Brexit range between 1.28% and 2.61% of GDP. Combining our reduced form results and estimates on the elasticity of income to trade in goods by Feyrer (2009), we find that Brexit would imply larger impacts on UK's income: a decrease by 3% in the "Norway" scenario and by 13% in the no-agreement case. A possible interpretation of the difference is that the reduced form estimates deliver a higher impact because they capture both the dynamic and static effects, while the structural model only accounts for static effects due to the increase in trade barriers (Dhingra et al. 2016).[11]

Our focus is on UK–EU trade relations, but Brexit will also impact trade relations the UK has with countries that have singed a PTA with the EU. What would be the trade effect if Brexit also implied the exit of the UK from all the EU's PTAs? The average number of provisions included in these agreements is around 14. The group of UK's non-EU PTA partners account for 14% of UK's total export of goods, of which the most important partners are Switzerland, South Africa, Turkey and Norway that together account for 11% of exports.[13] By exiting all the non-EU PTAs the UK would decrease its exports to these countries by 17% equivalent to $12.212 billion. Obviously, the UK could re-negotiate these agreements seeking deeper integration or decide to pursue deep trade agreements with other important trade partners such as the US, Canada, and China.

5   Conclusions

This paper studies the role of deep trade agreements in UK–EU trade relations. We first look at the impact that membership of the EU had on trade of the UK with its partners and then use this information to predict future trade relations based on different scenarios. We find that EU membership had a strong impact on UK–EU trade and that it contributed particularly to the rise of UK services exports and its integration in global value chains. While there is substantial uncertainty on the content of a future agreement between the UK and the rest of the EU, our scenario analysis indicates that there is a clear tradeoff between the depth of such agreement and the intensity of future UK–EU trade. In particular, a shallower agreement will have a stronger negative impact on UK's services trade and GVC integration which have relied more on the deep arrangements of the EU.

A number of questions remain open. First, the analysis does not account for the possibility that the UK after Brexit may choose to sign new trade agreements with other trade partners and for the EU to continue its process of "ever closer union" by further deepening its integration. Both scenarios would impact future UK–EU trade relations going forward in ways that are difficult to predict, as the effects will depend on the specific content of these agreements. But the tradeoff between PTA depth and trade intensity uncovered in this analysis will still likely delimit future policy choices. Policy makers can either choose to undertake more binding commitments in deep agreements that support more trade or opt for weaker commitments and less trade. Second, while our focus here has been on the complementarity between deep trade institutions and trade flows, it could be argued that a high level of trade integration requires some form of political integration for its legitimacy and long-run sustainability. Indeed, this complementarity between economic and political integration has been at the core of the European project (Padoa-Schioppa 1999). In light of this, deeper forms of agreements may be difficult to pursue outside the Union.

Notes

1. The distinction between "deep" agreements and "shallow" agreements, where the latter focus on tariffs and other border measures, was first introduced by Lawrence (1996).
2. The letter by the Japanese government on Brexit to the UK and the EU can be accessed at: http://www.mofa.go.jp/files/000185466.pdf.
3. The database is available on the World Bank website at http://data.worldbank.org/data-catalog/deep-trade-agreements.
4. Data from COMTRADE show that UK trade increased between 2011 and 2015, but it remains in the same order of magnitude. The UK exported 466 billion dollars and it imported 629 billion dollars in 2015.
5. Almost 80% of UK exports are made of domestic value added.
6. Since trade data from WIOD are limited to the 1995–2011 period, the deepest agreement in our sample is the EC (27) Enlargement with 41 provisions.
7. The results in the last columns of the table suggest that on average deep PTAs did not increase foreign value added in gross exports. This may be due to the fact that in our data we do not know the origin of foreign value added in the bilateral relationship.
8. Since the depth variable is normalized to be equal to 1 when the value of depth is 41, the maximum depth in our sample, we use the following formula to calculate the percentage change $\frac{\exp\left((.522+.129)*\frac{36}{41}\right)}{\exp\left((.522+.129)*\frac{44}{41}\right)} - 1 = -0.1193$.
9. The data on GDP are from the World Bank.
10. Based on estimates in Table 3, column 1 of Baier et al. (2008).
11. Baier et al. (2008) code the dummy EEA equal to 1 from 1973 onwards if one of the countries is in the EU and the other is in EFTA.
12. Similarly, a recent study by Kee and Nicita (2016) focusing on tariff changes finds that leaving the EU would lead to a 2% decrease in UK's exports in the short run.
13. Given the limited coverage of WIOD, we compute these statistics using data from COMTRADE.

References

Anderson, J. E., & van Wincoop, E. (2003). Gravity with gravitas: A solution to the border puzzle. *American Economic Review, 93*(1), 170–192.

Anderson, J. E., & van Wincoop, E. (2004). Trade costs. *Journal of Economic Literature, 42*(3), 691–751.

Antras, P., & Staiger, R. W. (2012). Offshoring and the role of trade agreements. *American Economic Review, 102*(7), 3140–3183.

Baier, S. L., & Bergstrand, J. H. (2007). Do free trade agreements actually increase members' International Trade? *Journal of International Economics, 71*(1), 72–95.

Baier, S. L., Bergstrand, J. H., Egger, P., & McLaughlin, P. A. (2008). Do economic integration agreements actually work? Issues in understanding the causes and consequences of the growth of regionalism. *The World Economy, 31*(4), 461–497.

Baldwin, R. (2010). *Sequencing regionalism: Theory, European practice, and lessons for Asia* (CEPR Discussion Paper 7852).

Brou, D., & Ruta, M. (2011). Economic integration, political integration, or both? *Journal of the European Economic Association, 9*(6), 1143–1167.

Campos N., Coricelli, F., & Moretti, L. (2014). *Economic growth and political integration: Estimating the benefits from membership in the European Union using the synthetic counterfactuals method* (CEPR Discussion Paper No. 9968).

Costinot, A., & Rodríguez-Clare, A. (2013). *Trade theory with numbers: Quantifying the Consequences of globalization* (NBER Working Paper 18896). National Bureau of Economic Research, Inc.

Dhingra, S., Ottaviano, G. I. P., Sampson, T., & Reenen, J. V. (2016). The consequences of Brexit for UK trade and living standards. CEP BREXIT Analysis No. 2, London School of Economics and Political Science, CEP, London, UK.

Feyrer, J. (2009). *Trade and Income—Exploiting Time Series in Geography* (NBER Working Paper 14910). National Bureau of Economic Research, Inc.

Head, K., & Mayer, T. (2014). Gravity equations: Workhorse, toolkit, and cookbook. *Handbook of International Economics*. Elsevier.

Hofmann, C., Osnago, A., & Ruta, M. (2016). *Horizontal depth: A new database on the content of deep agreements*. The World Bank: Mimeo.

Horn, H., Mavroidis, P. C., & Sapir, A. (2010). *Beyond the WTO? An anatomy of EU and US preferential trade agreements*. Blueprints. Bruegel. Accessed August 25.

Johnson, R., & Noguera, G. (2014). *A portrait of trade in value added over four decades*. Unpublished, Dartmouth College.

Kee, H. L., & Nicita, A. (2016). *Short-term impact of Brexit on United Kingdom export of goods*. Work in Progress. The World Bank.

Koopman, R., Wang, Z., & Wei, S.-J. (2014). Tracing value-added and double counting in gross exports. *American Economic Review, 104*(2), 459–494.

Lawrence, R. Z. (1996). *Regionalism, Multilateralism, and Deeper Integration*. Washington, DC: Brookings Institution Press.

Limão, N. (2016). *Preferential Trade Agreements* (NBER Working Paper 22138). National Bureau of Economic Research, Inc.

Mattoo, A., Mulabdic, A., & Ruta, M. (2016). *Trade creation and trade diversion in deep agreements*. Work in Progress. The World Bank.

Orefice, G., & Rocha, N. (2014). Deep integration and production networks: An empirical analysis. *The World Economy, 37*(1), 106–136.

Osnago, A., Rocha, N., & Ruta, M. (2015). *Deep trade agreements and vertical FDI: The devil is in the details* (Policy Research Working Paper Series 7464). The World Bank.

Osnago, A., Rocha, N., & Ruta, M. (2016). Deep trade agreements and global value chains. Work in Progress. The World Bank.

Padoa-Schioppa, T. (1999). *Reflections on the globalisation and europeanisation of the economy*. Lecture at the University of Göttingen, Göttingen. Available at http://www.ecb.europa.eu/press/key/date/1999/html/sp990630.en.html.

Silva, J. M. C. S., & Tenreyro, S. (2006). The log of gravity. *The Review of Economics and Statistics, 88*(4), 641–658.

Wang, Z., Wei, S. J., & Zhu, K. (2016). *Quantifying international production sharing at the bilateral and sector levels*. Mimeo: Columbia University.

WTO, World Trade Organization. (2011). *World Trade Report 2011—The WTO and preferential trade agreements: From co-existence to coherence* (Working Paper id: 4335).

Conclusions

Nauro F. Campos and Fabrizio Coricelli

Brexit is undoubtedly the result of a political decision, not necessarily reflecting a rational calculation of its economic implications. To be fair, the whole process of European integration since its start has been affected by political considerations. The primary initial motivation for the creation of the European Community was the objective of avoiding another war in Europe. Judged on this ground, the European Union has been a success.

N.F. Campos (✉)
ETH, Zurich, Switzerland
e-mail: nauro.campos@brunel.ac.uk

N.F. Campos
IZA Bonn, Bonn, Germany

N.F. Campos
Brunel University, London, UK

F. Coricelli
Paris School of Economics, Paris, France
e-mail: fabrizio.coricelli@gmail.com

F. Coricelli
Research Fellow at CEPR, London, UK

© The Author(s) 2017
N.F. Campos and F. Coricelli (eds.), *The Economics of UK–EU Relations*,
DOI 10.1007/978-3-319-55495-2_11

In times of rampant euroscepticism, it is also worth reminding that the integration in the European Union is the largest example of *voluntary* integration in history, bringing together 28 countries. Brexit represents the first exit from the EU, which so far has only see enlargements of its original area. Therefore, the uncertainty of the effects of Brexit both for the UK and for the EU is very high.

What is certain is that Brexit raises fundamental questions on the value of EU membership, as well as on the relative importance of political as opposed to purely economic integration. Indeed, the choice of leaving the EU comes with the simultaneous declared objective of remaining in the EU Single Market. These are complex questions, which the economics profession has largely neglected. This book is a first step in trying to fill the gap. It focuses on the economic consequences of Brexit, but it places Brexit in the broader context of the EU–UK relationship since UK entry in the EU in 1973.

A first fundamental contribution of the book is to allow EU integration a prominent role in explaining the UK performance in post-WWII period. Specifically, we provide evidence on the key role of EU accession in stopping the rapid UK relative economic decline during the 1950s and 1960s.

The second main intended contribution is the analysis of the relevance of political integration for economic performance. From the chapters on trade, FDI, finance and migration, it clearly emerges that in order to exploit the full potential for economic growth of the whole set of transactions in the four areas, a sufficient degree of political integration is needed. For instance, the nature of contemporary international trade among advanced economies is based on participation in so-called global value chains, which require deep agreements among nations, agreements that go well beyond those contemplated in the WTO. Trade between UK and EU is indeed mainly based on intermediate products, products that belong to different stages of production of a whole chain. The degree of deep integration achieved in the EU plays a crucial role in this type of trade. Arguing that the UK can easily replace trade with the EU with trade with other parts of the world, especially emerging economies like China, is ill founded because it misses the key point that the nature of trade with the EU is fundamentally different from trade with China.

Trade with the EU is mainly intra-industry whereas trade with China in mainly inter-industry. Moreover, intra-industry trade tends to have a larger positive effect on productivity than inter-industry trade. Trade in intermediate goods and participation in global value chains crucially modify traditional concepts of competitiveness based on real exchange rates. The benefits of the chain are related to the overall performance of the chain that involves various countries. As firms and countries in the chain are both sellers and buyers of products within the production chain, currency depreciation plays a marginal role for trade performance. Similar arguments are presented in the chapters on FDI, finance and migration. The picture that emerges is of key complementarities among different economic areas.

All in all, the idea that Brexit will strengthen the position of the UK as a global player, away from the "provincial" EU, is more political propaganda than serious economic analysis. The inter-linkages between UK firms and EU firms in value chains, the large flows of FDI from the EU and from the rest of the world but directed to the EU market, immigration of EU workers and, last but not least, a financial system that bases its global importance on trade in assets denominated in euro, they all testify of the deep integration of the UK with the EU.

Such deep integration is not independent of the degree of political integration characterizing the European Union. Whether the economic integration can be maintained without the political integration is perhaps the main question for assessing the economic effects of Brexit on the UK economy.

The analysis in the book suggests that the answer to the question above is likely to be negative as an exit from the EU is bound to reduce the degree of economic integration between the UK and the EU. However, the relationship between economic and political integration is highly complex and its analysis is still in its infancy. Therefore, this book should be considered as an initial contribution that paves the way for future research, which is required to provide a definite answer. The economic impact of political plus economic integration versus economic integration alone is a key area for future research. Even more, we need to better understand which are the mechanisms through which political integration produces distinctive effects on the economy. A main implication of political integration is that several decisions and regulations affecting the economy are transferred from the national authority to supranational institutions, EU institutions in our case. By its nature, this transfer entails loss of national power and loss of independence in national policies to achieve certain objectives. Whether this can bring economic benefits that are larger than the loss of policy instruments in the hand of nation states depends on the forces that dominate decisions at the national level. The power of local interest groups is certainly weakened by the transfer of authority from national capitals to Brussels. The resistance to complete the Single Market in the areas of services, for instance, testifies the power of local interest groups at the national level. These are complex issues and economic theory needs to make progress in analysing them.

Empirical analysis is also needed and should make use of methodologies that allow using relevant counterfactuals. This has been a major problem in the evaluation of the benefits of EU integration and it will continue to be a problem for the evaluation of key decisions such as Brexit. Ultimately, the question we need to answer to assess the economic impact of exit for the UK is to compare the actual performance of the UK as a non-EU member relative to "how the UK economy would have performed had the UK remained in the EU?" This is the same question we tried to answer to evaluate the economic impact of UK participation in the EU, by comparing the actual behaviour of UK economic indicators with those of a counterfactual, representing a virtual UK "outside the EU." Therefore, the great uncertainty surrounding the prospects for the life of the UK after the EU is of similar nature of the difficulties in assessing the economic impact of the UK participation in the EU, which is an event of the past. This is an instance that challenges the famous say that "economists are good at predicting the past." In contrast, we conclude that there are difficulties in predicting the future that is associated with the inability of properly assessing the past. This book contributes to this effort: without an anchor from an assessment of past evidence and an analysis of the main channels affecting the effects of EU integration, the debate on future costs and benefits of Brexit will be dominated by purely ideological views.

We began these concluding remarks by stating that Brexit was mainly a political decision. We do not want to give the impression that politics is necessarily irrational, in the sense of conflicting with economic implications. Indeed, economics is a discipline based on the study of outcomes affected by economic constraints but also by preferences. Even if one establishes that EU integration raises aggregate income per capita and productivity of member states, it does not follow that entry in the EU is optimal for every country, irrespective of the specificity of its preferences. One of the reasons for the existence of nation states is that, in principle, differences in preferences should be smaller within national borders, relative to differences across borders. Moreover, nations have developed redistribution mechanisms that permit to reduce economic differences across different groups of a society. In these areas certainly the EU implies significant costs, especially in its current form. It is unquestionable that in many countries local politicians use euroscepticism for their own short-term political benefits. However, issues related to different preferences, which may relate to the complex issue of "identity," and issues related to redistribution mechanisms are crucial themes that cannot be put in a generic basket of "populist" themes. Brexit could be an opportunity for the EU to seriously tackle these problems and realize that they are crucial for the survival of the EU project.

Index

Printed by Printforce, the Netherlands